Irish Townlands

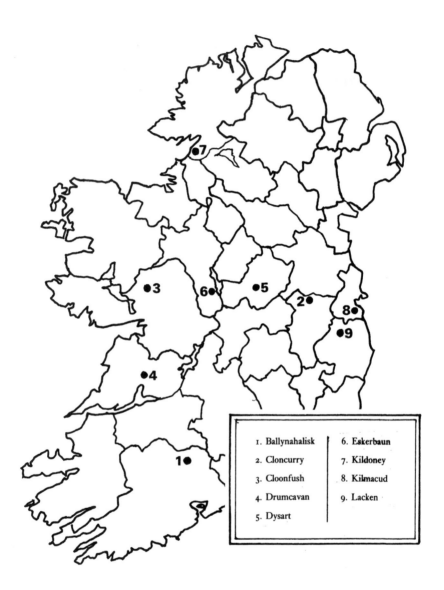

1. Ballynahalisk	6. Eskerbaun
2. Cloncurry	7. Kildoney
3. Cloonfush	8. Kilmacud
4. Drumcavan	9. Lacken
5. Dysart	

Townlands mentioned in this book

Irish Townlands
Studies in Local History

Paul Connell, Denis A. Cronin
& Brian Ó Dálaigh

EDITORS

FOUR COURTS PRESS

This book was set in 10.5 on 12 point Bembo for
FOUR COURTS PRESS LTD
Fumbally Court, Fumbally Lane, Dublin 8
Email: info@four-courts-press.ie
and in North America for
FOUR COURTS PRESS
c/o ISBS, 5804 NE Hassalo St, Portland, Oregon 97213

A catalogue record for this title
is available from the British Library.

ISBN 1–85182–319–0

Printed in Great Britain
by MPG Books Ltd, Bodmin, Cornwall

Contents

LIST OF ABBREVIATIONS   6

PREFACE   7

INTRODUCTION   9

Ballynahalisk, county Cork   14
Denis A. Cronin

Cloncurry, county Kildare   43
Karina Holton

Cloonfush, county Galway   69
Gabriel O'Connor

Drumcavan, county Clare   93
Brian Ó Dálaigh

Dysart, county Westmeath   113
Paul Connell

Eskerbaun, county Roscommon   141
William Gacquin

Kildoney Glebe, Kilbarron, county Donegal   164
Francis Hayes

Kilmacud, county Dublin   186
Charles Smith

Lacken, county Wicklow   203
Séamas O Maitiú

INDEX   221

Abbreviations

CDB	Congested District Board
CSORP	Chief Secretary's Office Registered Papers
DED	District Electoral Division
Griffith, *Valuation*	Richard Griffith, *Primary Valuation of Ireland* (1848–64)
HC	House of Commons
ILC	Irish Land Commission
IMC	Irish Manuscripts Commission
JCHAS	*Journal of the Cork Historical and Archaeological Society*
JGAHS	*Journal of the Galway Archaeological and Historical Society*
JKAS	*Journal of the Kildare Archaeological Society*
JRSAI	*Journal of the Royal Society of Antiquaries of Ireland*
Ms(s)	Manuscript(s)
NA	National Archives
NLI	National Library of Ireland
OPW	Office of Public Works
OS	Ordnance Survey
pos.	positive (microfilm)
PRIA	*Proceedings of the Royal Irish Academy*
PRONI	Public Record Office of Northern Ireland
RCB	Representative Church Body Library
RD	Registry of Deeds
RIA	Royal Irish Academy
TAB	Tithe Applotment Books
TCD	Trinity College, Dublin
UCD	University College, Dublin
VO	Valuation Office

Preface

This collection of essays arises out of the M.A. in Local History course offered by the Department of Modern History, N.U.I. Maynooth. In 1994 some members of the first group of graduates decided to meet on a monthly basis in order to share ideas about local history and to undertake a number of studies, beginning with one on townlands. They were subsequently joined by later graduates of the M.A. programme. This book is the first of what is hoped will be a number of local history studies.

The authors wish to thank Professor Vincent Comerford and the Department of Modern History, N.U.I. Maynooth for their encouragement and assistance. In particular they would like to acknowledge the guidance and unfailing support given them by Dr Raymond Gillespie.

They wish also to thank the staffs of the following institutions for their assistance and courtesy: N.U.I. Maynooth, Library; Trinity college, Dublin, Library; National Library of Ireland; National Archives of Ireland; Public Record Office of Northern Ireland; Valuation Office; Registry of Deeds; Irish Land Commission; Department of Folklore, University College, Dublin.

Introduction

PAUL CONNELL, DENIS A. CRONIN
and BRIAN Ó DÁLAIGH

The first edition of the Ordnance Survey series of six-inch maps of Ireland recorded a snapshot of the country's land divisions in the middle of the nineteenth century. Some of these divisions are well known and enduring, such as the county and parish. Others, like the barony and deanery, are falling into disuse. Townlands, however, because of their size, their association with family and with home place remain the most intimate and enduring of our land divisions. From early historic times a variety of land units have divided the Irish countryside into small viable agricultural units. The tate and sessiagh of Ulster and the cartron and gnive of Connacht and Munster are examples of such units. However, through repeated usage in land surveys and property transactions from the seventeenth century onwards, the townland gradually replaced all earlier units and in the last century was chosen by government as the basic administrative unit for the purpose of land valuation and census of population.

The strong attachment of family to townland is best appreciated through the examination of placenames. Many townlands are named after their principal families, like, for instance, Derryriordane and Derrynabourky, both in the parish of Inchageelagh, county Cork.[1] In areas of Anglo-Norman settlement the smallest divisions were named by attaching the element 'town' to the name of the colonising family: in west Dublin one finds the townlands of Huntstown, Warrenstown and Luttrellstown. It is sometimes posssible to see this name changing process in action; in county Wexford at the end of the thirteenth century the denominations of Ballydermod and Trillok were renamed Cushenstown and Rochestown respectively by their new Anglo-Norman owners.[2] The strong attachment of family to the townland unit continued well into the eighteenth century with the formation of such townlands as Lysterfield, county Roscommon and Mahonburg, county Clare.[3]

The Ordnance Survey recorded 62,205 townlands in all. The recorded history and provenance of individual townlands varies enormously. According to Reeves, townlands are 'the earliest allotment on the scale of Irish land divisions',

---

[1] Diarmuid Ó Murchadha, 'Gaelic land tenure in county Cork: Uibh Laoghaire in the seventeenth century', in Patrick O'Flanagan and C.G. Buttimer (eds), *Cork: History and Society* (Dublin, 1993), pp. 213–48; see map p. 215; **2** Billy Colfer, 'In search of the Barricade and Ditch of Ballyconnor, Co. Wexford' in *Archaeology Ireland*, 10, no. 2 (Summer 1996), p. 19. **3** On Lysterfield see William Gacquin, *Roscommon before the Famine* (Dublin, 1996), p. 26.

roughly equivalent to an intermediate grade of Irish and Anglo-Norman measures of land such as ballyboes, quarters, carucates and ploughlands.[4] He traces,
for instance, the proto-townland of *Ochter n-Achid* recorded in the Book of
Armagh before AD 800 'with all its appurtences, both wood, and plain, and
meadow, together with its habitation and its garden' to the modern townland of
Oughteragh in county Leitrim.[5]

The townland framework was present in many parts of the country by the
twelfth century, as a number of local studies have demonstrated.[6] But the majority
are recorded for the first time in the documents of the late sixteenth- and early
seventeenth-century land conquests. Some more townlands were creations of
the eighteenth and nineteenth centuries, most typically by improving landlords
or their agents. One unusual example is the townland name of Bleachyard
examined by Joseph McDermott in his study of Newport, county Mayo.[7]

What this evidence on the differing origins and development of townlands
suggests is that they were, above all, economically viable units, pragmatic mecha-
nisms for dividing land that evolved to suit the people that used them. It is their
continuity that impresses. The original townland framework remains despite many
changes over time. This framework was frozen in time by the cartographers of the
Ordnance Survey and the units they recorded have now largely ceased to evolve.

The recording of townlands by the Ordnance Survey was not in itself a perfect
undertaking. We know that in some cases the surveyors created new townlands
and subdivided others to suit their own purposes. In particular, they sometimes
gave townland status to demesnes, deerparks and large farms. They straightened
imprecise boundaries, extended boundaries in upland areas and transferred part
or all of some townlands into others.[8]

This mapping of townlands for the first edition of the Ordnance Survey maps
led to them being used as administrative units in order to make census-taking
more accurate from 1841 and to use as the basic framework in Griffith's *Valuation*.
In addition, Poor Law Unions and the later District Electoral Divisions were
created from groups of townlands. Townlands continue to be used as administrative units for census-taking and for postal addresses. But the townland is above all
a social unit, a division which evolved to suit the people who owned or occupied
the land. Boundaries were often recited from memory and the older inhabitants
consulted about them when disputes arose.[9] Because the townland is so linked

---

4 William Reeves, 'On the townland distribution of Ireland', in *PRIA*, vii (1862), pp.
473–96.   **5** Ibid., p. 480.   **6** For example, Liam Ó Buachalla's series on 'Townland
development in the Fermoy area, twelfth century to nineteenth century' in *Dinnseanchas*,
vols i and ii (1996–7).   **7** J.P. Mc Dermott, 'An examination of accounts of James
Moore Esq., land agent and collector of port fees at Newport Pratt, Co. Mayo, 1742–65'
(unpublished MA thesis, Maynooth College, 1994), p. 13.   **8** See Thomas McErlean,
'The Irish town land system of landscape organisation' in Terence Reeves-Smith and
Fred Hamond (eds) *Landscape archaeology in Ireland* (British Archaelogical Reports, British
Series 116, Oxford, 1983), pp. 315–40.   **9** Many instances of this can be found in
O'Donovan's OS Letters.

with the identity of people and their sense of community it is an appropriate unit for the local historian to study.

This book is an attempt to study a selection of townlands from different parts of the country. Their topographies, social structures, origins, and the histories of their communities may be similar or different to various extents, but in each case these elements combined to give a townland its particular character or personality. The locations chosen reflect the particular interests of the authors and illustrate different regional geographies. This collection of essays is not about the origin of townlands or their significance as territorial units but rather about the diversity of historical experience of different townland communities.

Frank Hayes in his essay on Kildoney, county Donegal, describes a coastal community whose members made a living from fishing and partnership farming. In sharp contrast is the townland of Kilmacud, county Dublin, described by Charles Smith, which details the experience of a community on the fringes of the urban environment of Dublin. In his study of Ballynahalisk, county Cork, Denis Cronin describes a community in a fertile river valley of Munster where people made their living largely from tillage and associated rural industry. Séamus Ó Maitiú tells the story of the upland townland of Lacken in county Wicklow, which, unusually has since lost one third of its land as a result of a hydro-electric scheme.

Some of these diverse experiences are explored thematically in this book. One theme which recurs in the essays is the way in which change is managed over the generations in the townlands. Some seem very closed to outside influence, like the townland of Cloonfush, county Galway examined by Gabriel O'Connor, which remained very close-knit for many years in spite of its close proximity to the town of Tuam. In another example of a closed townland, William Gacquin has demonstrated the high level of continuity among the occupying families of Eskerbaun, county Roscommon, from the Synge census of 1749 to the present day.

In his study of Dysart, county Westmeath, Paul Connell explores a large townland which constituted a single estate. Land ownership continued in the hands of the same family from the fourteenth to the twentieth century and the evidence of landholding also points to a high degree of continuity among tenants.

Some townlands appear more open to change, like Cloncurry, county Kildare, explored by Karina Holton, where the building of the Royal Canal led to a large influx of people into the townland. Brian Ó Dálaigh has demonstrated in his essay on Drumcavan, county Clare, that the Great Famine was a catalyst for change whereby the existing community of tenants was cleared and replaced by a new breed of commercial graziers.

Another theme explored is that of landlord intervention. This varied enormously from townland to townland. In Eskerbaun, for instance, the landlord intervened directly to create a more viable farming community out of an over-populated townland. This he did by encouraging some tenants to emigrate and by resettling others in a neighbouring townland, thereby creating larger and more economic holdings for those who remained. By complete contrast, Cloonfush shows little or no landlord influence because of its status as church land. The experience of most of the communities in these studies was of a distant landlord operating through the aegis of the land agent and middleman. As Brian Ó Dálaigh points out, it was almost a point of honour among landowners in Clare that they should never deal directly with their tenants.

The townlands studied in this book are spread over a wide geographical area, spanning most of the country. This geographical diversity coupled with a diversity of historical experience ensured that a wide range of sources were available to the various authors. Some of them had unique sources at their disposal like, for example, William Gacquin's use of the Synge Census for Elphin or Brian Ó Dálaigh's use of the Lucas farming diary. Not all the townland studies could draw on the rich vein of medieval material used by Karina Holton in her study of Cloncurry. There are a number of sources however, particularly nineteenth century material, which were used in most or all of these townland studies.

The nineteenth-century census material from 1841 onwards gave access to townland population figures and information on townland housing stock. In particular, the enumeration forms for the 1901 census and the 1911 census enabled a detailed study to be undertaken of townland population and occupancy, house by house. This census material was in many cases enhanced by the use of local church baptismal, marriage and death registers.

Two important sources for landholding patterns in townlands are the Tithe Applotment Books and Griffith's *Valuation*. The Tithe Applotment Books were drawn up in the 1820s and 1830s for the purpose of composition of tithes under the tithe reform act of 1823. Although the information given in these books varies from parish to parish they are a useful guide to landholding patterns in the early part of the nineteenth century.

Griffith's *Valuation* is an individual tenement valuation for the whole country begun by Richard Griffith, Commissioner of Valuation, in 1844 and completed in 1865. It became the basis for all local taxation including the county rate and the poor law rate, and also became the basis for the franchise for parliamentary and local elections. Its importance as a source for local history cannot be overstated. The picture it gives of nineteenth-century ownership and occupation of land and property is unique. Apart from the published version of the valuation, a further picture of local conditions can be garnered from original field books, tenure books, house books and other documents. Its value is even more enhanced by the fact that it was continually updated by the Valuation Office in Dublin. These updates, known as the cancellation books, enable the transfer of property to be established for each tenement right into this century. For the purposes of these townland studies the cancellation books were essential for the study of family names and for the study of continuity in landholding patterns.

Another nineteenth-century source used in a number of these townland studies was the papers of the Irish Land Commission which contain an enormous amount of material on local areas and estates gathered during the sale of estates in the late nineteenth and early twentieth centuries. Records of central administration now held in the National Archives were also used. These include the State of the Country Papers, the Outrage Reports, and the Chief Secretary's Office Registered Papers. These papers provide a further insight into local community life.

As well as these nineteenth-century sources there were other sources used from an earlier period by many of the townland studies. A number used the Books of Survey and Distribution. These are abstracts of surveys and changes in land ownership in Ireland during the period 1636–1703. They were used to impose the quit rent, a rent which was payable yearly on lands granted under the Act of Settlement of 1662 and the Act of Explanation of 1665. They constitute an official record of landed proprietors and their respective estates. Another such source used was the 1659 census. Available for most of the country it was drawn up in 1659 during the course of the Down Survey. It gives the names of the principal or distinguished occupiers of townlands under the title of 'Tituladoes' and records the number of males as heads of households, and unmarried females over eighteen, while dividing all into English, Irish or Scotch. To establish a rough estimate of total population historians use a multiplier of three.

The availability of all these sources enable us to compare and contrast the different townlands in this study and they help us to achieve a greater understanding of the diverse and common experiences of these townland communities.

What this collection of essays demonstrates is the importance of studying units like townlands with which people had a strong sense of identification. However, it is important that such studies should not degenerate into mere collections of individual facts. Rather they should explore something of the social world of townlands, their relationship with their hinterlands and their interaction with nearby urban communities. This can only be understood when local experiences can be compared and contrasted.

Ballynahalisk, county Cork

DENIS A. CRONIN[*]

The townland of Ballynahalisk (c.533 acres) lies in the valley of the river Funcheon, a tributary of the Munster Blackwater, about ten miles north of the town of Fermoy in north-east county Cork. Together with the smaller town-lands of Ballyvoddy and Ransborough it makes up a small civil parish called St Nathlash or Nathlash (c.1023 acres), now part of the united Catholic parish of Kildorrery centred on the village of that name about a mile and a half to the north. As part of the rich and rolling basin of the Blackwater it is located in one of the most fertile and prosperous agricultural areas of Ireland, and so provides a contrast with many of the other townlands examined in this collection.

The scope of this study allows only a limited examination of the history of the community in Ballynahalisk and its vicinity. The story of human settlement in the historical period is its over-riding theme. A number of elements within that story will help to illuminate the unique character or 'personality' of the com-munity in Ballynahalisk. These include the relationship between topography, settlement and agriculture in a Munster river valley, the rise and fall of a rural industry and its associated village settlement, and the relationship between different social groups and religious communities.

Ballynahalisk has only one natural boundary, the river Funcheon to its east and north-east. Its other boundaries are human ones, including the townlands of Carrigleagh to the west, Ballyvoddy to the north, and Lisnagourneen and Carrigdownane (Upper and Lower) to the south. The land rises from the river boundary, steeply at first from a picturesque glen called the Rock and then more gently, and extends over half a mile to the south-west. It has a height at the river of about 200 feet above sea level and rises to a height of about 300 feet at its western boundary. The fields are regular and mainly rectangular in shape, with their length on a north-east to south-west axis, mirroring the townland shape. Land quality, although relatively good, is best summed up in this description by the valuation officials in the 1840s:

> The whole of this parish [of Nathlash] is a dry poor sandy soil on a secondary limerock, which is in many parts too near the surface. It suffers

[*] I would like to record here my thanks to my father, Sean Cronin of Scart, Kildorrery for his great assistance to me in researching this study, which I dedicate to him. I am indebted also to the Casey/Vaughan families, present owners of Rockmills Lodge, for access to a number of deeds in their possession relating to their property.

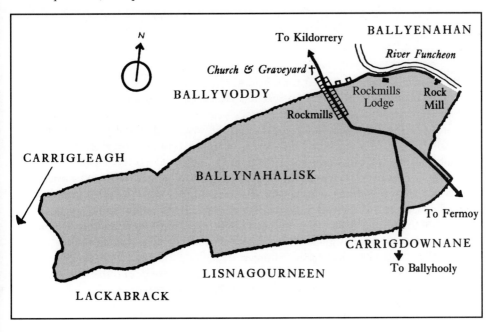

Ballynahalisk, county Cork, 1845, 533 acres.

for the want of water on the south west side, but it is otherwise con-
veniently situated as to roads, markets, shops etc. It produces good crops of
every sort and an excellent sheep grass but is too dry for dairy stock.[1]

Ballynahalisk today is a quiet rural backwater, with dispersed farm settlements
typical of north Cork farmland reached via by-roads and untarred 'boreens'.
Farming remains largely a mixture of stock-rearing and tillage. Near the eastern
border of the townland and also partly in the townland of Ballyvoddy is the
small hamlet of Rockmills. This once substantial village, originally called
Ballynahalisk, took its name from a large flour mill called the Rock Mill which
was built nearby on the river Funcheon about 1775. The mill went out of operation at the turn of this century and is now in ruins. The village of Rockmills
declined as the mill did and today it contains only a few families. At the northern
edge of the village, in the townland of Ballyvoddy, is a graveyard, within which
can be seen the ruined steeple of a Church of Ireland parish church.

    These features or landmarks of human settlement – farms, village, flour mill,
graveyard and church – will be used to examine the material and mental world
of Ballynahalisk and its vicinity up to the early twentieth century.

                                            I

It may be appropriate to begin this study by looking at the name of the
townland, since the link between place and name is central to any study of locality. The etymology of Ballynahalisk suggested by O'Donovan in the Ordnance
Survey namebook was *béal an átha loiscthe* (mouth of the burnt ford), indicating
a possible link between name and landscape. Because his sources were recent he
was careful to add that this was 'very uncertain'. Nevertheless, this explanation
seems to have been generally accepted by subsequent students of the locality.[2]

    Fortunately for the cause of accuracy, the medieval placenames of this corner
of county Cork have largely survived in Gaelic and Anglo-Norman manuscripts
and these sources point to an entirely different origin for the name, one which
suggests a much older provenance. *Echlasca Molaga*, a placename in a copy of a
twelfth-century manuscript (*Crichad an Chaoilli* or Topography of Fermoy) in
the Book of Lismore, has been identified as referring to the townland and its
vicinity, possibly to an area roughly contiguous with the three townlands of
Nathlash parish.[3] The meaning of *echlasca* is unclear: it may mean 'pools' or

1 VO, Field book for parish of Nathlash, District Electoral Division of Derryvillane,
Co. Cork.   **2** OS, Townland namebooks for Co. Cork, no. 35, p. 4 (in microfilm at NLI,
pos. 1037).   **3** Liam Ó Buachalla, 'Placenames of north-east Cork' in *JCHAS* lv (1950),
pp. 91–5.

'springs' (a link with the townland's topography) but it is more likely to have a meaning referring to horses–'horse switches' or possibly 'stables'.[4]

The appearance in this oldest placename of St Molaga, the district's most prominent local saint, connects Ballynahalisk with two local sites also dedicated to the saint (Labbamolaga and Templemolaga/Aghacross). This may indicate an early Christian ecclesiastical settlement or even pre-Christian sacred site in or near the townland, close to a fording point in the river Funcheon that linked it with the other sites a few miles to the north.[5] Taxation records of a small church at 'Achlyskmolaga' in 1292 and 'Athlyskemelag' in 1307 and the survival into the modern era of the small civil parish of Nathlash and its graveyard indicate the existence there of a medieval parish church.[6]

4 *RIA dictionary of the Irish language*, Vol. E (Dublin, 1932), pp. 31–2.   **5** These connections are discussed briefly in a recent study by Kenneth Hanley, Mairead Weaver and Judith Monk, *An archaeological survey of St Mologa's Church, Aghacross, Mitchelstown, Co. Cork* (Cork, 1995); a fascinating argument suggesting the survival of elements of the pagan worship of Lug in the cult of Molaga and other regional saints can be found in Padraig Ó Riain, 'Traces of Lug in early Irish hagiographical tradition', in *Zeitschrift fur Celtische Philologie*, xxxvi, 138–56.   **6** *Eighth report on the public records of Ireland* (1819), appendix 'Pope Nicholas' taxation, 1292', p. 65; H.S. Sweetman (ed.), *Calendar of documents relating to Ireland 1302–07* (London, 1886), pp. 277, 314.

By the fifteenth century the placename association with St Molaga appears to have been lost and the district was recorded as *Baile na nEchlusc* in a fifteenth-century Roche charter, a copy of which is included in the Book of Fermoy. Later corruptions of this name, including 'Ballenynathliske' and 'Banhalisk', are part of the process of evolution which led to its present name.[7]

This loss of the original sense of the townland name and its echoes of pre-Christian and early Christian times because of a series of corruptions over the centuries illustrates the many difficulties associated with the study of placenames. The link between the parish name of St Nathlash and the parish's patron saint, Nicholas, illustrates these difficulties further. Although Nathlash has sometimes been supposed to be an anglicisation of the Gaelic name, Nioclás (a supposition completely accepted by O'Donovan) it is far more likely to be a contraction of the medieval denomination of *(Baile na) nEchlusc*.[8] The earliest surviving reference to a parochial name of Nathlash seems to date back only as far as 1591, when it was bleakly described as '*E. de Neathlash – locus vastus et desertus vacat*'.[9] It would appear therefore that naming the parish 'St Nathlash' and invoking St Nicholas as its patron saint was an accidental consequence of losing its original meaning!

In the early Christian period the townland of Ballynahalisk formed a small part of the territory of *Caoille* or Fermoy, a fertile tract of north-east Cork about twenty-six miles by eighteen miles, bordered by the Galtee, Ballyhoura and Nagle mountains and including much of the middle Blackwater river. This area now largely corresponds to the baronies of Fermoy and Condons & Clangibbons. Although the region is defined by mountain ranges to the north, east and south, it is geographically quite an open one. Passage is easily made through mountain gaps, especially through the large Mitchelstown gap, into the nearby counties of Limerick and Tipperary, while the rest of county Cork and its other neighbouring counties, Kerry and Waterford, are also very accessible.

As a result, the region has never been isolated historically and was linked in particular with the rich lands to the north and east: from the early Christian period Fermoy was subject to the overlordship of Cashel and formed part of *Glennamhnach*, one of the sub-kingdoms nominally ruled from there. In the twelfth century its accessibility allowed it to be quickly penetrated by the first wave of Norman invaders. The lands passed from the O'Keeffe family and its satellites into the hands of the Flemings and later came by marriage to the Roche family to form the medieval lordship known as the 'Roche country'. This lordship survived repeated wars with its neighbours, rebellions against the crown and the lottery of natural extinction until the Cromwellian confiscations of the mid sevententh century.

---

7 *Irish Patent Rolls of James I* (IMC facsimile edition, Dublin, 1966), p. 209; Sir Wm. Petty, *Hiberniae Delineatio* (c.1685). **8** OS, Co. Cork barony and parish namebook, f. 240 (in microfilm at NLI, pos. 4924). **9** W.M. Brady, *Clerical and parochial records of Cork, Cloyne and Ross* (3 vols, Dublin, 1863), ii, 363.

Within this regional context, Ballynahalisk and its neighbourhood have always had a quasi-borderland status. Originally it was part of the borderland of the eastern of the two cantreds – or land divisions – of Fermoy. These cantreds are said to have been divided by a boundary ditch or bank called *An Claidh Dubh*, traces of which are believed to survive on the western boundaries of the townlands of Nathlash.[10] After the Norman invasion it stood on the borders of the ever-shifting territories of the Roche and Condon lordships. As early as 1295 the Condons were in dispute with Milo de Waleis over a site at 'Athlyskymeleth', while in 1321, this time in dispute with the Roches, they attacked the district and burned thirty houses and the church of Kildorrery.[11] This disputed and borderland status is reflected in Nathlash's position today – within the barony of Fermoy but bordering the barony of Condons and Clangibbons.

It is not possible to reconstruct how the land was settled or used during the Roche lordship but descriptions of it as 'plowland' indicate that at least some of it must have been tilled. We know that the area was in the heart of a grain-growing region regarded for centuries as the granary of Munster, of which the bard Aenghus Ó Dálaigh wrote, 'It is well for me that I eat not butter, for, if I did, [while I was in Roche's country] I could not get it.'[12]

It is not clear how soon after the Norman invasion *Echlasca Molaga* was subdivided into different townlands, but by the fifteenth century a denomination called *Baile na nAnnlonoc* had emerged which appears to correspond to the present townland of Ballyvoddy. This is confirmed by church records for 1774 which state that *Temple un Aunlaunogh* was an alternative name for Ballyvoddy and which refer also to a ruined church in the townland.[13] The Book of Survey and Distribution for county Cork records 'Morris, Lord Roche' as owner in 1641 of the townlands of 'Ballinballick' (Ballynahalisk) and 'Ballynawlon' (later renamed Ballyvoddy). After the Cromwellian confiscations ownership of these townlands diverged permanently, the former becoming the property of Captain William Harmer and Lord Kingston, while the latter went to Thomas Coppinger, William Radford and (by patent) Richard Nagle.[14] The old proprietors were never to regain these lands, despite a legal declaration, dated 27 July 1663, of a right to Ballinhalisk in favour of Patrick Roche. In 1667, under the acts of settlement and explanation which followed the restoration of Charles II, Captain Harmer was confirmed as owner of almost a thousand acres in Fermoy barony, including part of a 'plow' comprising 265 plantation acres in 'Ballinhalisk'.[15]

---

10 This tradition is referred to in a short piece by T.M. O'Driscoll in *JCHAS*, xxxvii (1932), p. 105; the later OS maps do trace and name such a boundary also but on the ground in Nathlash it is hard to distinguish from other field boundaries. **11** Diarmuid O'Murchadha, *Family names of county Cork* (revised ed., Cork, 1996), pp. 95–6, 276–7. **12** Aenghus O' Daly, *The tribes of Ireland* (facsimile ed., Cork, 1976), p. 65. **13** Eamon de hÓir, 'Liosta de Thailte Roisteacha 1461' in *Dinnseanchas*, ii, uimh. 4 (Nollaig, 1967), p. 108; Brady, *Records*, ii, 364. **14** PRONI, Annesley Mss., Books of Survey and Distribution, vol. xvii (Co. Cork, ii) [NLI, microfilm pos. 273]. **15** *Fifteenth report on the public records of Ireland* (March 1825), app. I, pp. 160, 224, 302.

By the early eighteenth century ownership of Ballynahalisk and some neighbouring townlands had come to John Bond, presumably by inheritance from the
family of Captain Harmer, judging by the use of Harmer as a Christian name in
the Bond family. Initially the Bonds lived on their estate at nearby Carrigdownane
but seem to have given up *de facto* ownership of much of their lands to middlemen during the eighteenth century. The family home at Carrigdownane was
sold to a family named Stannard as early as 1752 and renamed Stannard's Grove,
while various parcels of land were disposed of on long leases of three lives
renewable forever or for terms of 999 years.

These leases give some indication of how the townland was divided up and
of the different sizes of holdings in the eighteenth century. In the absence of
estate records they are the only such evidence available. The land was let out in
parcels of different sizes. For example, in 1788 Harmer Bond let about thirty-six
Irish acres to Richard Aldworth of Annesgrove around Aldworth's residence at
Rockmills Lodge. His son let nine acres called the 'Kiln Fields' to Hearman
O'Connell of nearby Snug Lodge in 1790 and a further fifty-one (plantation)
acres, known as the 'Demesne of Ballinahilisk', to Redmond Graham of
Millstreet in 1795.[16]

A similar process emerged in neighbouring Ballyvoddy. In the early eighteenth century ownership lay with George McQuay, who seems to have bought
it from Ebenezer and Bostock Radford, but by 1733 it was effectively in the
hands of the Kearney family by virtue of a lease from McQuay for three lives
renewable forever.[17] The Kearney family – who appear initally to have come
from Kilmallock in county Limerick – lived and farmed locally but sublet a
good deal of their holding. The benefits of these leases were divided up among
the family to satisfy its members at different times. One deed allows us to see
something of the patchwork of subdivisions in existence and the range of
different tenants, from cottiers to substantial farmers, that inhabited the townland
by the end of the eighteenth century. In 1795 Mary Kearney divided her one-
third share of the family holdings among two surviving sons, giving to James:

> … that part of Ballyvoddy in the tenancy of William Goold containing
> about one acre and a half held by David Sheehan, the house and garden
> containing about half an acre held by Richard Baker, and ten acres and
> twenty-six perches part of that part of Ballinvoddo in the tenancy of
> Nicholas Meade and partners to be divided from the residue of said
> Meade's farm

---

16 RD, 64/407/44411; 177/163/117888; 391/418/261759; 428/308/280244; 481/333/
317369. **17** RD, 516/484–5/338239.

and giving to Denis, who as eldest surviving son already held the bulk of the land:

> ... the residue of said Nicholas Meade's farm, containing about forty acres, and the said lands of Lackybrack, in the tenancy of John Blake, containing about twenty-three acres [and] the small spot of ground from the well to the ditch on the said William Goold's land ...[18]

One feature of landholding revealed by this document is that at least one farm in the neighbourhood was held in partnership. It is not possible to say if this indicates that in the late eighteenth century the townland was in transition from partnership or village farming to individually held farms. The evidence of the earliest list of landholders, the 1820s tithe applotment book, is ambiguous on this point: though individual farms were universal, many seem divided up among families.

In essence, land ownership in both townlands passed into the hands of new proprietors in the 1650s; these were confirmed in their ownership in the decades that followed; and by the early eighteenth century the land was let on long leases to middlemen who farmed part of the lands and relet the rest on shorter leases. This was a pattern very common in the eighteenth century in parts of county Cork and elsewhere where the landowner was unwilling to reside and supervise his estate.

This structure survived largely unchanged into the later nineteenth century. In Ballynahalisk the only significant change that occurred was at the top of the landholding pyramid when, during the crisis of the 1840s, the Bond family lands were sold in the court of chancery and were bought by Thomas Leader, a member of a prominent county Cork family and one of a new breed of landlord who was investing in encumbered estates.[19] The valuation office records of *c.*1850 record the terms under which land was held in the two townlands. In Ballynahalisk the new landowner, Thomas Leader, was not able to get immediate control of his lands, which were held in the main from a middleman at rents between 30*s.* and 35*s.* per acre for terms of three lives or for twenty-one or thirty-one years. In Ballyvoddy the Kearneys and their relatives the Keeffes held the lands on an old renewable lease at only 4*s.* 6*d.* an acre from the McQuays and relet portions at rents of up to 41*s.* an acre, usually for twenty-one years. Cottiers seem to have held their land at will.[20]

From the evidence of the eighteenth-century leases and elsewhere, the physical landscape of the area had largely taken its modern shape by the end of the eighteenth century. Though it was recorded in 1750 that the land around Farahy (about two miles from Nathlash) was 'open, dry and healthy, with good

---

18 RD, 481/217/316715; the Kearney connection with Kilmallock is established in RD, 339/541/229916.   **19** NLI, Transcript summary of the land commission records, E.C. 6223, box no. 5743.   **20** VO, Field book for parish of Nathlash; NA, Tenure book for parish of Nathlash, OL 6.0113.

sheepwalks, and is fit for sporting', enclosure soon became common. Townsend wrote in 1810 that the barony of Fermoy 'was formerly an open grazing country; it is now inclosed, tilled, and almost as full of inhabitants as the lands along the sea coast'.[21] Firstly, it seems, townland boundaries and, later, farm and field boundaries had been marked out – one deed, for instance refers to 'a straight large bounds ditch erected by ... Mr Bond' before 1789 – and there was in place a mixture of large and small farms and cottier holdings.[22] A village settlement had grown up in Rockmills and the existing road system was largely in place.

Although an early seventeenth-century reference to 'Roche's country of the fine roads' suggests that the region had long had a good road system, it is difficult to ascertain how or when it developed in the vicinity of Ballynahalisk.[23] Some of it may have been a consequence of the foundation of the Rock Mill and the need to transport both grain to the mill and flour to important markets, especially to Dublin and Cork. The high road and other minor roads linked Rockmills directly with neighbouring villages like Kildorrery, Glanworth, Farrahy, Shanbally-more, Castletownroche and Ballyhooly, and with the main towns of the region, such as Fermoy, Mallow and Mitchelstown.

The section of the high road from Fermoy to Kilmallock which runs through Rockmills is hard to date. It is likely to be a very old routeway but does not appear in the map which accompanied Smith's history of Cork in 1750. Yet there seems to be such a road recorded in the 1770s and its existence is certain in 1788. The development of Fermoy town led to more traffic on the route because it linked the town with Kilmallock and Limerick. John Anderson, founder of Fermoy town and a leading local moderniser, wrote in 1820 of having made great use in the past of grand jury presentments to make improvements to this road.[24]

This road system provides clear evidence that Ballynahalisk cannot be looked at in isolation from the district in which it lies. Its community was linked easily with its neighbours and therefore was part of a wider local and regional consciousness. A Bianconi car route which passed through Rockmills, for instance, brought the outside world into the community every week. The Catholic register for Kildorrery gives us a glimpse of the marriage horizons of the young in the early decades of the nineteenth century. Between 1803 and 1831, out of 96 marriages which involved at least one inhabitant of Nathlash, 52 per cent married within Nathlash parish, 17.7 per cent married within the parish of Kildorrery, 24 per cent married someone from a neighbouring area within a

21 Charles Smith, *The ancient and present state of the county and city of Cork*, edited reprint in *JCHAS*, i (1892), part iii, p. 318; Revd Horatio Townsend, *A statistical survey of county Cork* (Dublin, 1810), p. 451.   **22** RD 714/377–8/488913.   **23** O'Daly, *Tribes of Ireland*, p. 65.   **24** *JCHAS*, vol. i (1892), part iii, map facing p. 33; George Taylor and Andrew Skinner, *Maps of the roads of Ireland* (reprint Shannon, 1969, of 2nd. ed. Dublin, 1783), p. 124; RD, 395/275/261760; Niall Brunicardi, 'John Anderson's bankruptcy' in *JCHAS*, lxxxix (1984) p. 94.

radius of about eight miles and 6.3 per cent married someone beyond that.[25] Given that opportunities for travel were so limited at this time, the community, with the help of a good road network, was far from being an isolated one.

III

An important development that affected Ballynahalisk in the later eighteenth century was an industrial venture undertaken by a group of north Cork entrepreneurs. To encourage grain growing in the district and to take advantage of the bounties on corn going to Dublin, a flour mill was established beside the Funcheon about 1775 at the joint expense of Sentleger Lord Doneraile, Revd Edward Delaney and Richard Aldworth (who already owned a shooting lodge on the high ground above the river) on land leased by Chichester St Leger from Delaney. Delaney sold his share to his partners in 1780 and the St Legers in turn sold their half share to the Aldworths in 1787 for £4000.[26] The mill was said to be one of the biggest in the country before the turn of the century, with most of its produce going overland to Dublin to take advantage of the corn bounties. For example, in the year to June 1777 it is recorded that the mill sent the largest quantity of grain – 2372 hundred weights worth £652 16s. – from county Cork to Dublin. Its nearest rival in the county on that occasion, the large mill at Glanmire, near Cork city, sent 2089 hundred weights.[27] Aldworth's success sparked off a number of other milling projects in the district, and by 1810 there were five such mills operating within ten miles of each other. Although the Rock Mill was affected by this increase in competition, especially from a large mill in Fermoy, and by the withdrawal of the corn bounties after the Act of Union, it was reported that it continued to maintain 'its character and credit' well into the nineteenth century.[28]

Some immigration seems to have followed the success of the mill, leading to an increase in size of the village of Ballynahalisk (eventually to be called Rockmills) along the access road to the mill and along the adjacent high road from Fermoy to Kilmallock. The earliest evidence of a village at Rockmills comes from a 1788 deed which refers to the 'town and lands of Ballinehallisk' and an 1808 deed which refers to 'the several small plotts of ground and tenements in the village of Ballinahillisk'.[29] These deeds postdate both the foundation and heyday of the mill so it is hardly surprising that the village had developed by then, probably beside a small settlement already in place around the graveyard and a chapel. It is not possible to calculate what levels of permanent or seasonal employment were given by the mill as no records seem to survive.

25 Catholic marriage register, Kildorrery, Co. Cork (NLI, microfilm pos. 4994).   **26** RD, 394/83/259512.   **27** *Journal of Irish house of commons*, ix (1773–8), pt 2, dxiv.   **28** Townsend, *Statistical survey*, pp. 451–2.   **29** RD, 375/275/261760; 600/447/411351.

IV

In any attempt to analyse the impact of the Rock Mill on Ballynahalisk and to detail changes in landholding and farm size in the eighteenth and nineteenth centuries it is necessary to examine population change during the period. The earliest data which can be used as a starting point to estimate demographic change in the two townlands is a 1766 religious census which returned forty five households in the parish of Nathlash.[30] On this basis, using a multiplier of five per household, as commonly suggested by demographers, it can be estimated that the population of the parish was about 225. Calculated on a proportionate basis for all three townlands in the parish, the estimated populations of Ballynahalisk and Ballyvoddy in 1766 were 120 and 80.

Since the 1821 and 1831 censuses do not return Nathlash as a separate parish, estimation becomes difficult here. By comparing the (estimated) base figure of 200 inhabitants in 1766 with that of 829 recorded in 1841 a fourfold increase in population in seventy-five years is indicated. Much of this growth can be explained by a disproportionate expansion in population in the village of Rockmills, which grew from a very low base in 1766 to 165 in 1821 and to 461 in 1841.[31] It can be estimated that the rural population doubled during the period, thus implying a growth rate of about ten per cent per decade, well within the range of general estimates of demographic change at this time.

Figure 1 shows the population between 1841 and 1891 of Ballynahalisk, Rockmills and Ballyvoddy.

Figure 1 · Population change 1841–1891

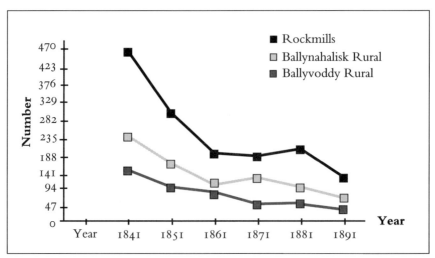

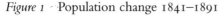

30 NA, M 5036a (transcript of religious census 1766), p. 223. **31** *Census of Ireland, 1821–41*, county Cork.

The 1841 census shows the population at its highest point. Subsequent figures indicate a picture of steady decline in population. The impact of the famine crisis of the late 1840s can examined by comparing the census return for 1841 with that for 1851.[32] In 1841 the population of the two townlands was 829 and a decade later it was 575, a decline of 30.6 per cent. The rural population of Ballynahalisk fell by 30 per cent and of Ballyvoddy by 23.7 per cent, while that of Rockmills declined by 33 per cent. This fall was very much in line with similar townlands in the vicinity: that of Scart fell by 27 per cent and of Oldcastletown by 32 per cent. But the general trend does mask features peculiar to certain areas and the individual circumstances of each townland had a major impact on its experience of the famine. Ransborough, the third townland of the parish, suffered a major clearance in its population, which fell 74 per cent in a decade from seventy to eighteen persons, apparently in response to the policy of its landlord, Kilner Brazier; having been in dispute with his tenants over rents, he seems to have taken the opportunity offered by the crisis to clear his lands; this small townland of 137 acres, which in the 1840s was divided into about ten farms, was by 1851 comprised of just one.[33] Similar clearances seem to have taken place locally in other crowded townlands, like Cullenagh to the north of Kildorrery and Ballyenahan, just across the Funcheon.[34]

What was the response of the local community to demographic change of the nature outlined above? What was the impact on land holding both of rapid population growth from 1766 to 1841 and of the steady decline that set in for the rest of the century? Some of the answers to these questions can be attempted by examining records of landholding, especially the tithe applotment books of the late 1820s/early 1830s and the land valuation documents of the late 1840s and 1850s (see Table 1).

Table 1 Farm size in Ballynahalisk *c.*1830 and 1851

Farm Size	c. 1830	1851
≤ 5 acres	1	0
6–10 acres	4	1
11–20 acres	4	3
21–50 acres	9	5
50+ acres	2	4
Total no. of farms	20	13
Mean farm size	26 acres	40.6 acres

32 *Census of Ireland, 1851,* county Cork, p. 82. **33** VO, Field book for St Nathlash.
34 *Census of Ireland, 1851,* county Cork, p. 82; The antiquarian J. Windele was distressed to happen upon the eviction of nine families from a farm at Ballyenehan held by the Hydes of Castlehyde near Fermoy. He fled the scene to seek out more old ruins! See 'Windele manuscripts' in *JCHAS,* ser. ii, vol. iii (1897), p. 377.

Virtually all the land of Ballynahalisk was rated for tithe (*c.*524 acres out of
531). There were forty-two cottier households and twenty farming households
returned.[35] Farm size ranged from the three acres held by Patrick Roache to the
ninety-five acres held by John Nagle. The mean or average size of farm holdings
was about twenty-six acres. It appears that a number of the holdings were held
by members of the same family, indicating that the response of some families to
the pressure on resources caused by population growth was to subdivide holdings.
Conor and Charles O'Brien shared forty-five acres equally between them;
Michael and William Burns held thirty-seven acres and twenty-one acres respectively; Edmund Roache held thirteen acres and Patrick Roache held three;
Maurice Sweeney held twenty acres and Bryan Sweeney held twenty-two. A
consecutive list of cottier households appears to include only the villagers in
Rockmills. It may be that rural labourers who sublet land from the farmers were
excluded from the tithe applotment (which may also explain the seven or so
acres not accounted for).

Table 2   Main landholders in Ballynahalisk *c.*1830 and *c.*1850.

Tithe	Applotment Book c.1830	Acres	Griffith Valuation c.1850	Acres
	Mrs Oliver	75	Sarah Oliver	69
	John Nagle	96	Johanna Nagle	98
	Daniel Hannan	49	Daniel Hannin	94
	John Stackpole	43	T.B. Leader [in fee]	37
	Michael Burns	37	T.B. Gardiner Esq	21
	William Burns	21	Charles Brien	67
	Bryan Sweeney	22	John Smith	14
	Maurice Sweeney	20	Edward Roche	26
	Conor Brien	21	Charles Conroy	12
	Charles Brien	21	David Keeffe	43
	Redmond Barry	21	Maurice Cronin	21
	George Smith	14	Charles Kearney	15
	James Graddy	13		
	Edmund Roache	13		
	Patrick Roache	3		
	Arthur Keeffe	13		
	William Jackson	9		
	Patrick Foley	9		
	David Sheehan	8		
	John Lundergan	7		

In the notebooks for the first valuation of tenements, carried out between 1848
and 1850, the number of farms listed had declined from twenty to seventeen and

35 NA, TAB, county Cork, parish of St Nathlash (on microfilm, film 12, 6E/10).

the mean size of farms has risen from twenty-six to thirty-one acres.[36] Although many of the tenant farming families listed in the tithe books continued to hold land some significant changes had occurred. Some farms remained unchanged, like the Smith farm of fourteen acres, or the joint Sweeney holdings. Other holdings appear to have declined in size, like the holding of Daniel Hannin, which went from forty-nine to twenty-nine acres. Some new tenants appeared – including Maurice Cronin (holding twelve acres) and Charles Conroy (holding seven acres), while others disappeared. A notable feature of this valuation is the way in which each tenant farmer is recorded as having sublet a little land to one or more labouring families, from whom he can be presumed to have received domestic and farm labour in return.

By the time that Griffith's *Valuation* was published in 1851 a more drastic process of consolidation had emerged.[37] There were now only thirteen farms remaining in the townland with a mean farm size of over forty acres. Two farming family names – Burns and Sweeney – had disappeared; some appear to have been reduced to cottier status – like Patrick Fitzpatrick, James Grady and Jerry Coghlan; while others, like Charles Conroy (from seven to twelve acres) and David Keeffe (from twenty-seven to forty-two acres) had increased their holdings. A number of holdings seem to have increased dramatically in size, especially that of Daniel Hannin (from twenty-nine to ninety-three acres) and of Charles Brien (from twenty-six to sixty-seven acres).

It would seem from these records of landholding that the famine period was one of great crisis in Ballynahalisk, with huge fluctuations in the fortunes of individual farming families. Some families were defeated by the crisis and either descended into the labouring class or left the area, while others were able to profit from it to increase the size of their holdings. The case of Charles Conroy is unusual. Recorded as a villager with no land *c.*1830, by *c.*1848 he held a small farm of seven acres, and by 1851 he had increased it to twelve acres. This acreage remained in the Conroy family into the early twentieth century. Indeed the most remarkable aspect of the shakeout in farm holdings was that, once the immediate crisis had passed, both the size of farms and the families who held them were to remain virtually unchanged for the remainder of the century. The community response to the famine crisis was to impose a far more rigid landholding structure that ensured family farms were rarely subdivided again. In most cases this appears to have been organised by passing them on to the eldest son.

If the famine crisis led to consolidation of family farms and to the virtual fossilising of farm size what impact did it have on the labouring class in Ballynahalisk and Rockmills? The famine followed much the same course in north Cork as it did in other parts of the country, hitting the cottiers and subsistence farmers hardest. In the year to December 1846 the number of inmates in Fermoy

36 NA, Tenure book for parish of Nathlash, OL 6.0113, pp. 7–20. **37** Griffith, *Valuation* (Dublin, 1851), Union of Fermoy, parish of Nathlash, pp. 175–6.

workhouse nearly trebled and as early as May of that year a deputation from the town to the lord lieutenant was arguing for aid for the labourers of the town and for the 'vast influx of labourers of the poorest-class from the country'. Towns and villages were devastated. In January 1847 Mitchelstown was described in the starkest of terms: its deserted streets gave it 'the appearance of a town infested with the plague. No business, no trade but coffin making.'[38] Fever was a menace in Kildorrery by April 1847, with some 'forty cases scattered around in different quarters' and to keep order the relief committee found it necessary to put 'iron bars and palings at the house for giving out the rations'.[39]

The evidence from Griffith's *Valuation* and the subsequent valuation records in particular is that the poor of Ballynahalisk, both urban and rural, suffered most from the famine and its aftermath. In 1851 ten houses in the townland were listed as unoccupied; in 1855 this had doubled to twenty, most of them in the village of Rockmills, and the process continued inexorably thereafter, particularly in the village.[40] Most of the cottiers from outside the village who had been renting small plots from the farming families in the 1840s had disappeared from the records by the late 1860s and had not been replaced.

This decline in population after the famine poses the question of what became of those who left. Emigration seems to have been the most likely route taken, but little is known today of the number or destination of most of those who left. People seem to have scattered widely throughout the English-speaking world: most information suggests that America was the most popular destination, with New York and Connecticut among the most favoured locations there. One account states that thirteen young people left Rockmills for New York on one day early in this century. Only one returned: defeated by the 'clocking-in' routine of factory work, he chose the poorer but relatively unpressurised world of Rockmills where 'a man could slip in for a pint in the middle of the day and no-one would bother him'.[41]

The opportunities offered by America attracted the adventurous and ambitious as much as the very poor. Younger children of farmers and shopkeepers no longer had any prospects of a share in the family property and were often anxious to be off, a desire which is summed up in the words of the popular song 'Muirisheen Durkin', said to be written by one of the Kearneys of Ballyvoddy to a farm workman:

---

38 *Cork Examiner.* (hereafter cited as *CE*), 16 Dec. 1846; *CE*, 4 May 1846; *CE*, 29 Jan. 1847. **39** NA, C S.O.R.P. 1847, Box 1449, H 4674, 5560. It is difficult to conceive how, in January 1847, a tea importer in Cork city, who distributed to grocers in the distressed small towns of the county, including E. McSweeney of Kildorrery, could claim in an advertisement that 'The Public will readily admit [that the] greatest difficulty in Ireland is that of getting GOOD TEA'(*CE*, 1 Jan. 1847). Clearly, the effects of the famine were not equally apparent to all and many of the better off members of the county Cork community continued to live as normal. **40** VO, Cancellation book for parish of Nathlash, county Cork. **41** Interview with Brigid Ryan of Rockmills, August 1996.

Goodbye Muirisheen Durkin, sure I'm sick and tired of workin'
No more I'll dig the praties, no longer I'll be 'fool.
As sure as my name is Kearney I'll be off to California,
Instead of digging praties I'll be digging lumps of gold.[42]

V

The story of the village of Rockmills correlates closely with the story of the
Rock Mill. Growing up along the post road from Fermoy to Kilmallock and
Limerick around the employment and service opportunities provided by the
nearby mill, the village prospered and declined in tandem with the mill. It never
became much more than a straggling hamlet. As a one-industry 'town' the
economics of milling were the reason for its existence and the most powerful
influence on its development; from the 1840s and probably much earlier, these
economics were negative. There is no evidence that the village was ever more
than a poor one. By 1840 the Ordnance Survey namebook's description of
Rockmills is of 'a large number of houses which composes the village, without
any public buildings, not even a post office. There are neither fair nor market
held here. The houses are only in middling repair. The inhabitants live poorly.' In
1850 it was said to be 'declining much in business and wealth'.[43] To counteract
the decline of the mill it needed another economic enterprise and a patron or
developer but got neither. The crossroads market village of Kildorrery, less than
two miles away, attracted most of the public and private investment that came to
the district. The mill owner (at first Aldworth and later Oliver) was not the main
landowner in the vicinity and Rockmills Lodge was usually only his second
home. Whatever hopes of developing the village community he may have had
(and Richard Aldworth's involvement in supporting a church and school in the
village indicates some interest), he did not even own the strips of land outside
his demesne wall on which the village developed.

The field book compiled by the valuation officers in 1848 recorded that the
mill was being rented by P.L. Lyster at £300 a year and was 'a very extensive
concern and in good repair, having a new water wheel of very great power …
and has abundant water to work it, driving six pair of stones, and all the
necessary machinery thro'out the year'.[44] In the first printed valuation it was
valued at £178, or over twice the value of the largest local farm (Johanna
Nagle's ninety-seven acres were worth £88).[45]

The rest of the mill's story is one of decline. By 1855 its value had reduced to
£160 and by 1863 to £110, after its then owner, Charles Oliver, complained that

42 Interview with Jack Walsh, formerly of Rockmills, November 1996. **43** OS,
Namebooks, county Cork no. 35, p. 7 [NLI, microfilm pos. 1037]; VO, Field book for the
parish of Nathlash. **44** VO, Field book for the parish of Nathlash. **45** Griffith,
Valuation, pp. 175–7.

he had paid £1500 for it and had laid out a further £1000 on improvements but
that its workload was reduced from seven pairs of stones to four. In 1869 its
value was further reduced, to £90, after further representations from Oliver:

> … now there is scarcely any wheat grown about and all the wheat grown
> has to be brought from Cork at great expense & the advantages that the
> Fermoy and Mallow mills derive from the railways enable them to
> monopolise almost all the trade of this country.[46]

Oliver leased the mill to at least three different tenants in the 1860s and tried to
sell his failing concern in 1870. Its value continued to reduce, to £60 in 1870
and to £40 in 1873 and it was reported as 'going rapidly to ruin, not likely to
be worked again'.[47] For a time a brief revival took place when the mill was
taken over by Patrick Mahony, an entrepreneur from nearby Kildorrery, and its
value increased to £60 in 1877. But the decline resumed as depression hit in
1879 and by 1891 the mill was worth only £20, being 'idle except for a month
in springtime when it is used for crushing oats'.[48] Thereafter it fell into ruin,
although the mill race was used for a brief time in the early 1900s as a hatching
station for salmon fry. This was a sub-station of a salmon hatchery further
downriver at Lismore which was under the supervision of C.D. Oliver, then
owner of the Rock Mill.[49]

As mentioned already, there are no records of employment to help gauge the
value of the mill as a local employer. Although it has been suggested that these
large corn mills did not employ more than a dozen workers it is likely that a
good deal of seasonal and casual work would have been available.[50] The very
existence of the village of Rockmills is an indication of the presence to some
degree of a rural proletariat which supplemented its income by working in the
mill or by offering goods and services to incoming farmers and carters. Lodgings
were a particular service on offer in the village; in the 1841 census twenty-seven
males in the town returned their occupations under that heading.[51] A note in
the census report of 1871 argues that a small increase in the population of
Ballynahalisk was 'chiefly attributable to more extensive employment being
afforded in a flour mill in the locality', although the valuation evidence above
appears to contradict this.[52]

VI

What was the relationship between the rural proletariat so clearly identified in
the sources and the farmers, the other major social group who lived in the

---

47 Cancellation book for parish of Nathlash. **47** Ibid. **48** Ibid. **49** C.D. Oliver,
Report on the salmon hatchery at Lismore, Annual Report on Fisheries, Ireland, 1902–3, pt ii,
app. xi, pt iii (1905). **50** L.M. Cullen, *An economic history of Ireland since 1660* (Dublin,
1972), p. 99. **51** *Census of Ireland 1841*, county Cork, pp. 180–1. **52** *Census of Ireland
1871*, county Cork, p. 179, footnote c.

locality? It is difficult to examine in detail what relations between these two groups were like for much of the period under study but there are undoubtedly some indications of tensions between them at times of agrarian crisis.

The border areas of county Cork were affected by Whiteboy activity in the early 1760s, causing the bishop of Cloyne to condemn 'the different bands of nocturnal rioters ... entirely composed of the loose and desperate sort of people, of different professions and communions' who roamed the countryside, implying that the more substantial people like the strong farmers were on the side of law and order.[53] The eruptions of 1798 also affected the district and local big houses became the focus of local discontent. A nephew of the owner of nearby Stannard's Grove, staying to prevent it being 'plundered of arms and property', was 'most barbarously murdered ... as he was fishing in the river Funcheon'. A surprise attack on the home of the Bowen family three miles away at Bowenscourt in Farrahy was anticipated and repulsed and the insurgents 'bolted back the way they had come', leaving one of their number dead in a pear tree outside the house. Years later it emerged that, as they returned home, they had secretly buried their dead leader in the graveyard at Rockmills (in the bag in which they had intended to carry home their booty!).[54]

There were widespread agrarian outrages in north Cork in the early 1820s and particularly in the baronies of Fermoy and Condons & Clangibbons, sparked mainly by a severe downturn in agricultural prices. Protest was expressed by opposition to tithes and to any diminution of the traditional rights of small-holders and labourers. The countryside was in a state of near anarchy for several years. 'Not a night passes without burnings in some direction, within view of this post', complained the local magistrate from behind the walls of Bowenscourt.[55] In March 1822 it was reported that 'a large body of insurgents appeared at Mr Aldworth's gate at Rockmills and swore several of the inhabitants of the village and neighbourhood' to obedience to their emblematic leader, Captain Rock.[56]

A notice posted in Rockmills in September 1824 clearly laid out the agenda (as well as the methods) of 'General Rock':

> ... no man is allowed to take tithes or overhold any farmers or dispossess poor families, until the year 1825 is over. You are hereby required to take notice ... you do not give up your tithe or tithes. I will visit you with a sufficient force to devour you and every one of you. We will not be going to the trouble of hanging or burning, but finish you off, the same as Thomas, Margaret and Henry Mansfield Franks if you put me to the disagreeable necessity ...[57]

---

53 NA, M 5036a, pp. 545–55. **54** *Saunder's Newsletter*, 23 March 1798, quoted in Col. J. Grove-White, *Historical and topographical notes etc.* (photographic reprint, Birmingham, Alabama, 1969 of 4 vols, Cork 1905–1925), iv, 226; Elizabeth Bowen, *Bowen's Court* (London, 1942), pp. 159–60. **55** NA, State of the Country Papers (hereafter cited as SOCP), 2512/13. **56** NA, SOCP 2345/32. **57** NA, SOCP 2616/38.

These threats would have been taken seriously by the farmers for whom they were intended, as the reference to the Franks family underlines. The Protestant family's house at Lisnagourneen – Thomas Franks was a land agent for Lord Kingston – was attacked five times in the month of January 1822, apparently by tenants whose cattle had been seized in lieu of rent; it was again raided in December and the attackers burned thirteen acres of oats, six acres of wheat and three acres of hay; and in 1823 all three members of the family were brutally murdered in their home.[58] In January 1824 the Frazier family farm in Ballyvoddy was attacked by a number of local labourers, including one armed with a bayonet, and was destroyed by fire.[59] In November, the house of Ballyvoddy's most prominent landholder and middleman, Michael Kearney, was set on fire and his barn, containing 'the produce of two and a half acres of barley, seized from one of his tenants last week for rent', was destroyed.[60]

The influence of the Catholic clergy on the farmers and their advocacy of the methods of the Catholic Association, along with the detrimental effect the disturbances were having on farmer prosperity, came to weaken the rural front against tithes. One report from north Cork suggested that a 'temporary and partial disunion has commenced between the farmers and the labouring classes, the latter being still discontented and ready for any innovation...'. An incident in Ballynahalisk in 1825 seemed to confirm this belief, in which a farmer called James Fox repulsed an attack on his home by armed men and was recommended for an award of ten pounds 'as the best species of encouragement to effectual personal resistance amongst the farmers to the system of robbery which exists solely among the labourers'.[61]

During the famine of the late 1840s evidence of similar tensions can be seen between the farming and labouring classes. The propertied classes, overwhelmed by the crisis, squabbled over who should pay to alleviate it and stoutly defended their respective interests. At meetings of Fermoy Union the landlords claimed they could give no more without bankrupting themselves and the middle classes argued that, while at least the labourers could draw a day's pay, 'the farming class were placed between two fires as it were, the demand for labour on the one hand, and the demand for rent on the other'.[62] There is evidence of considerable insecurity among the farmers on the ground. At the petty assizes held in Kildorrery during the height of the famine in 1847, for instance, one entire session was taken up with vociferous complaints from farmers against the poor who were stealing their turnips from the fields. A story surviving in the folklore of Ballynahalisk in the 1930s tells of a poor man caught stealing turnips by a farmer in the neighbouring townland of Derryvillane, who was arrested and sentenced to six months in prison, while his wife and eight children were left to die in their house. Unsurprisingly the Rock Mill features in the folklore of the famine, most poignantly in the story of an employee caught stealing flour who

58 NA, SOCP 2345/32, 2347/49; NA, M 2631, ff 13–14.   **59** NA, SOCP 2614/8.
60 NA, SOCP 2617/33, 39.   **61** NA, SOCP 2617/49; 2726/7.   **62** *CE*, 4 Sept. 1846.

jumped in despair onto the revolving mill wheel. Incidents like these help to explain the view taken of many farmers by the head of the Kildorrery relief committee, who wrote angrily to the government about the failure of the well-to-do farmers to help the poor, and described local jobbers and middlemen 'as cruel as they are worthless and selfish'.[63]

For the hard-pressed farmers of the Kildorrery area the years immediately after the worst of the famine brought little improvement and so, suffering from rampant sheep-stealing and heavy poor rates, they were not inclined to come to the aid of those even poorer than themselves; thus they were reported in the *Cork Examiner* in 1849 as refusing 'to give any sort of relief to the poor creatures who crawl about demanding it'.[64]

The relationship between the farming and labouring classes in Ballynahalisk becomes less easy to trace after the crisis of the famine. The balance of economic power in the countryside swung decisively in favour of the strong tenant farmers but for the smaller number of labourers who remained there was more certainty of regular work. It would seem that Ballynahalisk settled into a more balanced and more predictable pattern of life, punctuated by various local social, economic and political events. When the farmers bought out their farms under the Wyndham land act early in the twentieth century they merely sealed the local dominance that they held after the famine.

VII

The latest sources within the ambit of this study which can be used to recreate the social structure of the locality are the census returns of 1901 and 1911.[65] The most noticable feature of the class structure of Ballynahalisk and Ballyvoddy in these census returns is its continued division into two main social groups, namely a farming/shopkeeping class (or rural middle class), and a lower economic class made up of agricultural labourers, servants and other workers (or rural proletariat). As might be expected, close analysis of the 1901 census return for Ballynahalisk shows a clear gap between the groups in terms of housing quality and educational attainment.

According to the census of 1901 Ballynahalisk had 108 inhabitants, of whom 58 were females and 50 were males. There were twenty-eight households, ranging in size from a single person (four households) to eight people (one household) and averaging just under four people per household. Ten of these

---

63 *CE*, 30 Oct 1846, quoted in J.S. Donnelly, *The land and the people of nineteenth-century Cork* (London, 1975), p. 87; UCD, Folklore Commission, S. 375, p. 207; Mountmorres, Dean of Cloyne to govt., 1 Aug 1846 (NA, Outrage Reports, county Cork 1846, 6/21689).   **64** *CE*, 14 May 1849, quoted in J.S. Donnelly, *Nineteenth-century Cork*, p. 88. **65** NA, 1901 and 1911 census, county Cork 293/12 (Ballynahalisk) and 290/13 (Ballyvoddy).

households were returned as headed by a female and eighteen by a male. The balance of males and females by age group in the townland is shown below (Table 3). Males outnumber females in age groups up to nineteen years of age and again in the age group 50–9 but females predominate in all other age groups. This is probably due to male emigration in the younger age groups as well as to higher male mortality in the older age groups.

Table 3   Male/Female Balance by Age Range 1901

Age Range	No. of Males	No. of Females
0–9	12	10
10–9	11	10
20–9	9	11
30–9	2	7
40–9	3	4
50–9	9	6
60–9	4	6
70+	0	4

Out of the twenty-eight households returned in the census nine belong to the middle class and the remaining nineteen belong to the proletariat (including ten households dependent on income from agricultural or domestic labour). This ratio of one farming family to two labouring ones, incidentally, is the same as that recorded in the tithe applotment book about seventy years earlier.

A number of indicators can be used to separate these groups, especially housing quality and educational standards as measured by literacy. For the purpose of examining housing the population can be divided into three groups: A represents the middle class, B the agricultural labourers and C the general workers and craftsmen (which include two tin vendors, a hive-maker, a gardener and a carpenter).

Table 4   Mean Housing Standards by Social Group in 1901

Group	Rooms Occupied	Front Windows	Housing Class
A	4	3.125	2.125*
B	2.9	2.2	2.5
C	2	2	2.83
*1 = 1st class, i.e. best housing.			

These figures, not surprisingly, show a considerable gap between the housing standards of the middle and lower classes; more unexpected is the difference in housing between the agricultural labourers and general labourer/artisan group. The relative poverty of the latter category may be explained by the more precarious and casual nature of its employment.

Literacy returns can be used directly as a measure of educational attainment and indirectly as a likely indicator of relative social position. The literacy rate among the farming and shopkeeping families is 91 per cent for persons over seven years of age. The rate of literacy among labourers and artisans is much lower at only 57 per cent.

Both levels bear witness to the success of the national school system by the early twentieth century. An increase in literacy in Nathlash is recorded in the census reports from 1841. In 1841 only 33 per cent of those aged five or over in the parish were returned as literate; this figure rose to 56 per cent in 1881 and to 70 per cent in 1891.[66] This improvement can also be measured in Ballynahalisk by age group in 1901. While only 40 per cent of people who give ages of fifty years or over are returned as fully literate (able to read and write), this figure increases to 62.5 per cent of people between the ages of thirty and forty-nine and to 92 per cent of those aged ten to twenty-nine.

The state of the Irish language in the townland in 1901 can also be traced on the basis of age groups. Nobody is returned as Irish-speaking only. In all, 23 per cent of the population claim an ability to speak Irish. Of those who are listed as aged fifty or over 50 per cent claim to be bilingual but only 6.25 per cent (that is, one person out of sixteen) of those aged between thirty and forty nine make the same claim. In the age group between ten and twenty nine the bilingual return rises slightly to 10 per cent. An interesting (if statistically insignificant) factor in this age group is that all those who are returned as speaking Irish are from farming, not labouring, backgrounds, a possible pointer to the success of the Irish-Ireland movement among the rural middle class.

VIII

One feature of the locality that remains to be examined is the question of whether it was open or closed, that is whether immigration was a regular feature in the life of the community. Reference has already been made to the open nature of the area in geographical terms and in respect of land ownership from early Christian times, both of which suggested a considerable degree of openness. But did this extend to the occupying community, whether farmers, labourers or craftsmen?

The marriage patterns for the early nineteenth century already examined above give one indication of the extent of the community's horizons. An examination of surname survival can be another form of evidence. A number of sources give lists of surnames of households in these two townlands, from the 1766 religious census to the 1911 census. There are thirty-five different surnames among the forty-five households listed in Nathlash in 1766.[67] Those appearing more than

66 *Census of Ireland 1841, 1881, 1891*, county Cork.   **67** NA, TAB for St Nathlash, microfilm 12 6E/10; NA, 1901 census, county Cork, 290/12–13; NA, 1911 census, county Cork, 293/12–13.

once are (O')Brien, Keeffe and Norry (three times each), and Carroll, Connor(s), Curtin and Hennessy (twice each) and it is interesting to note that (assuming Norry to be a version of Norris) all of these survive in the wider parish of Kildorrery today. Out of these thirty-five surnames listed in 1766 only six occur in all lists up to 1911 (viz. O'Brien, Meade, Nagle, Roche, Sheehan and Sweeney), an indication of considerably more change than continuity. Two tables can be drawn up using the 1766 and 1911 lists as respective starting points to measure the rate of surname change.

Table 5   1766 Surnames Recurring to 1911 (%)

Year	No. of Surnames	% Re-occurring
1766	35	100
c.1830	12	34
1851	14	40
1901	9	26
1911	8	23

Table 6   1911 Surnames Recurring to 1766 (%)

Year	No. of Surnames	% Re-occurring
1911	27	100
1901	26	96
1851	14	52
c.1830	11	41
1766	8	30

The evidence of these tables points to a considerable turnover in surnames during this period, even allowing for continuity via the female line. It suggests a relatively open society with changeover in property occurring frequently. Taking a narrower perspective, that of farming families with over five acres of land, who might be expected to have the biggest stake in continuity, an examination of landholders from the 1830s tithe lists to the census of 1911 suggests a significant changeover in holdings over seventy-five years – not all of which can be acc-ounted for by consolidation and amalgamation of holdings. In Ballyvoddy only two farming surnames, Kearney and Meade, survived; likewise in Ballynahalisk, only two surnames, Nagle and Roche, survived without interruption. Some cross-townland movement seems to occur, with the Cronin family crossing from Ballyvoddy to Ballynahalisk and the Stackpoles going the opposite way, but this does not go anywhere near explaining the rate of change.

However it is important not to set too much store on this evidence in itself, especially in the key area of farm holdings. While it seems clear that there was a good deal of fluidity up to the 1840s, from the immediate post famine period to the early twentieth century there occured a very marked continuity in the holding of land. Of the thirteen farms listed in Griffith's *Valuation* or in the 1850s revisions eight were still held in the same family name (Kearney, Smith, Cronin, Gould, Conroy, Brien, Roche and Oliver) in 1901 and most of the rest appear to have changed only through marriage or inheritance by maternal relatives.

The information given on individuals' birthplaces in the census of 1901 and 1911 is another indicator of the open or closed nature of the townland. Although a clear majority of the inhabitants appear native to the area, a significant minority was born outside the vicinity. Daniel Dineen, agricultural labourer, was a native of Bandon and John Grace, agricultural labourer, came from county Limerick, as did Catherine Murphy, a seventy-two year old widow. One farmer, John Caughlin, was born in Kerry, while his wife and eldest (fourteen year old) son were born in West Cork. He appears to have been at one time an RIC officer in the locality.[68] In all there is evidence of immigration in five out of twenty-seven households (18.5 per cent). By 1911 this number increased to eight out of twenty-five households (32 per cent), including the return of Joseph Jackson, agricultural labourer, born in county Dublin, who seems to have married a local woman, and the O'Briens, Patrick and Ellen, a young farming couple, who appear to have immigrated from county Limerick.

IX

What indications are there of the religious life of the community? The place-name connections with St Molaga and the survival of the placename *Temple an Aunlaunogh* in Ballyvoddy into the eighteenth century indicates that one or both of these townlands held an ecclesiastical site, most probably where the graveyard is sited.[69] In pre-reformation times surviving references to the area seem to refer to an area roughly contiguous with the later civil parish of Nathlash, like a reference to 'Atlysmolag' in a fourteenth-century plea roll. On the evidence of medieval taxation rolls it held no more than a small parish church, worth two marks in 1292, only half the value of nearby Cachoyrdunan (Carrigdownane).[70] It is likely that the medieval parish church and adjacent graveyard survived into the modern era and was appropriated, even if nominally, by the Established Church.

Nevertheless, the area seems to have continued as a Catholic centre during penal times, still largely organised around the old medieval parishes. There are contemporary records of a Catholic mass house in both Carrigdownane and in either Nathlash or Templemologa in 1731, and of one in the townland of Ballyvoddy in 1762, possibly near the graveyard at Rockmills.[71] In 1752 John

68 Interview with Jack Walsh, Nov 1996. **69** Liam Ó Buachalla, 'An early fourteenth-century placename list for Anglo-Norman Cork' in *Dinnseanchas*, ii, uimh. 2 (Nollaig, 1966), pp. 39, 43. **70** *Eight report on public records of Ireland* (1819), appendix 'Pope Nicholas taxation, 1292', p. 65. **71** 'Report on the state of Popery' in *Archivium Hibernicum*, ii (1913), p. 119; NA, M 5036a, p. 541.

O'Brien, bishop of Cloyne and Ross and a native of Ballyvoddy, erected a gravestone there 'over the remains of his parents' which can still be seen. This graveyard apparently continued in use as a Catholic one until a Protestant church was built within it in 1812, reinforcing the likelihood of the site being that of the old medieval parish church. William Lyne was recorded as 'Popish priest' at 'Ballynahaless' in 1760 and as late as 1820 Revd James Lane is recorded as living or serving in Rockmills.[72]

A survival of popular religion recorded in the folklore was the holy well called 'Kearney's Well' near the bank of the river in Ballyvoddy, water from which was said to cure eye ailments. An echo of the old placename link with St Molaga can be heard in a legend about a trout living in this well which was similar to one about St. Molaga's Well at Aghacross, a couple of miles to the north.[73]

In the nineteenth century the local centre of Catholic worship moved north-wards from Rockmills. This was in part due to the increasing importance of the crossroads and market village of Kildorrery; the Catholic chapel for the area in the early nineteenth century had been sited on the border of the townlands of Scart and Meadstown, equidistant from both Rockmills and Kildorrery but in the late 1830s a new chapel was built in Kildorrery itself.[74] Although its position can be explained by the central geographic and economic position of the village in the Catholic parish of Kildorrery, perhaps an element of religious tension was also responsible for the abandonment of Rockmills to the Established Church. One can only speculate on the reasons for the takeover of the religious centre of Rockmills by the Protestant community; an intention by the Aldworths to create a little Protestant haven around their demesne looks most likely.

Earliest references to a post-reformation religious infrastructure suggest that Nathlash was not fertile for Protestant settlement. During the seventeenth century it appears to have been subsumed into neighbouring parishes, usually Carrigdownane, and was served by an absentee. A visiting bishop recorded the 'church and chancel down' in 1615; late in the century it was reported that both Kildorrery and Nathlash were 'out of repair since the rebellion of 1641'; and a visitor to the area in the 1840s reported a local tradition that the Protestant population of Carrigdownane had been murdered at that time.[75]

The hearth tax return of 1762 gives a total of four Protestant families in Carrigdownane, while the religious census of 1766 records only one Protestant family, that of Michael O'Brien, living in Nathlash itself. In 1785 only six

72 W[illiam?]. C[arrigan?]., 'The old priests: gleanings from documents in the P.R O., Dublin, pt ii', in *JCHAS*, ser. ii, vol. iv (1898), p. 214. **73** UCD, Dept. of Folklore, S. 375, pp. 163–7. **74** Samuel Lewis, *Topographical dictionary of Ireland* (2 vols, London, 1837), ii, 88, states that the chapel near Kildorrery was about to be rebuilt; by 1839 the village contained a 'very handsome R.C. chapel'; cf. OS field book quoted in Col. J. Grove-White, *Historical and Topographical notes*, ii, 286. **75** M.A. Murphy (ed.), 'The Royal Visitation of Cork, Cloyne, Ross and the college of Youghal' in *Archivium*

Protestants were recorded as living in the parish and by 1805 this number had fallen to two.[76] A remarkable increase in the local Protestant population, or hopes of one, seems to have led to the building in 1812 of a church in Rockmills capable of accommodating one hundred people. This apparent explosion in the Protestant population can be partly explained by a need to cater for a wider catchment area than Nathlash alone – Carrigdownane, for example – but it is nevertheless puzzling. Some hint is given by looking at who sponsored the building: Richard Aldworth, mill owner and prominent resident of Rockmills Lodge – although not owner of more than seventy statute acres in Ballynahalisk – who obtained a gift of money from the Board of First Fruits for building the structure and who fitted out the interior at his own expense.[77] Perhaps encouraging Protestant immigration to the locality was part of the role he saw for himself as a well known 'improver' and loyalist stalwart.

The parish register, which began on 18 Oct 1812, is now the best indicator of the size and structure of the Protestant community centred around Nathlash (Table 7).

Table 7   Numbers of Baptisms, Marriages & Deaths in Nathlash, 1812–76

Decade beginning	Baptisms	Marriages	Deaths
1812	13	6	4
1822	29	9	*c.*12
1832	22	4	1
1842	14	4	4
1852	10	5	3
1862	7	1	2
1872	4	0	1

On the evidence of this register the community seems to reached a peak during the 1820s and 1830s and it declined steadily after that.[78] This is confirmed by other sources, which report a Protestant congregation of sixty-two in 1834 declining to twenty-six (with an average of nine monthly communicants) by 1860, to thirteen by 1871 and to only four by 1881.[79] The church building, with the

Hibernicum, ii (1913), p. 199; Brady, *Records*, ii, 363; Anon., 'Irish rivers–no. iv, the Funcheon', in *Dublin University Magazine*, xxix (1847), p. 184; no depositions are recorded from either Nathlash or Carrigdownane according to the list of Cork depositions drawn up by Nicholas Canny in the appendix to his article 'The 1641 depositions ...' in Patrick O'Flanagan and C.G. Buttimer (eds), *Cork history and society* (Dublin, 1993), pp. 281–307. **76** NA, M 5036a, pp. 223, 541; Brady, *Records*, ii, 365.   **77** Brady, *Records*, ii, 366.   **78** NA, M 2631 ('extracts' from register 1812–76 by Col. James Grove-White).   **79** Brady, *Records*, ii, 365–7; Guy's *Cork and Munster directories* 1871, 1881.

exception of the steeple, was demolished in 1889, the remaining few Protestants having abandoned it over ten years previously for the church at Farrahy, near Bowenscourt, about three miles away. It seems unlikely that there were ever more than a few Protestant families resident in the parish itself.

The most convincing indication of this is found in the parochial school return of 1824 – on the face of it the highest point of Protestant worship at Nathlash – when only eight of the seventy one children (eleven per cent) attending school in the village of Rockmills were members of the Established Church.[80]

It is difficult to find any documentary evidence to explain why the Protestant community based around Nathlash declined so precipitously after the 1830s. The decline of the flour mill may offer a partial explanation, as may the general decline in population through emigration after the famine. The strong recovery in Catholic prestige and economic power during the nineteenth century may also have helped to reduce Protestant numbers. Interdenominational rivalry seems to have been a significant feature of life in the Blackwater valley from the early eighteenth century as a relatively numerous and cohesive Catholic gentry resisted a militantly Protestant settlement.[81] This hostility was probably replicated among tenant farmers and labourers and may have made widespread Protestant settlement more difficult. Echoes remained in the folklore collected in the 1930s of a belief that the local Church of Ireland leadership had attempted on occasion to coerce Catholics to convert. One story tells how a Catholic woman resisted proselytism by reciting aloud the rosary at a Protestant service she was obliged to attend.[82]

It can be argued that a strong thread of religious hostility became apparent during periods of agrarian and political unrest in the vicinity of Rockmills. There is some evidence of sectarianism in the 1820s, in particular during the period early in the decade when the sectarian milleniarism associated with the so-called 'prophesies' of Pastorini overlaid the Rockite movement. In one infamous case, a group of soldiers' wives in transit were stopped and raped just outside Kildorrery in February 1822 in what appears to have been primarily a 'political' action by Rockites, who seem to have specifically sought out Protestant victims. Other, more everyday, instances of sectarian feeling were reported: two men were arrested in a public house in Kildorrery on the day after Christmas 1823 for singing a ballad which included a call to 'tear Orangemen and Protestants to pieces'; and a notice posted on the gates of Bowenscourt in June 1824 warned that 'Capten Rock is going to comence to kill all the Protestants [he] will find [and] burn them alive in their houses'.[83]

80 *Second report of the commissioners of Irish education enquiry*, appendix (parochial abstracts), HC 1826–7 (12).   **81** The strong Catholic landlord presence even at the height of the penal laws is discussed in detail by L.M. Cullen, 'The Blackwater Catholics ...' in O'Flanagan and Buttimer (eds), *Cork: history and society*, pp. 535–84.   **82** UCD, Dept. of Folklore, M. 1086, p. 209.   **83** J.S. Donnelly, 'Pastorini and Captain Rock' in Samuel Clark and J.S. Donnelly (eds), *Irish Peasants: violence and political unrest 1780–1914* (Manchester, 1983), pp. 114, 123, 134–5.

But the balance of evidence suggests that class motives were at least as important in these outbreaks as sectarian ones. One spokesman for the Whiteboys in 1786 probably expressed the exasperated feelings of many of the peasantry of the district thus:

> The luxurious parson drowned in the riot of his table the bitter groans of those wretches that his proctor fleeced, and the poor remnant of the proctor's rapine was sure to be gleaned by the rapacious priest … Thus plundered by either clergy, we had reason to wish for our simple druids again.[84]

X

One incident which might be said to sum up many of the themes that have been explored in this study, including those of class, religion and emigration, and also to illustrate the fierce love of place among the community there is worth recounting. A story is told of 'the tyrant George Bunloe', a local Protestant squireen who took pleasure in humiliating his social inferiors. One day he tried to horsewhip a group of men from Rockmills whose game of road bowls blocked his way but he was pulled from his horse and thrashed by one of their number. The miscreant was sheltered locally, dressed up as a priest and smuggled out of Queenstown, never to return to Ireland. The following verses from a local song give voice to his sense of loss on hearing from home:

> When after years of weary toil in a far off distant land
> How cheerful was that welcome news from a fond and cherished land
> Where the river Funcheon proudly flows in majestic rippling rill
> Where the blackbird sings his merry notes in the glens of sweet Rockmills
>
> Rockmills it was a sporting spot as well you understand
> Such festive dance and jubilee was not throughout the land
> At Clifford's reel and jig house where oft times I did stray
> But like a midnight vision it now has passed away.[85]

Like the emigrant represented in this song people from Ballynahalisk and Rockmills remembered and still remember with most fondness not the ills that beset them but the simple pastimes they enjoyed together, such as road bowling,

---

84 Copy of letter from Whiteboys to Rt. Hon. Silver Oliver in Theophilius [Patrick Duigenan], *An address to the nobility and gentry of the Church of Ireland* (2nd ed. Dublin, 1787), p. 110. 85 Interview with Jack Walsh, November 1996; UCD, Dept. of Folklore, S. 375, p. 159. The reference to George 'Bunloe' appears to be to George Bond Low, a local landowner who was active against agrarian societies during the Tithe War.

throwing weights over the mill, carrying weights across the stepping stones, fishing, storytelling, singing and dancing. They enjoyed a strong and vibrant community life and Rockmills remained a noted centre for crossroads dancing until the advent of dance halls. In 1914 the area is said to have fielded a junior hurling team which reached the Cork county championship final.[86]

Like the emigrant's vision, much about the area has now passed away. In particular, its population today is much smaller than it was even in 1901 as ever-increasing farm mechanisation encouraged an increase in farm size and at the same time reduced the labouring population to a very small number. But a community still remains that recognises itself as the heirs, in many cases literally, of those who once lived there. It continues to live off the same land, and recognises the same landmarks as those who have gone. Although, as ever, the people identify with the larger communities of parish, diocese, county or nation, they know too that they belong to a townland called Ballynahalisk and a village called Rockmills.

86 UCD, Dept. of Folklore, S. 375; Interview with Jack Walsh, November 1996.

Cloncurry, county Kildare

KARINA HOLTON

INTRODUCTION

Travellers on the N4 route from Dublin to Galway are for the most part un-
aware of the history and significance of the area surrounding the small crossroads
one mile east of Enfield. Cloncurry is situated on the northern edge of Kildare
along the border with county Meath. The area has had a long and chequered
past, its documented history extending from the early Christian period to the
modern day, including Anglo-Norman settlement, growth and decline in the
Middle Ages, connections with the Ormond estates, and later ownership by the
Aylmer and Lawless families. The area is distinctive in that its medieval past is
documented in detail in an extent taken in 1304 which was subsequently
published in *The Red Book of Ormond*.[1] Today, all that remains of its past are the
physical ruins and the earthworks in its fields. The Anglo-Norman motte still
stands close to the ruins of the old parish church and graveyard, while the sunken
or hollow way nearby, with its cross base of possible medieval origin, is the only
visible evidence of what was once a thriving and populous community.

The name Cloncurry refers to three different entities – the manor of Cloncurry,
the civil parish of Cloncurry and the townland of Cloncurry. It is with the
townland of Cloncurry and neighbouring Ballyvoneen and Ballinakill that this
essay is concerned. Now comprising some 163 acres, it is known from the Civil
Survey that Cloncurry once included the townlands of Ballyvoneen (636 acres)
and Ballinakill (619 acres) which lie to the south and southeast respectively. The
present townland of Cloncurry forms part of Kildare's northern border with
county Meath. It is bounded on its western and northern sides by the Ballycarn
river, a tributary of the Blackwater, which, while initially flowing westward,
turns sharply to the south at the north western edge of the townland. The river
forms the county boundary with Meath at this point. This boundary is an
ancient one and was described by Geoffrey Keating as follows:

> *ordained in the beginning, to wit, as the river Liffey goes from Dublin to the river
> Rye and from that westward to Cloncurry in Uí Faoláin and from Cloncurry in
> Uí Faoláin westward … to the confluence at Clonard …*[2]

Due to its strategic location, straddling as it did the ancient kingdoms of Meath
and Leinster, Cloncurry has enjoyed a long and varied history.

1 *The Red Book Of Ormond*, ed. Newport B. White (Dublin 1932), pp. 27–34. **2** 'A
fragment used by Keating' in *Archivium Hibernicum*, i (1912), pp. 1–10.

ORIGIN OF THE TOWNLAND NAME

The name Cloncurry derives from the Irish *Cluain Conaire*, usually translated as
the meadow of Conaire or Conary. Unfortunately the identity of Conary has
been lost through the centuries. Early documents refer to the area as *Cluain
Conaire Tomain*. It is thought that this is an allusion to Maoinean or Ninian, a
saint who is reputed to have built a monastery in Cloncurry in the early fifth
century. The *Martyrology of Donegal* lists the 16th of September as the feast of
Maoineann, bishop of Cluain Conaire.[3] The name Cloncurry is spelt in many
different ways in various medieval documents. Some of the most frequently used
versions are Clonconry, Cloncunry and Cluncunneri.

Cloncurry is also known as Cloncurry-Offelan (Uí Faoláin). Uí Faoláin refers
to both the territory which comprised most of the northern half of the present
county of Kildare and the tribe who ruled that territory. While the name of the
area has been anglicized as Offelan or Ophelan, the family name became Magelan
or McGelan.

The Cloncurry area has been documented as early as the sixth century. In
AD 590 Bran Dubh McEaghagh, king of Leinster, defeated the Uí Neill in battle
on the hill above *Cluain Conairi Tomain*.[4] The Ulster Annals record a great royal
meeting at Cluain Conaire Tomain between Feidhlimidh, king of Cashel, and
Niall, king of Ireland, in 837. In the year 870 the death of Colgu, abbot of
Cloncurry, was also recorded.[5]

LAND QUALITY

The land lies at approximately 260 feet above sea level and today is fertile and
productive. In the Middle Ages the entire manor of Cloncurry (approximately
4000 acres) supported an estimated population of some 2000 people.[6] The
Extent of 1304 gives us a detailed account of how the land was farmed and of
the farming methods used at that time. Most of the land in the manor was in
tillage. A three-course rotation of cultivation was employed – fallow in the first
year, wheat in the second and oats in the third. A team of eight oxen would
plough twenty-five acres per season with the land being ploughed three times
for wheat and once for oats. The corollary of the manor being able to support
2000 people was the labour required for tillage production. The Extent refers to
people being required to sow and weed the crop, to scare the birds, to mow, tie

3 *The Martyrology of Donegal – A Calendar of the Saints of Ireland*, ed. John O'Donovan,
(Dublin, 1864), p. 249. **4** 'The Annals of Tigernach', ed. Whitley Stokes in *Revue
Celtique*, xvii (1896), p. 159. **5** *Annals of Ulster*, ed. William M. Hennessy and B.
MacCarthy (4 vols, Dublin, 1887–1901), i, 341, 385. **6** J. O'Loan, 'The Manor of
Cloncurry, county Kildare and the Feudal System of Land Tenure in Ireland' in
Department of Agriculture Journal, lviii (1961), pp. 14–36.

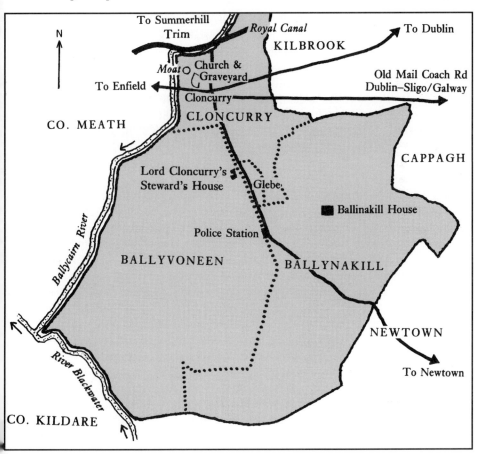

To Summerhill
Trim

Royal Canal

To Dublin

KILBROOK

N

Moat

Church &
Graveyard

Old Mail Coach Rd
Dublin–Sligo/Galway

To Enfield

Cloncurry

CLONCURRY

CO. MEATH

CAPPAGH

Lord Cloncurry's
Steward's House

Glebe

Ballinakill House

Police Station

Ballycairn River

BALLYVONEEN

BALLYNAKILL

NEWTOWN

To Newtown

River Blackwater

CO. KILDARE

Cloncurry, Ballinakill and Ballyvoneen, county Kildare, 1838, 1418 acres

and stook the straw, cart and stack in the haggard, thatch the stack, thresh and winnow. As well as the tillage, there was a small amount of pasture and meadow, while some of the land was scrubby and could not be used for anything.[7]

By the middle of the fourteenth century, many manorial settlements had declined as a result of the wars and upheavals in the country. The ensuing decades brought further war and neglect. An Inquisition dated 1657 stated that thirteen acres of glebe land in Cloncurry parish, which had been worth £40 in 1640, was worth only £11 seventeen years later.[8] In 1654 the Civil Survey recorded that the soil in the barony was generally low and wet and was 'indifferent good for corne and cattell'.[9] By 1833, the land in Cloncurry was mainly in pasture, while much of Ballyvoneen was described as moory or wet pasture. Ballinakill was used for both tillage and pasture land.[10] A Government survey of Irish bogs undertaken in the early nineteenth century shows that large parts of the town-lands of Ballyvoneen and Ballinakill were subject to flooding in winter time.[11] During his years as landlord in the first half of the nineteenth century, Valentine, Lord Cloncurry, had made great efforts to improve his whole estate. He began draining, building, planting and cultivating with the intention of '... surrounding [himself] with a prosperous and happy tenantry who occasioned [him] no uneasi-ness and put the state to but small cost for soldiers, police and lawyers'.[12] Lord Cloncurry was also involved in several agricultural societies and in the 1830s began to experiment with growing flax. It is known that he had samples of New Zealand flax sent to him by the marquis of Anglesey in June 1830.[13] In fact, a large field in Ballinakill is still known locally as the Flax Field. The *Parliamentary Gazetteer of Ireland* in 1846 observed that the '... general surface [of Cloncurry townland] is freely interspersed with bog, has a cold and tame appearance and prevailingly consists of poor or at least inferior soil'.[14] Today the land is used mainly for tillage and cattle fattening. Local drainage and modern agricultural methods have now rendered the relatively shallow soil quite fertile.

RELIGIOUS HISTORY OF THE TOWNLAND

The ecclesiastical history of Cloncurry begins in the era of St Patrick, when Ninian, a follower of St Martin of Tours, settled in the area sometime in the

7 Ibid.   **8** RCB Library, Mss Box N.2.24, Inquisitions, Kilcock Parish, f. 15.   **9** Robert Simington (ed.), *The Civil Survey ad 1654–1656*, vol. viii, County of Kildare, (Dublin, 1952), p. 197.   **10** NA, TAB, Parish of Cloncurry, County of Kildare (Great Cloncurry).   **11** Map of N.W. Kildare appended to *The First Report of the Commissioners appointed to enquire into the Nature and Extent of the Several Bogs in Ireland and the Practicability of Draining and Cultivating them*, vol. 1, A–H (Dublin, 1810).   **12** Lord Valentine Cloncurry, *Personal Recollections of the Life and Times with extracts from the Correspondence of Valentine Lord Cloncurry* (Dublin, 1850), p. 216.   **13** Letter from Marquis of Anglesey, quoted in *Life and Times of Lord Cloncurry*, p. 338.   **14** *The Parliamentary Gazetteer of Ireland 1844–45* (Dublin, 1846), i, 430.

early fifth century. It would appear that a monastery existed in Cloncurry until at least the year 869, when the death of Colgu, Abbot of Cloncurry, was recorded in the Annals.[15]

The Mac Fhaoláin family (anglicized as Magelan or Mackelan) feature prominently in the political and ecclesiastical history of the area. This family were without doubt connected to the Ui Faolain dynasty which originally ruled the area. They had adopted the tribal name from an ancestor named Faelan, who died in 737 and who was son of Murchadh Mor, king of Leinster. Apparently the then leaders of the Ui Faolain territory, refused to submit to the Anglo-Normans on their arrival. In *The Song of Dermot and the Earl* the unknown raconteur claims

> The greater part of Leinster
> Made peace in this manner
> MacDonnchadh did not come in ...
> Nor the traitor Mackelan
> Who was king of Offelan.[16]

The Mackelan family were closely connected with the church of Cloncurry before and during the early years of the Anglo-Norman settlement in the area. Flanagan suggests that Cloncurry was the Eigenkirche (principal church) of the family in the pre-Norman period.[17] It is possible that the family used Cloncurry as their principal residence because the location had been a religious and historical site for many centuries. This may account for the fact that the Anglo-Normans later established it as the centre of the manor.

The prominence of the Mackelan family in the local and diocesan church throughout the thirteenth century may suggest that there was a certain amount of continuity with the early or pre-invasion Irish church. Cornelius Magelan, who had been associated with the church at Cloncurry, was consecrated bishop of Kildare in 1206. He had been rector of Cloncurry and afterwards was archdeacon of Kildare. He was bishop for sixteen years until his death in 1222. Tradition states that Cornelius was buried at Cloncurry although there is no physical or documentary evidence of this. A mandate passed in 1217 prevented Irishmen from being elected as bishops, and so Cornelius was the last native Irish man to hold the episcopal office in Kildare for several centuries. Cornelius was succeeded in Cloncurry by his brother, Fin, who later became canon of the Kildare cathedral chapter.[18] Another brother, Felix, is mentioned as being one of two vicars in the church of Cloncurry.

15 *Annals of Ulster*, iii, 385.   **16** *Song of Dermot and the Earl – An old French Poem*, ed. Goddard H. Orpen (Oxford, 1892), p. 65.   **17** Marie Therese Flanagan, 'Henry II and the kingdom of Ui Faelain' in John Bradley (ed.), *Settlement and Society in Medieval Ireland* (Kilkenny, 1988), p. 236.   **18** *Register of the Abbey of St. Thomas, Dublin*, ed. J.T. Gilbert (London, 1889), p. 301.

On their accession to tenure in the area, the Anglo-Norman de Herefords established a church at Cloncurry and granted it and all its ecclesiastical benefices to the canons of the abbey of St Thomas in Dublin. The canons of St Thomas, well known for their hospitality to guests, were granted permission to convert Cloncurry for the reception of the poor and other guests. For example, John de Sandford, the archbishop of Dublin, stayed at Cloncurry on the night of 6 May 1290, while en route to Athlone.[19] Sometime in the late thirteenth century, the canons of St Thomas conceded ownership of their lands at Cloncurry to three local men, though they did retain a small amount of land for themselves on which they could build and maintain a haggard.[20] By 1328 a certain William of Cloncurry had become abbot of St Thomas' abbey in Dublin.[21] His elevation to the abbacy in Dublin may be an indication of the status of Cloncurry at this time.

By the year 1302, Cloncurry had become a deanery in the diocese of Kildare. The church there had been dedicated to Saints Mary and Martin by the Anglo-Normans. This dedication occurs throughout the documents which deal with Cloncurry in the *Register of St Thomas Abbey, Dublin*. However, in a papal letter of April 1491, the church is referred to as the parish church of St Ninian.[22] A similar reference occurs in a papal letter dated August 1504,[23] and again in State Papers dated 1564.[24] It is not clear if the same establishment is being referred to throughout these documents.

Due to the limitations of the available sources, it is not possible to give a detailed listing of the clergy who served Cloncurry. It is known, however, that the parish was served by Roger Walshe, who died in 1347 and was replaced by Walter Aleyn. John Broning was created vicar of Cloncurry in 1403. By 1547 the parish was being served by Nicholas Walsh.[25] He was succeeded by William Weldon in 1557.[26] Upon the death of William Weldon in 1564 the position of vicar was filled by Robert Cusack. In 1571 the rectory was leased to Anthony Lowe, for a period of forty years. This lease carried the stipulation that Lowe could only let this land to persons of the English nation or to those born in the Pale.[27] An Inquisition dated 1657 denotes that the civil parish of Cloncurry was served by Mr Christopher Golburne. The church itself had fallen into disrepair by this time.[28]

19 H.S. Sweetman (ed.), *Calendar of Documents relating to Ireland, 1285–1292*, (London, 1875–80), p. 273.   **20** *Register St Thomas Abbey*, p. 100.   **21** Aubrey Gwynn, 'The early history of St. Thomas Abbey, Dublin' in *JRSAI*, xxiv (1954), pp. 1–35.   **22** W.H. Bliss, J.A. Twemlow and C. Johnson (eds.), *Calendar of Papal Letters, 1484–1492*, (London 1883), p. 399.   **23** *Calendar of Papal Letters, 1503–1513*, p. 297.   **24** Fiants – Elizabeth, No. 706, *Appendix to 11th Report of the Deputy Keeper of the Public Records in Ireland*, p. 110. **25** Fiants – Edward VI, No. 217, *8th Report of the Deputy Keeper of the Public Records in Ireland*, (Dublin, 1876) p. 47.   **26** *Calendar of the Patent and Close Rolls of Chancery in Ireland of the Reigns of Henry VIII, Edward VI, Mary and Elizabeth*, 3 vols, ed. James Morrin (Dublin, 1861), i, p. 412, no. 164.   **27** Fiants – Elizabeth, No. 1821, *Appendix to 12th Report of the Deputy Keeper of the Public Records in Ireland*, (Dublin, 1889), p. 48.   **28** RCB Library, Mss Box N.2.24, p. 15.

We find the first reference to a post-reformation Roman Catholic presence when, in 1704, the Catholic community in the parish of Cloncurry was ministered to by a Revd Laurence Welsh. He had been ordained to the priesthood in Kilkenny in 1680.[29] The *Report on the State of Popery* recorded in 1731 that Cloncurry had a mass house which was served by Revd Andrew Egan. There was another priest called John Cormick who said private masses in peoples' houses.[30] By 1766 the parish of Cloncurry had two Protestant and 133 Popish families.[31] This implies a population of about 730 persons.[32] In 1804, Charles Lindsay, the Protestant bishop of Kildare, recorded that the church at Cloncurry had fallen in 1799 and was now listed as a ruin.[33] The rector was Revd Dixie Blundell, who resided in Dublin. Parochial duties were performed by Revd John Williamson.[34] Revd Blundell was replaced in 1811 by Revd Archibald Douglass.[35]

With the settlement of the Anglo-Normans in Ireland came the introduction of the larger religious orders here. In the fourteenth century the order of Our Lady of Mount Carmel established over thirty houses in this country, including one at Cloncurry. A licence for the foundation of the Carmelite friary in Cloncurry was granted to John Roche by Edward III in 1347.[36] Very little more is known of John Roche or his motive in seeking the licence. Nothing is known either of the life of the friary. It was reputedly burned to the ground in 1405 and later rebuilt by the local people.[37] In the description of the dissolution of the monasteries in November 1540, it was indicated that there were no buildings on the site. The timber on the land was said to be worth 6s. 8d. and was given to a William Dixon. There were also ten acres and three cottages which were held by Sampson.[38] However, in an Inquisition taken in 1543, we have a seemingly contradictory reference when it was found that the Prior of the monastery of Cloncurry was seized of a belfry, chapter house, dormitory, hall, two chambers, a kitchen, an orchard, three cottages and ten acres of arable land.[39] In January 1544 William and Edward Dixon of Ballyskeagh, county Meath, purchased the Carmelite friary of Cloncurry. Edward Dixon had died by 1560 and there were tithes of 18d. outstanding in respect of the late house of the monks of Cloncurry.[40]

29 *A List of the Names of the Popish Parish Priests as they were registered at a General Sessions of the Peace, county Kildare, 14th Day of July, 1704* (Dublin, 1704).   **30** 'Report on the State of Popery' in *Archivium Hibernicum*, iv (1915), p.161.   **31** Ibid., Appendix I, p. 270.   **32** Using 5.42 as a multiplier, see K.H. Connell, 'The Population of Ireland in the Eighteenth Century' in *Economic History Review*, xvi (1946), pp. 111–24.   **33** Raymond Refausse, 'The visitation note book of Charles Lindsay, bishop of Kildare, 1804–8' in *JKAS, xvii* (1991), p. 133.   **34** Nicholas Carlisle, *A Topographical Dictionary of Ireland* (London, 1810).   **35** John C. Erck (ed.), *An Ecclesiastical Register of the names of the Dignitaries and Parochial Clergy*, (Dublin, 1830), p. 102.   **36** Bodleian Library, Oxford, Ms Rawlinson, Class B, Fo. 53. *Rotulorum Patentium Hiberniae* 21, Ed III, (1347).   **37** Revd P. R. McCaffrey, *The White Friars – An Outline of Carmelite History* (Dublin, 1926), p. 369.   **38** *Extents of Irish Monastic Possessions 1540–1*, ed. Newport B. White (Dublin, 1943), p. 172.   **39** Revd M. Comerford, *History of the Dioceses of Kildare and Leighlin* (Dublin, n.d.), p. 160.   **40** *Fitzwilliam Accounts 1560–5, (Annesley Collection)* ed. A.K. Longfield (Dublin, 1960), pp. 22–3.

In 1566, the friary with one messuage, one cottage and thirty-five acres of land was granted to Richard Slayne for twenty-one years. A further Inquisition carried out in March 1611, found that the late Andrew Forster of Ballineskeagh was seized of the church, hall and dormitory together with ten acres of land and other buildings pertaining to the monastery of Cloncurry.[41]

All of these Inquisitions and grants are in marked contrast to the report of 1540 which stated that there were no buildings extant at the time of the dissolution. It would appear that there were buildings on the site of the monastery for at least fifty years after the dissolution. However, a list of Carmelite houses compiled in 1645 does not include Cloncurry,[42] while in the Civil Survey of 1654–6 Edward Foster of Cloncurry is listed as the owner of the 'Abby of Cloncurry' together with ten acres of land.[43] Some sources assert that the monastery buildings still existed in some form as late as 1737.[44]

LAND OWNERSHIP

In the late twelfth century, the cantred of Ui Faolain in which Cloncurry is situated had been granted to Adam de Hereford by Strongbow, in reward for services rendered. Adam was dead by 1216, leaving his heir, Stephen, a minor. Stephen later married the niece of the archbishop of Dublin but the marriage did not produce an heir for Stephen. His sister, Auda, married William Pippard and their daughter, Alice, became Stephen's heir. On her father's death in 1228, Alice married Ralph FitzNicholas.[45] Their son Ralph took the name Pippard and he inherited all the Pippard and de Hereford estates. Ralph's son, John, married Matilda, daughter of Sir Theobald le Botiller. They held the manor of Cloncurry by 1290. They in turn granted Cloncurry to Sir Theobald le Botiller in 1297. Cloncurry continued to be a part of the Ormond estates throughout the fifteenth and sixteenth centuries. The entire lordship of Cloncurry was conveyed to Richard Aylmer of Lyons in May 1558.[46]

In the Civil Survey of 1654, the townland of Cloncurry consisted of some 460 Irish acres. The lands were owned by George Aylmer who declared himself

41 *Inquisitionum in Officio Rotulorum Cancellariae Hiberniae asservatarum Repertorium*, (London, 1826) i, No. 21.   **42** Petition of Irish Carmelites to the Nunzio, in Revd Patrick F. Moran, *Spicilegium Ossoriense, being a Collection of Original Letters and Papers illustrative of the History of the Irish Church from the Reformation to the year 1800* (Dublin, 1874), p. 294.   **43** *Civil Survey, Kildare*, p. 198.   **44** Aubrey Gwynn and R. Neville Hadcock, *Medieval Religious Houses in Ireland* (London, 1970), p. 288. The location of the Carmelite monastery is not remembered today.   **45** E. St. John Brooks, 'The Family of Marisco' in *JRSAI*, lxii (1932), p. 57.   **46** Revd Matthew Devitt, 'The Barony of Okeathy' in *JKAS*, viii (1915–1917), p. 487. Richard Aylmer of Lyons had married Elinor, only daughter of Margaret, sister of Piers, Earl of Ormond. Their son George, was granted lands at Cloncurry and Trim. For further information see Hans Hendrick Aylmer, 'The Aylmers of Lyons, County Kildare' in *JKAS*, iv, no. 3 (1904), pp. 179–83.

a Protestant. However, it was known that he had 'consorted with rebels', had regularly attended mass and had raised his children as 'papists'. The ten acres attached to the Abbey of Cloncurry belonged to Edward Foster, a papist.[47] In the summary of Cloncurry parish it is stated that most of the inhabitants of the area were either dead or had been transplanted to Connacht.

The *Books of Survey and Distribution* date from the 1660s and create an official record of land owners and their estates at that time. The Kildare books show that the lands of Cloncurry, which had belonged to Edward Foster and George Aylmer in the Civil Survey, were now held by Thomas Aylmer and Katherine Wogan.[48]

The census of 1659 records a population of eighty-nine in Cloncurry, eighty-five of them Irish and the remainder English.[49] The principal persons of standing in the townland were Richard Thompson and Joseph Thompson. An Inquisition set up to report on the churches of Kildare in 1657 listed the same Richard Thompson of Cloncurry as a witness.[50] Petty's map of 1685 depicts a row of some nine or ten houses situated along the road to the south of the crossroads at Cloncurry.[51] It is not possible however, to tell from the map whether these houses are in a habitable state or in ruins. Netterville's 1752 map depicts a similar pattern in the village. These houses are two storeys high, with three large windows across the top. They are uniform in design and scale.[52] This 1752 map also shows an area called 'The Green' lying south of the village. This Green was about one acre in size and today, the remains of a stone cross base can still be seen at its western end. The word AMEN is carved in relief onto the cross base. It is possible that this may have been a wooden wayside or market cross. The location of the Green suggests that there may still have been a substantial settlement in Cloncurry in the first half of the eighteenth century.

In the early medieval documents there is no mention of a castle at Cloncurry. The first reference to a castle occurs in 1414, when Thomas Harbrig was appointed by the earl of Ormond as constable of his castle at Cloncurry.[53] An Inquisition dated 1637 states that Richard Aylmer was seized of a castle and various land holdings at Cloncurry.[54] The Down Survey map depicts a castle in the vicinity of Cloncurry but its exact location is not certain. The Civil Survey records that in 1656 'there is upon the aforesaid lands of Cloncurry one Castle which is valued to bee worth fourty pounds sterling'.[55]

47 *Civil Survey, Kildare*, p. 200.   **48** 'Books of Survey and Distribution' in *JKAS*, x (1922–8), p. 200.   **49** *Census of Ireland c.1659*, ed. S. Pender (Dublin, 1939), p. 406. **50** RCB Library, Mss Box N.2.24.   **51** Kildare County Library, William Petty, *Hibernia Delineatio*, 1685.   **52** NLI, Aylmer Estate Maps, Map 21 f [50] (4), Netterville's map of Michael Aylmer's land in Cloncurry in 1752.   **53** E. Curtis (ed.), *Calendar of Ormond Deeds*, (Dublin, 1932–70), iii, no.8.   **54** *Inquisitionum in Officio Rotulorum Cancellariae Hiberniae Asservatarum, Repertorium*, (London, 1826), i, no. 87.   **55** *Civil Survey*, Kildare, pp. 197–203.

Noble and Keenan's map of 1752 shows a castle or fortified house about one kilometre southwest of the church.[56] This building however, is not shown on Taylor's map of 1783.[57]

Travellers in the early eighteenth century observed that there were no enclosures or trees to be seen in the vicinity of Cloncurry.[58] Charles Etienne de Coquebert, who passed through the area in the early 1790s, referred to the fact that by standing on nearby Cappagh hill (which lies to the southeast of Cloncurry) it was possible to see the Wicklow mountains to the south east and the city of Dublin to the east.[59]

During the early eighteenth century, Cloncurry townland continued to be a part of the Aylmer estate. In 1732 Michael Aylmer inherited the family estates while still a minor, following the deaths of his father and elder brother. The main tenants of Michael Aylmer in Cloncurry in 1752 are listed in Table 1.[60]

Table 1   Tenants of Michael Aylmer in Cloncurry, Ballyvoneen and Ballinakill, 1752

Tenant	Townland	Acreage
Luke Maly	Cloncurry	43
Bartle Smith	Cloncurry	14
Denis Magauen	Cloncurry	13
Peter Coffey	Cloncurry	11
Charles Aylmer	Cloncurry	10
Mr. Coates	Ballyvoneen	111
Denis Magauen	Ballyvoneen	148
Charles Aylmer	Ballyvoneen	108
Thomas Ryan	Ballinakill	340

By the end of the eighteenth century, Michael Aylmer was in serious debt. He was forced to sell off his estate at Lyons in Newcastle, county Dublin, which had belonged to his family for almost 500 years, as well as all his lands at Cloncurry. In December 1790, the estate of Cloncurry was purchased from the Aylmer family by Sir Nicholas Lawless, subsequently created Lord Cloncurry. The purchase price was £25,365.[61] A rental dated 1793 shows that Charles Aylmer

56 Noble and Keenan, *Map of Kildare, 1752* in Kildare County Library.   **57** Alex Taylor, *A Map of the County of Kildare by Lieut. Alex Taylor of His Majesty's 81st Regiment, 1783*, in Kildare County Library.   **58** Thomas Molyneux, 'Journey into Connaught – April 1709' in *The Miscellany of the Irish Archaeological Society* (Dublin, 1846), i, 162.   **59** Síle Ní Chinnéide, 'An Eighteenth Century French Traveller in Kildare' in *JKAS*, xv (1971–6), p. 384.   **60** NLI, Netterville's Map 21 f [50] (4).   **61** NLI, Cloncurry Papers, Ms. 5657. Nicholas Lawless was born in the 1730s. He was educated at Rouen in France. As an adult he settled in France, where, as a Catholic, he could live in freedom. He soon continued to hold 107 acres at Ballyvoneen. By then the Ryan family had increased their holding from the original 340 acres in Ballinakill. They had acquired Denis Magauen's 148 acres in Ballyvoneen as well. Arthur Coates still held 112 acres in Ballyvoneen. Aylmer held a lease of three lives, dated May 1776, while the others had ninety nine year leases.[62]

By 1797, the Ryans had again increased their holding size by acquiring another fifty acres in the townland of Cloncurry. Thomas Ryan was now acting as agent to Lord Cloncurry, and as the local magistrate. In July 1795 he had been seriously injured while returning from Naas court. He was ambushed by several armed men and was shot in the head and neck. Despite his injuries, he managed to gain entry to his house in Ballinakill. The ambush party surrounded the house and tried unsuccessfully to burn it down. The following week the Lord Lieutenant issued a proclamation offering a pardon to anyone who would supply the names of the attackers to the authorities.[63]

As the local magistrate, Ryan worked closely with Lord Cloncurry's son and heir, Valentine, in bringing a certain Captain Frazer to trial for a murder committed in Cloncurry. This notorious incident followed the passing of the insurrection act in 1796 under which martial law was declared in nearby Carbury. An army camp had been established there under the command of Captain Fraser. While passing through Cloncurry one evening, Fraser observed that Christopher Dixon, an old local man, was outside mending a cart wheel. Despite Dixon's justified pleas that Cloncurry was not subject to curfew, Fraser arrested him. While the party was stopped at the turnpike, Dixon attempted to escape. However, he was followed and stabbed many times by the soldiers and subsequently died from the wounds. Thomas Ryan and Valentine Lawless were both so incensed by the murder that they rode into the army camp demanding the arrest of Fraser, who refused to submit. Later, however, Fraser rode into Athy led by a marching band and gave himself up for trial. He was acquitted by the judge, Lord Norbury.[64]

became disenchanted with life in France, however, and returned to Ireland having converted to Protestantism. He purchased estates in Limerick, Kildare and Dublin. He also entered the banking, woollen and blanket trades, thus greatly increasing his wealth. A popular ballad of the period stated:

> 'Cloncurry, Cloncurry, Come here in a hurry.
> And tell why you laugh at the squire.
> Now although he's tossed high, I defy you deny,
> That blankets have tossed yourself higher!'

Quoted from 'Miscellany', *Leinster Leader*, 10 Sept. 1983. **62** NLI, Cloncurry Papers, Ms. 5659. **63** *Freeman's Journal*, 13 August 1795. **64** Lord Norbury instructed the jury that 'Fraser was a gallant officer, who had only made a mistake; that if Dixon was as good a man as he was represented to be, it was well for him to be out of this wicked world; but if he was as bad as many others in the neighbourhood, it was as well for the country to be quit of him.' Quoted from *Personal Recollections of the Life and Times of Valentine Lord Cloncurry* (Dublin, 1850) p. 40.

In December 1799, the first Lord Cloncurry died while his son, Valentine, was in prison in London on charges of treason related to the 1798 rebellion. Ryan was forced to manage the estate until Valentine's release in 1802. He was described as a 'very capable man in every respect'.[65] In 1803 Ryan held over 580 acres in total between Cloncurry, Ballinakill and Ballyvoneen and had become a trusted friend and confidant of Lord and Lady Cloncurry. Three years later in 1806, Lord Cloncurry discovered that his wife had been 'compromised' by Sir John Piers, a gentleman who had attended school with him. A trial ensued, and Lady Cloncurry was dispatched back to her family in England.[66] For many years afterwards she continued to correspond with Thomas Ryan to enquire after her children and to beg for tokens by which to remember them. Apparently Ryan never made this correspondence known to his employer.[67] By 1812 it would appear that Ryan had fallen into debt and he received many admonishments from Lord Cloncurry to put his affairs in order.[68] Ryan's death in 1814 may indicate that he had been having difficulties managing his finances due to age or infirmity. His widow continued to hold their land after his death.

Throughout the early nineteenth century, Aylmer's and Coates's holdings remained unchanged. Bartholomew Smith continued to hold his fourteen acres in Cloncurry, while Luke Maly's widow, Mary, held their forty two acres in the village.[69] In 1823 the Inn holding at Cloncurry had been transferred to Christopher Donegan.[70] Edward Ryan had taken over his father's holdings at Ballinakill and Ballyvoneen.

Early in the nineteenth century a tree planting project was begun in Kildare. By 1808 Thomas Ryan had planted 4,000 trees in Ballinakill. By 1827 Thomas Kearney, Ryan's successor in Ballinakill, had planted 79,000 more. Sam Coates had planted 4,000 trees in Ballyvoneen by 1834.[71] This tree planting on such a vast scale divided up what had been large swathes of land into smaller, more compact holdings, and analysis of the Tithe Applotment Books of the early 1830s proves this was the case in Cloncurry and Ballyvoneen.[72]

The Tithe Applotment Books of 1833 show the whole of Ballinakill occupied by Thomas Kearney, who had leased it from Edward Ryan. Ballyvoneen is occupied by three families, namely Doran, Coates and White. Edward Doran had leased Michael Aylmer's holding of 107 acres.[73] The small area of glebe land sandwiched between Cloncurry and Ballinakill was occupied by Bridget Dunn,

65 Quoted in a letter to Valentine, Lord Cloncurry from Cooper Crawford, in *Personal Recollections of the Life and Times of Lord Cloncurry*, p. 81. **66** NLI, Pamphlets, P.1426, *A Correct and Full Report of the Trial of Sir John Piers for Criminal Conversation with Lady Cloncurry, Feb. 19, 1807*. **67** William John Fitzpatrick, *The Life, Times and Contemporaries of Lord Cloncurry* (Dublin, 1855), p. 301. **68** NLI, Cloncurry Papers, Ms. 8492. **69** NLI, Cloncurry papers Ms. 5659. **70** NLI, Cloncurry Papers, Ms. 8283 (3). **71** E. McCracken, 'A Register of Trees, County Kildare, 1769–1909' in *JKAS*, xvi (1977–86), p. 48. **72** Tithe Applotment Books, Kildare county Library. **73** NLI, Cloncurry Papers, Ms. 5662.

Edward Hart and Richard Drennin. There were three families listed in Cloncurry, namely Harris, Ryan and Geraghty. Geraghty had taken over the Inn holding in 1831 from Christopher Donegan.[74] Rent rolls from 1826 show that Michael Donegan was in arrears and his plot appears to have been sublet by November 1830.[75] The land was divided into three main categories: 514 Irish acres of arable, 156 acres of pasture and 184 acres of moorland and bog. All of the land in Cloncurry was in pasture. Land in the nearby townlands of Cappagh, Ballycahon and Grange was mostly in tillage. A total of £19 5s. 8d. was due to the vicar. Rental amounts did not increase during the 1830s.[76]

By the mid 1830s many of the larger tenants were in arrears with their rent. By May 1836, Ryan was in arrears by one full year's rent. In May 1837 the representatives of John Geraghty were also in arrears. Edward Doran who had taken over Michael Aylmer's 107 acres, was in arrears by 1837. In May 1838 Samuel Coates took over the lands previously held by Thomas Ryan.[77] This period of financial difficulty was referred to in the Poor Law Inquiry for the area. It was stated that, at this time, the locals who had previously contributed generously to the education of children in the area, were no longer in a position to do so as many of them were impoverished.[78]

Field Books for February 1840 show one large dwelling house in Ballinakill worth £53. This house was occupied by Thomas Kearney. A small Police Barracks in Ballinakill was worth £6. There were three houses in Ballyvoneen. The largest house was occupied by Samuel Coates and was worth £25. The second house was occupied by Edward Doran, a herdsman to Lord Cloncurry, while the third was lived in by Edward Robinson, a policeman. This house was later occupied by James Murphy, another herdsman.[79] Day books from 1842 onwards show Edward Doran of Ballyvoneen paying a half yearly rent of £69 11s. 0d. During the years 1842 to 1844 the payments were at irregular intervals of the year, while from 1 November 1845, payments were recorded on a regular basis at the beginning of May and November.[80] The area referred to as glebe land in the Tithe Applotment Books was no longer differentiated as such in the 1840s. It had been assimilated into the townland of Cloncurry.

When the Commissioners for Inquiring into the State of the Poorer Classes in Ireland sat in the early nineteenth century, Thomas Kearney was among the panel selected to give information for the local area. It was stated that for many widows in the locality, the only means of income open to them was to keep 'shebeen houses'. One labourer in the area stated that he had come from Longford in his youth to work on the canal. When work became scarce he was unable to provide for his family. He stated that he and his neighbours 'are in our

74 NLI, Cloncurry papers Ms. 5694.   **75** NLI, Cloncurry papers Ms. 5662.   **76** NLI, Cloncurry papers Ms. 5664.   **77** NLI, Cloncurry papers Ms. 5664.   **78** Revd Martin Brenan, *Schools of Kildare and Leighlin, AD 1775–1835* (Dublin 1935), p. 249.   **79** VO, First valuation, perambulation & field books for county Kildare, Barony of Ikeathy and Oughterany, Parish of Cloncurry.   **80** NLI, Cloncurry papers Ms. 12818.

cabins, lying like brutes on straw and chaff on the ground'. Others claimed that part of the problem lay in the fact that the majority of landlords were absentees. Work was difficult to find for these labourers and they would consider themselves lucky to have two days employment in any week. Most labourers were unemployed from the middle of November to the middle of April. The unemployment was blamed on the amount of land that was given over to pasture in the area. So extreme was the situation that canal boats were sometimes attacked and looted. One infamous incident occurred on 25 May 1837 when about twenty local men attacked a canal boat and threatened and beat the boatman. This incident necessitated the protection of the boat and its crew by the constabulary at Cloncurry. They were unable to provide such protection, however, and requested the assistance of the constabulary at Enfield and Kilcock.[81] Locals were also known to cut away the embankments of the canal at night in order to create employment for themselves in repairing them the following day. During the 1840s, it was reported by the Quaker relief committee that in the adjacent parish of Hortland there were thirty or forty families in need of aid.[82] The fact that no relief was given in Cloncurry, Ballyvoneen and Ballinakill suggests that the people in these townlands were not in need of assistance. They were, for the most part, large tenant farmers. Analysis of the data from Griffith's *Valuation* shows that in the 1850s, in the three combined townlands there was approximately one family per sixty six acres, while in nearby Kilbrook the average holding size was only seven acres.

In Griffith's *Valuation* the 181 acres of Cloncurry were valued at £204 2s. 0d. This included four acres owned and occupied by the Midland and Great Western Railway and Royal Canal Company, five acres belonging to the M.G.W. Railway & R. Canal Co. occupied by William Hare, and one acre of graveyard. There were thirteen houses in the village, two of which were vacant. The majority of the land was owned by the representatives of John Geraghty, with Lord Cloncurry owning fifty three acres (which was also held by the Geraghty family).

All of the 590 acres in Ballinakill were leased by Thomas Kearney from Lord Cloncurry; he kept 131 acres for himself and relet the other 459 acres. Most of Kearney's holding was occupied by his herd, Thomas Kenna. There were only two other tenants in the townland, Hugh Kilroy who occupied a house and garden, and the constabulary force who maintained the barracks nearby. This constabulary barracks is first mentioned in Griffith's *Valuation*. It was located in Ballinakill. The staff comprised a constable, two 'effective subordinates and one sickly subordinate about [to] be discharged with gratuity.'[83]

The 612 acres in Ballyvoneen were entirely owned by Lord Cloncurry. There were three houses and three tenants listed, holding plots of 185, 248 and 178 acres each. The only surname that is listed by Griffith and common to previous

81 NA, Outrage Papers, Kildare 1837 f.8902C.   **82** *In Time of Want: Quaker Relief in county Kildare during the Famine*, Kildare Famine Commemoration Committee, ii, Kildare county Library, (1996).   **83** NA, Outrage Papers, Kildare, June 1837 f.9077C.

lists of tenants is that of Mary Ryan. This lady, a widow, owned several houses, gardens and plots of land in neighbouring townlands. Throughout the 1850s, James Murphy, who lived in Ballyvoneen and was employed by Lord Cloncurry as a herdsman, fell into arrears with his rent. Lord Cloncurry's other estates in Lyons and in Abington, county Limerick were allowing their tenants abatements in rent at this time, but there was no such allowance in place in Cloncurry.[84] This fact further reinforces the supposition that the tenants in Cloncurry, Ballinakill and Ballyvoneen were much better off than their counterparts on Lord Cloncurry's other estates.

Using Griffith's *Valuation* and records from the Valuation Office, it is possible to trace ownership of the various plots of land in the three townlands through- out the latter half of the nineteenth century (see Appendix 1). It is interesting to note that Lord Cloncurry took over as occupier of many of the holdings during the final decade of the century. Whether as landlord he was clearing the land, or whether these changes were effected as a result of decreasing population is not certain. The available evidence would suggest the latter. However, it was reported in the local newspaper that in June 1881, following an eviction, effigies of Lord Cloncurry, his agent and the agent's wife were paraded through the nearby townland of Kilbrook on the backs of three asses and were later consigned to flames amid the ruins of the eviction.[85]

In 1826 and again in 1846, it was remarked upon that Cloncurry village consisted of a few thatched cabins.[86] The population of Cloncurry decreased from thirteen households in 1851 to seven in 1901, a reduction of almost fifty per cent, while Ballinakill decreased from four households in 1851 to one in 1901. Ballyvoneen also decreased from three in 1851 to one in 1901. This is in striking contrast to the adjacent townland of Kilbrook (406 acres) which supported fifty eight households in 1851 and which continued to sustain a large population throughout the second half of the nineteenth century.

Table 2   House numbers in Cloncurry, Ballyvoneen and Ballinakill

Townland	1833	1840	1851	1901	Decrease (1851–1901)
Ballinakill	1	2	4	1	75%
Ballyvoneen	3	2	3	1	66%
Cloncurry	3	3	3	7	46%

(source: VO Records and 1901 census)

84 NLI, Cloncurry papers Ms. 5666. Lord Cloncurry gave £200 to his agent in Abington to be distributed to tenants in need there. Later in 1848, in a published address to his Limerick tenants, Lord Cloncurry criticised the Government for its failure to improve the situation. See Fitzpatrick, *Life … of Lord Cloncurry*, p. 518.   **85** *Kildare Observer*, 7 August 1881.   **86** J.N. Brewer, *The Beauties of Ireland, being original Delineations, Topographical, Historical and Biographical of each County* (London, 1826), ii, 64; *The Parliamentary Gazetteer of Ireland 1844–5*, i, 430.

EVIDENCE OF AN OPEN OR CLOSED SOCIETY?

Much change occurred in the townlands in the fifty years after the famine. During the period from 1860 to 1880, the birth rate for the Cloncurry area averaged two children per year with a peak of four children born in 1878.[87] By the census of 1901 there were seven houses in Cloncurry and a total population of thirty-eight. Four of the seven were owner-occupiers, while Lord Cloncurry owned the other three. In Ballyvoneen there was only one dwelling house, occupied by the Kelly family and owned by Lord Cloncurry. In this house there was a room called the Lord's Room. This room was reserved for Lord Cloncurry whenever he stayed in the neighbourhood.[88] There was also only one house in Ballinakill, which was occupied by Catherine Dawson. The turn on the road nearby is still called Dawson's Turn. Therefore, this was not the former residence of Thomas Ryan and Thomas Kearney, which seems to have been demolished at this time. The vast majority of the inhabitants of the area had been born in Kildare. The Kelly family of Ballyvoneen had transferred from Manor Kilbride in Wicklow as stewards to Lord Cloncurry.

Thornton, the shopkeeper, had been born in Mayo. He ran a shop at Cloncurry crossroads along with his nephew, John Boggan. In the Kenny household, the husband was born in Westmeath and his wife was from Wicklow. Their two grandchildren, who were from Dublin, were registered in the census but it is not certain whether they lived with the grandparents or were merely on a visit.

Figure 1   Birth rates for the combined townlands of Cloncurry, Ballyvoneen and Ballinakill, 1863–1880. (Source: Parish Registers, Kilcock, NLI)

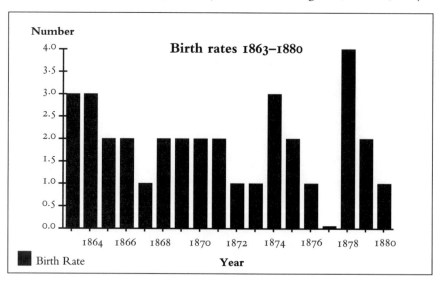

87 NLI, microfilm pos. 4207, Parish registers for Kilcock R.C. Parish, county Kildare.
88 Interview conducted with Sean Gorman, October 1996.

The Feeney family lived at Cloncurry crossroads. Their ancestors had originally moved here from the west of Ireland. John Feeney's wife, Christina, was a Dixon from nearby Kilbrook. On the night of the census, her brother, Matthew Dixon, was in the house with them. The earliest reference to the Feeney family is found in the Grand Jury Presentment Books in 1867. Patrick Feeney was employed to mend the road from Cloncurry crossroad to Newtown. In 1880 John Feeney was employed to do the same task.[89]

Thomas Walsh was married to a woman from Kilcock. Both himself and his son, John, were listed as coopers. The family had come from Donadea. They worked on the Aylmer estate. The Monaghan family also resided at Cloncurry crossroads in a small building which later became known as The Hall. They were listed as farm servants.

Farming related occupations were the most common ones returned in 1901. This included farmers, farm servants, stewards, shepherds and labourers. There was also a cooper and a shopkeeper. Several of the women are listed as seamstresses or dressmakers. This may be indicative of the fact that the women in the homes needed to supplement the family incomes by engaging in cottage type industry. Analysis of the age profile of the 1901 population for the three townlands shows that almost 40 per cent were aged twenty or below. One third of the people were aged between twenty and fifty, while there were two people aged over eighty.

Figure 2   Profile of age range of population of Cloncurry, Ballyvoneen and Ballinakill from 1901 Census

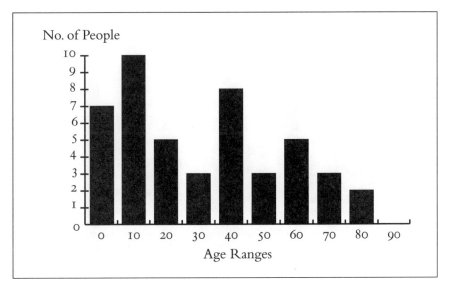

---

89 Kildare County Library, Grand Jury Presentment Books, Kildare, 1838–1893. The Grand Juries were the precursors of Kildare County Council.

By 1911, the population of Cloncurry had fallen by 26 per cent to twenty eight persons. Two new houses had been built and there were two uninhabited houses. Two families had moved into the area. One of these was Sarah Boggan, a widow from county Meath, who lived with her two sons, who had been born in Kildare. The second family was the Murrays, who had also moved from Meath, and whose three children had been born in Kildare. They were carpenters by trade. The Harris family, who were included in the 1901 census and who have lived in the area from the end of the seventeenth century to the present day, are not listed in the 1911 census. Examination of the local graveyard shows that the husband, wife and mother-in-law all died in 1902, leaving three children, the eldest of whom was a mere four years old. These children were taken to be reared by relatives in Prosperous, explaining the absence of the family name in the area in 1911.[90]

Occupations listed in 1911 were again predominantly agricultural in nature, although there were also two carpenters and a cooper. Thornton, the shopkeeper from Mayo and his nephew, seemed to have moved on. The 1911 census for Ballyvoneen shows just one family, that of Thomas and Bridget O'Brien, a newly married couple, who were both born in county Meath. In Ballinakill, James Dawson and his sister, Lizzie, continued to live in the old police barracks, the only inhabited house in the townland. An analysis of the age profiles for the three townlands in 1911 shows that almost one half of the population was aged between twenty and forty.

Figure 3   Age profile of population of Cloncurry, Ballyvoneen and Ballinakill, 1911 Census

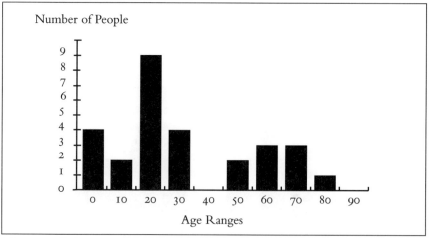

The overall demographic trend of ever decreasing population has been the pattern in Cloncurry since the peak during the Middle Ages. Yet, local lore claims that there are some families in the locality who can claim ancestry from

90 Interview with Michael Harris, Cloncurry, October 1996.

these medieval inhabitants. The large pasture lands of the Aylmer and Cloncurry estates, the transplantation of people in the 1640s to Connacht, and the nineteenth century levels of poverty and emigration, were possibly the main reasons for the continued decline. Coupled with this was the fact that despite the long history of settlement in the area, Cloncurry never attained the status of a substantial urban centre, the commercial focus of its inhabitants being on Kilcock, or, following the construction of the railway, on nearby Enfield. Its location on the railway, canal and main western route has ensured that its population has always possessed a certain transitory aspect. The migration of workers into the area during the periods of railway and canal construction combined with the fact that several people married partners from outside the immediate area, has ensured that the society has remained open and subject to continual change.

INDUSTRY AND COMMERCE IN THE AREA

Throughout the centuries, trade and industry have always formed part of the life of the Cloncurry area. Records of industrial and commercial activities survive from as far back as the Anglo Norman era. During this time small manorial villages were sometimes granted charters conferring rights and privileges on the inhabitants. Most important among these privileges were the granting of holdings to the burgesses. Many of these burgesses were artisans or petty merchants. There were 112 burgesses in Cloncurry according to the Extent of 1304. Merchants from Cloncurry were also enrolled in the Dublin Guild of Merchants intermittently throughout the thirteenth century. Adam the baker of Cloncurry was enrolled in 1230; Walter, cleric of Cloncurry, enrolled in 1238; Jacob of Cloncurry in 1248 and Walter, cleric of Cloncurry in 1250.[91]

It is known that there was a water mill in the medieval village of Cloncurry. In 1304 the site of this mill was held by William Blundo. All the inhabitants of the town and the manor were obliged to have their corn ground there. A certain 'Thom the miller' is listed in the Extent of 1304.[92] There was also a medieval market in Cloncurry village. This market is referred to in the Justiciary Rolls in the year 1298.[93] The area called 'The Green' on Netterville's eighteenth-century map of the area is likely to have been the location of the market place. The presence of the stone cross base at this location supports this interpretation, but there is some uncertainty as to the medieval origin of this cross base. The inclusion of 'The Green' in Netterville's mid eighteenth-century map suggests that this area continued to be a trading centre throughout the later middle ages.

---

91 *The Dublin Guild Merchant Roll c.1190–1265*, eds Philomena Connolly and Geoffrey Martin (Dublin, 1992), pp. 62, 74, 88, 89.   **92** *Red Book of Ormond*, pp. 27–34.   **93** James Mills (ed.), *Calendar of Justiciary Rolls, Ireland, Edward I*, (Dublin, 1905), p. 198.

During the late eighteenth century the Royal Canal was extended through the Cloncurry area. Great difficulties were encountered during the course of the construction. These resulted in considerable delays and ever-increasing costs. The stretch of land that runs from Cappagh bog to Cloncurry bridge is underlaid by fine running sand. When the water eventually entered the newly built section, the banks collapsed into the channel.[94] Dry walls were suggested by the engineers in order to alleviate the problem, and by 1799 the Royal Canal Company was eventually able to extend its passenger service to Cloncurry.[95] Workers came from all over the country to seek employment on the building project with payments averaging 9s. per week.[96] Some of the men who came into the area to work settled locally. The commercial impact of the canal on the local area is difficult to judge. However, in 1812, after an incident on the Grand Canal in which potatoes were stolen from a canal boat, Lord Cloncurry declared that 'whatever effect the canal may have farther from Dublin, it does not raise the price of provisions in this neighbourhood'.[97]

Valentine, the second Lord Cloncurry, was an active opponent of the construction of the Royal Canal. As a director and shareholder in the Grand Canal (and someone through whose lands the Grand Canal passed), he thought that use of a parallel canal would draw much business from it. By 1827, however, he was suggesting the construction of a ship canal from Kingstown to Galway Bay which would pass through Cloncurry. This waterway was intended to considerably reduce the time taken to travel to the Americas and the West Indies. It would also provide employment to local people and would serve as a useful resource for national defence in time of war. The estimated cost amounted to five million pounds, but the government refused to assist financially.[98]

So-called 'Fly Boats' were introduced on the Royal Canal on 30 July 1833, in order to reduce the time of the journey. These boats were towed by two horses galloping at speeds of approximately twelve miles an hour. It was discovered, however, that the sections of the canal at Cappagh bog and at Cloncurry were unsuitable for this new innovation, as the towpaths were not substantial enough to support the horses and the clay banks were being eroded by the currents caused by the boats. In order to pass through this section of canal the horses had to walk, thus lengthening the time taken to complete the journey.

In the following year a new venture was established on the canal bank at Cappagh. The project was set up by Charles Wye Williams and aimed to convert wet peat into fuel by mechanical methods. Cappagh was chosen for the factory as it afforded immediate transport to Dublin. Locals were employed and wages

94 Ruth Delany, *Ireland's Royal Canal 1789–1992* (Dublin, 1992), p. 47.   **95** Peter Clarke, *The Royal Canal – The Complete Story* (Dublin, 1992), p. 51.   **96** *Appendix to First Report from the Commissioners for inquiring into the State of the Poorer Classes in Ireland* (Dublin, 1835), p. 299.   **97** 'Minutes of the Grand Canal Company, vol. 46, 10 March 1812', quoted in Ruth Delany, *Ireland's Royal Canal 1789–1992*, p. 59.   **98** *Life and Times of Lord Cloncurry*, p. 365.

of 8*d.* to 10*d.* a day were paid. Unfortunately the manufacturing process soon proved too expensive and various other methods were tried. None were successful however, and the project was abandoned after about five years.[99]

As mentioned above, there was a shop at Cloncurry crossroads run by Thornton and later by his nephew Boggan. This shop ceased trading sometime between 1901 and 1911.[100] In the 1860s there was a public house across the road from the shop. This was owned by a man called Byrne. Peter Byrne is listed as occupier of that site in 1866. The pub was knocked sometime in the 1880s. The local people shopped for everyday items at Boggan's shop and later at Dixon's shop in nearby Kilbrook. A fair was held in Enfield every three months. Fairs were also held at regular intervals in Kilcock, Johnstownbridge and Hortland.[101] Most of the necessary services were available in Kilcock. The midwife lived there, as did the local doctor. While Enfield was nearer geographically, Kilcock seemed to be the focus of activity for the inhabitants of Cloncurry.

Cloncurry's location on the main east-west artery has contributed to its longevity. The old road to Dublin lay south of its present location, and traffic was forced to climb Cappagh hill, which is quite a steep gradient. In winter time the hill was almost impassable with mud or ice, a difficulty reputed to have been sometimes added to by locals eager to hire out teams of horses. In the early nineteenth century this road was replaced by the present road to the north, which is situated on level ground. Old maps also depict a road which was situated south of and parallel to that old Dublin road. This road, shown on the 1752 map, is located in the area thought to be the site of the original Anglo-Norman settlement at Cloncurry.[102] All that remains of this roadway today, is a long depression which can be traced through several fields. This depression or 'hollow way' is typical of a deserted medieval village and in places, the banks on its side rise to heights of one and a half metres above its base. There were also several small roads which criss-crossed the main Dublin road and which led from Cloncurry, Kilbrook and Cappagh into nearby Meath. However, parts of these roads have disappeared or been rerouted, as the original routes have been severed by the canal and railway. Aerial photographs and local lore suggests that the courses of the Blackwater river and its tributary the Ballycarn river have been altered in two places, but there is no indication of a reason for this. The Ballycarn river forms part of the county boundary with Meath at the north western corner of the townland of Cloncurry. Today the river flows due west and then turns sharply south. Further south there is evidence that the Blackwater may also have been altered.

---

99 John Cooke, 'Bog Reclamations and Peat Development in County Kildare' in *JKAS*, xiv (1964–70), p. 597.   **100** Interview conducted with Mrs Keoghegan, October, 1996.   **101** Thomas Rawson, *Statistical Survey of the County of Kildare with Observations on the Means of Improvement* (Dublin, 1807), pp. 1–238.   **102** NLI, Netterville's Map 21 f 50 [4]. See also John Bradley, 'The Urban Archaeological Survey of county Kildare' (Unpublished report, 1986) Kildare county Library.

EDUCATION

There was a school established at Cloncurry by 1731. The teacher was Patrick Ryly, a Catholic. It was set up to teach English to young children. It would appear to have been the only school in the parish at that time. By 1796 the local school for Cloncurry was situated in Newtown. The first teachers there were Joseph and Catherine Dunne. Their salaries were paid by subscription and were supplemented by the Society for the Education of the Poor in Ireland. The children were also expected to pay one penny per week. By 1823, however, such was the state of impoverishment, that many of the generous locals who had contributed willingly to the school, were now unable to do so. The administration was forced to apply to the Kildare Street Society for financial assistance. Many of the clergy were reluctant to apply to this charitable institution for help, due to its insistence on biblical study. The administration of the local school registered their objections to this regulation, but acknowledged the society's readiness to help them financially. Comerford records in his *History of the Dioceses of Kildare and Leighlin*, a statement by Lord Cloncurry that Revd Francis Haly, Parish priest of Kilcock and Newtown, had succeeded in carrying out the regulations required by the society, while at the same time protecting the consciences of his flock. According to Lord Cloncurry, the bible had been read aloud after the school children had been absented from the school at Newtown! Haly indignantly denied the allegation and Cloncurry later apologised for the scandalous misstatement.[103]

During the 1820s enrolments averaged about 104 children. In 1823 it was noted that many of the children were kept at home by their parents during the spring and harvest to the detriment of their education. Children of poor people were sometimes forced to absent themselves for want of food or clothing.[104] Text books used in the school included the *Dublin Reading and Spelling Book, Gough's Arithmetic* and the *History of Voyages*. Children in the area were also expected to attend Christian Doctrine classes in Newtown church throughout the year on Sundays and holydays. Throughout the 1850s enrolments in the local school averaged some 130 children.[105]

CONCLUSIONS

One of the interesting features of Cloncurry is the extent to which it has been influenced by human structures and infrastructure, such as the manor, the church, the road to the west, the canal and the railway. Cloncurry was not a closed community. We see clear evidence of new blood being brought into the

---

103 Comerford, *Collections Relating to the Dioceses of Kildare and Leighlin*, p. 168. **104** Brenan, *Schools of Kildare and Leighlin*, p. 249. **105** *Appendix to 18th, 19th and 20th Reports of Commissioners of National Education in Ireland* (Dublin, 1852–4).

community, often because of the structures based there, or the infrastructure which goes through it. It is interesting to trace the reasons for new families and new names moving into the area: the presence locally of Norman names such as Ledwidge, Fowler and Adams, probably there since the manor of the 1300s, the people who came for the building of the canal or the railway, or the families who had a connection with the stagecoach which changed horse teams at nearby Cappagh. Even though strictly outside the remit of this historical study, Cloncurry is also characteristic of locations which have seen huge Land Commission inspired influxes in the last two generations. The once large tracts of land in the townlands of Ballyvoneen and Ballinakill have now been divided into smaller holdings and many of their owners moved here from Mayo in the 1920s and 1930s. The population of these two townlands has increased significantly as a result. Several of the families registered in the 1901 and 1911 censuses have died out. The descendants of others are still living in the community.

It is also interesting to speculate as to why Cloncurry never developed into a proper village or town. We know of its importance to the local Uí Faoláin or Magelan clan, and its nurturing of a medieval village and Anglo Norman church and monastery. Yet, there always seems to have been a reason why it never developed an urban settlement role. In the Middle Ages it had a church, monastery and perhaps even an inn. But the suppression of Henry VIII greatly reduced the importance of these. Equally, it is known that the confiscation and redistribution seem to have greatly disrupted the local societal structures, even if only certain members of the community were displaced. Then, in the eighteenth century, Cloncurry was turned into a set of three townlands dominated by large tenant farmers, many not living on the land in Cloncurry.

Cloncurry has long been the location of a junction or crossroads with the main road to the west, but it is known from Netterville and other maps of the 1700s that the road north to Baconstown in Meath, or south to Newtown, was never an important artery. So, like many pre-reformation Christian settlements and in common with so many locations of Protestant churches, Cloncurry remains a rural community. History proves that one could hardly have expected anything different.

GLOSSARY

Extent: A survey of a manor containing details of the buildings, agricultural practises and rents and obligations due from tenants.

Messuage: a house or holding.

Occupants of plots of land based on information from Griffith's *Valuation* and from Valuation Office Cancellation Books.

Ballinakill

1ABac Thomas Kearney (1851) – William Kenna (1860) – James Kenna (1880) – Lord Cloncurry (1892) – Simon Hannon (1901) – Christopher Hannon (1905).
2b Hugh Kilroy (1850)
2c Constabulary Force (1851) – Vacant (1860) – Patrick Hanlon (1866) – House fallen (1884).

Ballyvoneen

1 James Murphy (1850) – James Eivers (1863) – Matthew Coates (1866) – Lord Cloncurry (1884) – House fallen by 1901.
2a Samuel Coates (1851) – Matthew Webb (1864) – William Webb (1869) – Lord Cloncurry (1882).
2b Samuel Coates (1851) – Matthew Webb (1864) – William Webb (1869) – Lord Cloncurry (1882).
3 Margaret Doran (1851) – William Kenna (1865) – James Kenna (1882) – Lord Cloncurry (1884).

Cloncurry

1 James Keogh (1851) – Michael Geraghty (1860) – James Eivers (1863) – John Feeney (1865) – John Feeney Jun. (1901).
2a, 2b Midland & Great Western Railway Co. (1851).
3 William Hare (1851) – Thomas Hare.
4 Richard Harris (1851) – Michael Harris (1860) – Anne Harris (1863) – Joseph Harris (1882) (1901).
5 Richard Harris (1851) – Michael Harris (1860) – Anne Harris (1863) – Joseph Harris (1882) (1901).
6 Graveyard.
7 John Geraghty (1851) – Michael Geraghty (1860) – James Eivers (1863) – Matthew Coates (1866) – Henry Clifden (1869) – Lord Cloncurry.
7a Michael Connaughton (1851) – Peter Byrne (1860) – Henry Clifden – John Halligan (1882) – Thomas Halligan (1885) – Lord Cloncurry.
7b Patrick Finn (1851) – Edmund Harte (1860) – Lord Cloncurry (1882).
7c Denis Holton (1851) – Thomas Monaghan (1860) – Pat Monaghan (1882) – Lord Cloncurry (1899).

7d   Margaret Levin (1851) – Margaret Ledwich (1860) – Pat Monaghan (1882) – 1901.

7e   Jane Kelly (1851) – Richard Molloy (1860) – Patrick Molloy (1863) – Patrick Ennis (1882) – James Ennis (1885) – William Kelly – Lord Cloncurry (1906).

8a   Thomas Monaghan (1851) – Thomas Dunne (1897) – Lord Cloncurry (1899).

8b   Vacant (1851) – John Feeney (1860) – Marcella Malone (1865) – 1899 House fallen.

8c   Vacant (1851) – Garrett Kenny (1865) – 1927 House fallen.

9   Bridget Dunne (1851) – Patrick Feeney (1860) – House in ruins (1878).

APPENDIX 2

NAME	AGE	OCCUPATION	COUNTY OF BIRTH
1901 Census: Ballyvoneen			
William Kelly	66	Steward	Wicklow
Catherine Kelly	46	Steward	Wicklow
Margaret Kelly	68	Steward	Wicklow
Mary Redmond	14	Domestic Servant	Kildare
1901 Census: Ballinakill			
Catherine Dawson	80	Seamstress	Kildare
James Dawson	46	Shepherd	Kildare
Christopher Dawson	36	Shepherd	Kildare
Lizzie Dawson	49	Seamstress	Kildare
1901 Census: Cloncurry			
Joseph Harris	38	Farmer	Kildare
Anne Harris	71	Farmer	Kildare
Anne Harris	36	Farmer	Kildare
Anne Harris	3	Scholar	Kildare
James Harris	1	Scholar	Kildare
Patrick Hareis	6 months	Scholar	Kildare
Thomas Murray	20	Farm Servant	Meath
John Feeney	46	Farmer	Kildare
Christina Feeney	45	Seamstress	Kildare
Mary Feeney	87	Seamstress	Kildare
Laurence Feeney	16	Scholar	Kildare
John Feeney	14	Scholar	Kildare

Patrick Feeney	12	Scholar	Kildare
Maly Feeney	11	Scholar	Kildare
Thomas Feeney	6	Scholar	Kildare
Anne Feeney	4	Scholar	Kildare
Matthew Dixon	50	Visitor\Labourer	Kildare
Thomas Walsh	55	Cooper	Kildare
Ellen Walsh	45	Dressmaker	Kildare
Mary-Anne Walsh	22	Apprentice Dressmaker	Kildare
John Walsh	17	Apprentice Cooper	Kildare
Patrick Monaghan	67	Farm Servant	Kildare
Anne Monaghan	65		Kildare
Patrick Monaghan	24	Farm Servant	Kildare
William Monaghan	20	Farm Servant	Kildare
Francis Thornton	70	Shopkeeper	Mayo
John Boggan	26	Shopkeeper	Meath
Garret Kenny	70	Agricultural Labourer	Westmeath
Elizabeth Kenny	63		Wicklow
William Daly	4	Scholar	City of Dublin
Gerald Daly	2	Scholar	City of Dublin
James Ennis	50	Labourer	Kildare
Mary Ennis	47	Kildare	
Margaret Adams	45	Kildare	
Patrick Ennis	17	Labourer	Kildare
John Ennis	15	Labourer	Kildare
Catherine Ennis	15	Scholar	Kildare
Joseph Ennis	11	Scholar	Kildare

Cloonfush, county Galway

GABRIEL O'CONNOR

I

An article in the *Tuam Herald* in January 1915 reported the sale of the Marshall Day property in Cloonfush to the Congested Districts Board.[1] The matriarch of the family had died in Terenure, County Dublin, in November 1913, leaving personal effects of £1,216. Her lands were then available for distribution among her tenants. What was intriguing about this item was the emphasis put on the friendly relations that existed between the owners of this estate and their tenantry. The claim that there was never any friction and never an eviction on Day property is well supported by local folklore. There was great resentment against their local clergy for not allowing them to attend their landlord's funeral.[2] However the peasant society of this townland settlement had very little contact with landlords or any outside destructive forces to their ancient way of life.

It is obvious that there was something different about this townland and its inhabitants. The history of Cloonfush is not a tale of benevolent landlords and subservient tenants. No landlord ever lived there. At times the inhabitants were unsure who their landlord was. Yet a very ancient community stubbornly survived here until post famine emigration gradually dispersed them, their way of life and their mentality. The sale notice of 1915 marked the death of the old community.

The earliest evidence of habitation can be traced back with certainty to the fifth century. This townland is located in the parish of Tuam, barony of Clare, approximately two miles west of Tuam town. The area, as surveyed in 1843, measures 398 acres. The topography identifies the townland as a unique feature of the local landscape. Its remoteness, created by natural barriers of water, marsh and bog, marks its identity as clearly as if it were an island. The Fair Maps of 1838, drawn just before the first major drainage of the Clare river, confirm this isolation.[3] The only entry was through bogland to an island of hills and green pasture. Yet this community lived within two miles of the market town of Tuam. However, these inhabitants were not transformed by the intrusion of commerce. Their material life and mentality changed very little until the twentieth century.

Even before the famine of the 1845, the physical isolation of this townland was coming to an end. The first of the major drainage schemes on the Clare

---

1 *Tuam Herald*, 23 January 1915; NA, Calender of Probate, Letters of Administration of 8 January 1914. vol. 1913–14, D. **2** James (O'Shaughnessy) Donnellan, Cloonfush, Co. Galway, in conversation with author, 15 Oct. 1994. **3** OS, Fair plans of Tuam and district (twelve sections), B269 OS 1838.

river, undertaken in the 1850s by the Commissioners of Public Works, lowered the bed of the river.[4] A new road had also been constructed by the county grand jury and provided access to Cloonfush from the Tuam Galway road at Clashroe.[5] Remarkably, the track of the ancient road is still visible, as it runs west through the townland of Killaunty to the Weir Road and on to Tuam.

The name of the townland has never been a source of controversy, as it is generally agreed that it has remained unchanged for at least 1,500 years and contemporary ecclesiastical evidence supports this. Yet the interpretation of its name is still able to cause disagreement in this quiet locality. Dr Joyce described a *cluain* as a fertile piece of land surrounded by bog or marsh on one side and water on the other.[6] This translation from the Gaelic is both apt and acceptable. What is not universally acceptable is the translation of *fush*. John O'Donovan visited the townland in 1838 and he translated the name as 'The Meadows of the Stay or Rest', a place of retreat.[7] Evidence of an early Christian settlement there helped support his view, which was further reinforced by subsequent ecclesiastical historians. He ignored a stubborn local folklore that insisted that the name of their townland translated as 'The Meadow of the Lark'.[8]

The archaeological and historical research on Cloonfush recorded by O'Donovan in the county Galway field books stands as a lasting tribute to the meticulous observation and research of both the man and his department.[9] The ruins of the early Christian settlement, a '*cillian*' or children's burial ground and a trig station are described. He mentioned that the land quality was a mixture of good, rough and bog. What was most surprising was that his hand written report actually stressed that 'the proprietor of this townland is not known'.

John O'Donovan's reconstruction of life in the fifth and sixth centuries, was compiled from isolated passages from the Benignus (Benen) manuscript and isolated passages from the lives of other saints.[10] Very little information on St Jarlath, the founder of the townland's monastic settlement has survived.

Jarlath belonged to the native race known as the Conmaicne of West Connacht. They were divided into three families, the Conmaicne Mara (modern Connemara), the Conmaicne Cuil-Fola (county Mayo), and the Conmaicne Chinealdubhain (who controlled the area later called the barony of Dunmore). Jarlath was descended from the Dunmore Conmacs. Early Irish saints generally founded their churches in their own tribal land. The Strafford Survey of 1636 placed the townland originally in Dunmore barony.[11] Since the early eighteenth century it is in the barony of Clare.

---

4 *Tuam Herald*, 14 July 1855.   **5** OS, Townland Survey Map of Co. Galway, 1841, sheets 29, 43.   **6** Galway City Archive, letters containing information relative to the Antiquities of the Co. of Galway collected during the progress of the Ordnance Survey, unpublished manuscript p. 27.   **7** Ibid., pp. 26–31.   **8** James (Shaughnessy) Donnellan and others, Cloonfush, Co. Galway, in conversation with author 15 October 1994.   **9** VO, Field books, O'Donovan, Cloonfush, Co. Galway, 1839.   **10** Revd J. Healy, *Ireland's ancient schools and scholars* (3rd ed, 2 vols Dublin, 1897), i, 541.   **11** *Book of Survey and Distribution*, Co. Galway, ed. R.C. Simington (Dublin, 1962) p. 290.

St Jarlath was trained by St Benen at a church founded for this purpose at Kilbannon, to the north west of Tuam. As St Benen died in 468 it is probable that the first church of St Jarlath was founded by that date at Cloonfush.[12] St Jarlath left Cloonfush, in advanced old age, as a result of a dream. It was suggested that he should travel eastward, and, where his chariot wheel broke, he was to build an oratory and remain there. Both wheels broke in Tuam, where he established a church about AD 540.[13]

The departure of St Jarlath certainly did not end the monastic settlement in the townland. Apparently it flourished as a school or college for at least 300 years. It attracted scholars from all over Ireland and even foreign dignitaries are mentioned. St Brendan, who subsequently founded Ardfert and Clonfert, and St Colman of Cloyne, were educated in this townland. Dr Healy, in the late nineteenth century, identified the old churchyard as being the site of the ancient college and he also claimed that he discovered the track of the old causeway that connected the church to that college.[14] The early ecclesiastical settlement was constructed of timber and the present stone archaeological remains would suggest that the college of Cloonfush survived for centuries. Yet the absence of a round tower, in contrast to its parent foundation in Kilbannon, also suggests that it was abandoned as a monastic settlement by the ninth century. As Tuam grew into a major ecclesiastical centre of seven churches, it became the object of plunder and the ravages of war.[15] The Danes burnt Tuam on numerous occasions between 835 and 984 and reputedly sailed by Cloonfush to get there, yet the only entry in the annals during these silent centuries is a solitary sentence recording the death of the archdeacon of Tuam in 1294, by drowning at Cloonfush, 'where there was an abbey and celebrated school in the sixth century'.[16]

The order of saints that came to this townland had some bishops but were mainly presbyters.[17] They refused the company of women and separated them from the monasteries in a separate habitation. The clergy of this Second Order were Gaelic.[18] St Jarlath of Tuam was specifically mentioned as being of this order. Also, these ecclesiastical settlements were self sufficient and seem to have been bound by vows to cultivate the land for the use of the poor.[19] A close relationship existed between the monastic settlement and the lay community.

There is evidence in Cloonfush of the existence of a *sean bhaile*, an ancient village that stood outside the boundary of the ecclesiastical settlement, until at least the seventeenth century. The entire village was moved to its present location, less than a quarter of a mile from the original site. The reason for the relocation, whether because of plague or otherwise, remains a mystery.[20] Another question

12 W.M. Hennessy (ed.), *The Annals of Ulster* (5 vols, Dublin, 1887–1901) i, 467.   **13** VO, Field book, Cloonflush, Co. Galway, 1839.   **14** Healy, *Ireland's ancient schools and scholars*, i, 541.   **15** Monsignor Dalton, *History of the archdiocese of Tuam* (2 vols, Dublin, 1928) i, 57. **16** Oliver J. Burke, *The history of the Catholic archdiocese of Tuam* (2nd ed., Dublin, 1882) p. 81. **17** James Stuart, *City of Armagh* (Belfast, 1819), p. 79.   **18** Ibid.   **19** Ibid.   **20** James Donnellan, Cloonfush, Co. Galway, in conversation with author, 17 October 1994.

raised is why the landscape, as shaped by human habitation, is different in this locality? An archaeological survey undertaken in 1902 details the numerical density of raths and lisses in the neighbourhood of Tuam.[21] Yet this feature of an ancient system of farming is not to be found in this townland. A very different landscape, shaped over the centuries by the descendants of the _sean bhaile_, can be seen in Cloonfush.

II

If the fifth-century monastic settlement had any enduring influence in shaping the structure of the community initially, no tradition of craft or business has survived in this townland. Despite its proximity to the extensive markets of Tuam and the port of Galway, there is no evidence of the intrusion of commerce affecting or transforming the traditional habits of this apparently closed community. How did such a social cohesion survive for so long? To answer this question, curiosity is focused on the power brokers who controlled the destiny of this quiet obscure townland, whose inhabitants existed without the shadow of spire, castle or local magnate of any kind. John O'Donovan failed to name the proprietor, while the valuers of the primary valuation even used an incorrect surname. Ownership of Cloonfush does not appear in nineteenth century property lists of landowners of over one acre. Land ownership in Ireland was always a complex issue, but an excellent example of its complexity is to be found in the surviving records of this hidden townland.

The evidence is strongly in favour of church ownership since the fifth century. The only question to challenge this was a reference to a grant of two quarters of land to the archbishop of Tuam in return for land on which to build the 'Wonderful Castle' in the town, by the O'Connors in 1161.[22] The area may correspond, yet there is no supporting evidence to connect this grant with Cloonfush. All subsequent grants to the Tuam archdiocese are well documented, yet this townland is not mentioned.[23] However, concrete evidence of long term church ownership is supported by Strafford's Survey of Connacht of 1636. The Connacht baronies were carved out by the lord deputy in 1585. The barony boundary followed the tribal boundary, not the physical boundary of the river Clare.[24] Cloonfush was listed as belonging to 'the See of Tuam'. The area was described as two quarters and the number of profitable acres was stated to be 215. In 1585 a quarter was equal to 120 acres, so this raised a question as the townland area is almost 400 acres statue measure. Apparently a quarter was an uncertain quantity,

---

21 Dr T.B. Costello, 'Tuam raths and southerains' in _JGAHS_, 2, no. 2 (1902) p. 109.
22 M.W. Hennessy (ed.), _The Annals of Lough Cé_ (2 vols, Dublin, 1871), i, 1161.   **23** H.S. Sweetman (ed.), _Calender of Documents relating to Ireland, 1252–84_ (London, 1877).
24 _Books of Survey and Distribution, Co. Galway_, ed. R.C. Simington (Dublin, 1962), p. 290.

a measure of value and not of actual acreage. It was relative to the number of cattle a standard quarter could carry. So the townland had the cattle carrying capacity of two standard quarters. Griffith's *Valuation*, 200 years later, actually reflected this quarter valuation in Cloonfush.[25]

The effects of the Reformation were late in coming to the west. In 1561 the Jesuit Fr Wolfe visited Tuam and found that the monasteries and lands were still in Roman Catholic hands.[26] It was not until 1573, under Archbishop Lally, that ownership of Cloonfush became the property of the Protestant Church. An important clause, imposed under the acts of settlement and explanation that followed the 1641 rebellions, was written into the instruments of title by the state. It stipulated that church lands could only be leased. Lease maps would have been drafted, usually on the arrival of each new archbishop and an example of this is the James Morris map of 1720 which numbers and lists the town properties of the archbishop. Notably, only one road out of the town is marked with a cross and this indicates the 'Killaunty' road, the old road to Cloonfush.[27]

III

Relations of several archbishops were listed as leaseholders on the abstract of title for this townland, but the earliest surviving lease was contained in the will of Isabella Marshall, dated 13 January 1829.[28] Her maiden name was Medlicott, a family which had acquired extensive estates in Sligo, Newport and Mayo. Her 'title' originated in her husband's will with grants of lands in Kilbannon, Cloonfush, Newport and Kilmore. The lease obtained by her deceased husband, John Marshall, in the previous century from the archbishop of Tuam was an example of an interesting circumvention of the law. Church land legally belonged to the crown and technically could only be leased, yet this Marshall lease gave security and title to the family almost as binding as a sale. Under this lease, an annual 'head rent' with 'renewal fines' was due each time the lease was renewed, which was to be on the death of the archbishop. However the 'head rent' was fixed initially at £100 yearly to the see of Tuam in respect of all lands held by the Marshall family. This land, shown in a lease map drafted by G. Browne in 1783, included four townlands, including Cloonfush, with a total acreage of 1,250 acres. The total stated income from tenants amounted to £1,000 per annum.[29] Rents paid by tenants in Cloonfush averaged £283 11s. 10d. per annum during the years from 1850 to 1868. When it is considered that the lessors retained 116 acres

25 Griffith's *Valuation*, Co. Galway, Barony of Clare, Union of Tuam.   **26** Oliver Burke, *The history of the Catholic archdiocese of Tuam* (Dublin, 1882), p. 87.   **27** James Morris maps, 5 July 1720, 'Drawn for his grace, The Lord Archbishop of Tuam in 1720' (copy by John Burke, 1863, in Tuam Library).   **28** NA, ILC, Prerogative will, 21 January 1830, Records of Court of Prerogative, transcript of will attached to CDB record no. 9927.
29 NA, ILC, Abstract of Title, Estate of John Marshall Day, CDB record no. 9927.

of grazing land, which was farmed by a herdsman, this left about 282 acres of mixed land and bog at rents that averaged £1 per acre. In 1845, when the Devon Commission inquired about the rent of 'average good land' in the district, it was informed that 15s. to 30s. was the usual. It was clarified that 30s. was considered, even for excellent tillage land, to be a very high price.[30] It appears that the Marshall Day family were able to command substantial rents for below average quality land. Yet the landlords held the respect and affection of their tenants. Rents were never changed and the landlord never interfered. This allowed the community to protect its interests and retain its own identity.

An unusual aspect of Isabella Marshall's will was the way the property was protected in the interests of the family. This also ensured security and stability in the townland. All descendants were to share in the family fortunes regardless of seniority by birth or gender. Isabella left the entire estate on her death in 1830 to her one remaining daughter, Christianna.[31] The will specifically excluded Christianna's husband, Robert Day, from any property rights. It stipulated that she inherited the property 'as if she were an unmarried women, free from all control and interference whatsoever of her husband and not to be in anywise subject to his debts or other incumbrances'. If he outlived his wife and if by her death she had not by deed divided the assets of the estate among her children, then that duty fell to him. Robert Day BL was a very prominent man in legal circles in his own right, yet safeguards to protect this family's interests from an unscrupulous husband were normal legal precautions. The principal Day residence was in Kerry. They owned several houses in Dublin and subsequently their son resided in Milford Lodge, on the Weir Road, Killounty, on the outskirts of Tuam.

Christianna died in June 1863 and she left the estate to her four children. She had two sons, William and John and two daughters, Elizabeth and Isabella. William inherited Kilbannon and Ballybane and John acquired Cloonfush and Newpark. Both had to pay the renewal fines and head rent for the entire property to the see of Tuam. This left William with an annual income in excess of £500. John had to pay the greater part of the head rent and renewal fines which amounted to £81 18s. 2d, which left him with an annual income of over £200 out of Cloonfush.

Elizabeth received the income from named tenants in Kilmore, who paid a combined rent of £119 per annum. Her inheritance was free of all head rent and renewal fines but was also protected from control, debts or engagements of any man or men with whom she might intermarry.[33] Kilmore was an adjoining townland, yet rents here were substantially lower per acre, as head rent and renewal fines were paid out of the income from Cloonfush.

---

30 *Commission of inquiry into the state of the law and practice in respect to occupation of land in Ireland* [Devon Commission], Minutes of evidence, Pt. 11 HC 1845, [616] Witness no. 526 (John Nolan) question 11. 1845, Tuam. **31** NA, ILC, Abstract of Wills, CDB 9927 (p. 5). **32** NA, Calender of Grants of Probate 1864, p. 46. **33** NA, ILC, Abstract of Wills, CDB 9927.

The youngest daughter, Isabella, had obviously married a man of substance and on her marriage to Dr Maybury of Kerry a substantial dowry was charged to the Day estate. However, Dr Thomas and Isabella Duckett Maybury must have been surprised by their unusual inheritance. They received the remainder of Kilmore, where the tenancy and representatives of John Cullinan paid a rent of £20 8s. 0d. per annum. These lands were free of head rent and renewal fines but carried debts of £750 paid to William and Elizabeth.[34] These lower rents may have been a factor that influenced at least two of the core families from Cloonfush to resettle in Kilmore after the famine.

The Marshal Day family never became directly involved with the management of the estate. The rent collector actually resided three miles away in Kilbannon. They were not improving landlords and never attempted to regulate any aspect of the life of the community. The only evidence of concern was expressed by William, on behalf of his family, at a meeting of the Drainage Commissioners held at Galway on 28 June 1855. The cess had been raised in Cloonfush as a result of the River Clare drainage and the Commissioners' valuer had admitted that too high an increase had been placed on the townland. In his lengthy complaint about this gross injustice he took the part of the proprietors. He never even mentioned the tenants who paid cess, as well as their rent, on the remaining area of the townland. William's address was given as Leinster Square, Rathmines, Dublin.[35] The Church of Ireland see of Tuam never had any contact with the townland, although the church retained turf-cutting rights recorded, without explanation, as the 'Robinson Line'. However this right was never used. In fact the only visitors ever mentioned, arrived annually, on 6 June after 1817, when the students of St Jarlath's seminary and their professors visited the ancient monastic site in commemoration of their patron saint. These excursions ended after a drowning accident in the Clare river in 1913, which claimed the lives of two students.

John Marshall Day only enjoyed his inheritance of Cloonfush for four months. He died intestate and a bachelor on 2 November 1863. However, the Mayburys moved quickly and in January 1864 Isabella Maybury of Tralee took out letters of administration and was granted probate as John's lawful sister and surviving next of kin. William had also died twelve days before John.[37]

IV

In 1869, the Westminster parliament under Gladstone passed the disestablishment act. The Representative Church Body was established to regulate the affairs of

---

34 NA, ILC, Abstract of Wills. CDB 9927. **35** *Tuam Herald*, 14 July 1855, letter to the editor from William Marshall Day. **36** James Donnellan, Cloonfush, Co. Galway, in conversation with author 15 Oct. 1994. **37** NA, ILC, *Calendar of Grants of Probate*, 4 January 1864. CDB record no. 9927.

the Church of Ireland and all church lands were taken over by the Comm-issioners of Church Temporalities. Because of the complexity of the Day lease, there was no question of disposing of the property directly to tenants, even if they had the deposit required. The Cloonfush lease was dealt with in July 1876.[38]

William had four children, who were minors, so his widow, Frances Benmina Day (Chambers), became the guardian of his estate. The children's names were Robert, John, Christina and Marion. William's two sisters, Elizabeth and Isabella were still alive. Elizabeth had no children but Isabella had one son, a minor, Named Robert Marshall-Maybury. So, with the agreement of the family and the Commissioners, Frances Benmina Day became the representative of the family and 'testamentary guardian' of all five minors. She purchased the entire estate as originally leased in 1783. In order to obtain the deposit, she sold her husband's government stock for £1, 660 8s. 11d., only half its stock value. The balance of the purchase price of £4,786 10s. 6d. was to be repaid to the treasury in sixty-four six-monthly instalments.[39]

This conveyance was registered in January 1881. A second deed was also registered in the Registry of Deeds, dated in July 1885.[40] This finally cancelled the original lease and John Brown map and an agreement of declaration of trust was made between the seven family members.

Robert, an engineer, died in March 1900. His address was given as 'late of Cook Street Hospital, Dublin'. Probate was granted to his brother, Dr John. Robert, a bachelor, left effects worth £1,673 8s. 11d.[41] Frances Benmina Day died on 28 November 1913.[42] Probate of her personal effects was also granted to Dr John. This simplified the position and made it possible for the Congested District Board to acquire, under the 1903 and 1909 land acts, the entire Day estate. The Congested Districts Board had no option but to pay all the debts on the estate. The dowries alone amounted to £5,600. Dr William retained a small portion of land, which he sold. The sale was completed in the office of Sutton and County Solrs on 3 December 1914. Dr John Marshall Day, head of a fever hospital in Dublin, finally severed the family connection with Cloonfush.[43] The family's ownership had ensured that this small settlement and the continuity of their lifestyle had survived into the twentieth century.

V

Estate records and account books did not list individual tenants until after 1843.[44] The absence of any 'Big House' ensured that casual observers of the upper leisured class never visited Cloonfush. The road into the townland was a cul-de-sac, which guaranteed its privacy. Yet one traveller's account in the early

38 Ibid.   **39** Ibid.   **40** RD, registered on 31 August 1885, book 36. no. 76.   **41** NA, Calender of Probate, registered 24 July 1905.   **42** NA, ILC, Copy of Probate in CDB record no. 9927.   **43** NA, ILC, CDB record no. 9927.   **44** NA, ILC, CDB record no. 9927.

nineteenth century described the area outside Tuam on his way to Headford as 'the most horrible imaginable'.[45] Another visited the hamlets surrounding Tuam and described the appalling living conditions of the peasantry.[46] The *Parliamentary Gazetteer* listed the principal hamlets, including Cloonfush. The description of the habitations suggested that none of the ten mentioned varied in standard. The houses were in general sheer huts, 'the lowest and most miserable abodes of squalidness and destitution'.[47] The landscape where these hamlets were situated was described as being on ground 'that contains many swells, undulating ridges and variously shaped hillocks, and possesses numerous little districts of pleasant ornate wood and especially tillage cultivation; yet it aggregately presents a dismally bleak, morassy and repulsive appearance'.[48]

Two young Frenchmen visited Tuam in August of 1835. They described a hamlet, which they called Village X, which was a short walking distance from the town. Alex de Tocqueville and his companion, Gustave de Beaumount, described houses 'made of sun dried mud and built with walls to the height of a man'. The roofs were of thatch so old, 'that the grass that covered it merged with the pasture'. The dwellings had no windows or chimneys and daylight and smoke entered and exited through the door. The only furniture described was a rickety, wooden stool and a turf fire between four stones. The inhabitants were described crowding to the door in surprise. Images of the pig, the dunghill, the bare heads and feet of the people and numerous healthy idlers, were painted. The men appeared to be civil and, in the presence of these gentlemen, the women 'curt'sy and cross themselves'. However, contrary to this travel writer's usual practice, there was no title or date for this entry. De Tocqueville did not arrive in Tuam from Galway until noon on 4 August. He can be located in Castlebar, thirty-six miles away, on the following day.

Internal dating of the Tuam episode indicates that it took place on a Saturday and a Sunday.[49] Yet, despite inaccuracies, his description supports the available evidence. Henry Coulter visited 'suburbs' outside Tuam a quarter of a century later and he was also shocked at the squalor, dirt and discomfort of the hovels. 'These are neither water nor airtight and are unfit for the habitation of human beings.'[50] Three hamlets, including Cloonfush, were within walking distance of Tuam. Although the *Parliamentary Gazetteer* correspondent was the only one to specifically name the townland, all the descriptions would suggest that the habitations in Cloonfush (and adjacent hamlets) were different from and much poorer than those in other parts of the country. The mud and rags covered an almost invisible community. There was no social or material distinction within the townland and this was a distinctive enough feature to be mentioned by Mr Williamson, the valuation official, who visited Cloonfush in 1834.[51] The first

45 Caesar Otway, *A Tour in Connaught* (London, 1839), pp. 177–86. **46** Alex de Tocqueville, *Journey in Ireland* (reprint, 1990), pp. 106–11. **47** *Parliamentary Gazetteer of Ireland* (1846), vol. 4, pp. 398–407. **48** *Parliamentary Gazetteer*, vol. 4, p. 399. **49** De Tocqueville, *Journey in Ireland*, p. 107. **50** *Saunder's Newsletter*, Winter, 1861/62. **51** VO, valuation map of 1838, shows the position of the disorganised cluster of cabins located in the centre of the townland, stamped with its own identity. This was not a plantation village. This was the home of an extended family unit. Cloonfush was a cohesion of people and place, who lived, loved and died, on the outskirts of another world.[52]

The tithe records for Cloonfush are available and at first glance looked to be a disappointing source, but yet had their story to tell. The Established Church Commissioners to whom the tithe was to be paid in 1831 were the Revd John O'Rourke and the Revd Thomas Browne. The tithe was a church tax on produce only, and the area on which tithes were due in this townland amounted to 180 acres. However, the total tithe due was a mere £6. This low value is misleading and is only partly explained by the fact that these tithes on church lands were paid to the vicar in Tuam exclusively.[53] Another intriguing arrangement to emerge from these records was that the entire community was represented by Roger Forde (and Co.), who paid the tithes on their behalf. This confirms what was already suggested in the Day family records in connection with rents, that one head man represented the townland. The potential income of the village, based on over 180 acres of produce, is possible to estimate. The rents from 282 tenanted acres of Cloonfush (the Days retained 116 acres for grazing) amounted to £1 per acre. Yet prices for produce was remarkably high. In 1824 a stone of potatoes sold for 5d. per stone or 2½d. cwt. sold for £1. Oatmeal cost 13s. per cwt. Oats sold for 7s. per cwt. So, less than three cwt. of oats per acre paid the rent. Pork sold for 18s. and 4d. per cwt. Wool per stone sold for 15s. and 4d. The large area of bog was extremely valuable as baskets of turf were in great demand, as the income from tolls of the Tuam Corporation show. Eels and salmon were harvested from the Clare river.[55] Their proximity to the Tuam markets, where they could sell geese and eggs, reveal an economy that left its hardworking inhabitants poor and struggling but considerably better off than many of the town poor. The farming enterprises in Cloonfush were very labour intensive but were also diverse. This system, combined with a fixed rent paid through one representative, gave them collective security. A partnership system of farming survived in this townland perhaps much longer than would have been expected. The functional interdependence of arable, meadowland and rough grazing were reinforced with turf-cutting and eel-fishing and its economy was shaped by its proximity to a thriving market centre in Tuam. The famine of 1820 was not severe in this area, and this is supported by correspondence from Archbishop Kelly in 1822.[56] In fact market prices in Tuam were exceptionally high, as food was particularly scarce in West Galway and Mayo.[57]

Field/book, Cloonfush.   **52** VO, Primary valuation map, no. 184, sheet 29, Co. Galway.
53 NA, TA survey 1824–44, vol. 2, no. 10–16, Cloonfush, parish of Tuam, 1831.   **54** *Tuam Gazette*, 7 August 1824.   **55** James Donnellan, Cloonfush, in conversation with author 15 Oct. 1994; Tuam Town Hall, minutes of Tuam Town Commissioners, 1843.   **56** Irish Studies Library, Armagh. Collection of Dr Oliver Kelly letters, 1822, to Famine Inquiry, London Tavern.   **57** Ibid.

There was no attempt to rationalise the land system in this townland until the Congested Districts Board purchased the property in 1913.[58] Neither the Established Church nor the Marshall Day family ever interfered, nor were there any evictions or change of tenants that could have threatened this community of kinship groups and connected families. Their culture and identity remained intact. This was an ancient hamlet, without any public house, school, church, forge, or shop. Cloonfush had all the essentials within the townland to sustain its way of life. It is more than probable that a dramatic rise in population in the years before the famine of 1845, rather than starvation, was the principal factor responsible for the disintegration of this community.

There are no population statistics available for Cloonfush until 1841. The figures for the parish of Tuam rose rapidly from 7,804 in 1821 to 14,219 by 1831. It is reasonable to assume that there was a corresponding rise in the number of inhabitants in this townland beyond the barrier of its limits for economic survival. In 1841 the population reached 209 inhabitants living in thirty-four houses.[59] This meant a density of over six people per thatched cottage of no more than two rooms. It also gives a person to land ratio of one inhabitant to a little over an acre of 'mixed' land. The population of the townland was reduced to 145 inhabitants by 1851. However, the decline may well be because of economic factors rather than the result of starvation and disease. There were two active relief committees based in Tuam and the workhouse, which was opened in 1846, provided outdoor relief on a very intensive scale.[60] The population of Tuam rose considerably between 1841 and 1851. Yet there is no evidence that any inhabitants from this townland moved to Tuam. The records show only one birth in the workhouse in 1850 where the mother had a Cloonfush address.[61] So who were the people who disappeared during that decade? It appears that eight houses were unoccupied by 1851, yet the number of inhabitants per house in the occupied houses remained almost the same. Comparing the lists of families in residence before and after the famine reveals that eight families have vanished.[62] An example of one such family is that of Michael Burke. The parish birth records lists his children as Patrick, Mary, Catherine, a second Patrick, Bridget, a second Bridget, Honor, Thomas, a third Patrick and finally Winifred. These children were all born between November 1811 and July 1827.[63] Two to three years separated each birth. Catherine married a Bermingham of Cloonfush, Mary and Honor also married within the townland, but the two surviving sons and remaining daughter do not appear on any register again. The mother of these ten children was Margaret Ford, a native of the townland. Another indigenous family gone by 1851 were the Kilgarriffs. John Kilgarriff was born in October 1801. He married Bridget Bermingham, also from the townland, and they had

---

58 NA, ILC, CDB 9927. **59** *Census of Ireland*, 1841. **60** Tuam Library, Minutes, Tuam Poor Law Union, Book 3, 1845. **61** Catholic birth register, parish of Tuam, 12 September 1850. **62** Catholic marriage register, parish of Tuam. 1799–1900. **63** Catholic birth register, parish of Tuam, 1799–1900.

three sons and two daughters. The youngest two sons were born in 1844 and the last in January 1847. Yet, by 1851 this family was also gone. The other missing families are named Connor, Keane, Foley, Raftery, Keenan and MacManus. These were similar in structure to the Burke and Kilgarriff families, but left no identifiable family connections behind.[64] However, a strong Cloonfush connection with Wigan, Wrexham and Warrington in Britain, the Bronx in the USA and the British army was well established during the second half of the nineteenth century.[65] It is more than probable that these missing families formed the nucleus of the first 'pioneers' from Cloonfush to establish 'colonies' abroad, which attracted and offered a base for the youth of the townland for generations. So emigration of entire families from a townland that could no longer sustain them began and continued.

An examination of the Catholic marriage register between 1799 and 1901 is reasonably accurate for this townland as the 1901 census indicates that the inhabitants were all of that persuasion. During the first half of the nineteenth century a maximum of twenty different surnames can be linked with Cloonfush. Peter Crisham was married to Catherine Ford. Margaret Ford was married to Mark Corcoran. Mary Shaughnessy was married to Andrew Cullinan. Walter Cullinan was married to Mary Reilly.[66] They were in fact a large extended family community.

By 1851, of the forty-eight named tenants in the townland, twelve were Shaughnessy, seven were Ford, seven were Higgins, three were Thorntons, and three were Reillys. Church records show that the remaining surnames of Roche, Foley, Crisham, Bermingham and Ryan also had some connections.[67] This would suggest that a mainly closed society, based on kinship, existed until 1851.

The decline in population continued during the twenty years that followed the famine. The number of inhabitants in the townland was 127 people living in twenty-four houses by 1861. This had dropped to 103 people living in twenty- two houses by 1871. The population density had improved to 4.68 people per house. There was also by 1871 nearly three acres of tenanted land per inhabitant. The twenty years after the famine may have been economically advantageous for beef and butter exports, but tillage farming barely survived, as the weekly market reports in the *Tuam Herald* clearly illustrate. On average prices were 20 per cent less than the 1824 prices for oats, barley and potatoes.[68] The period of economic decline from 1841 to 1871 reveals a slight pattern of change in the population structure. Up to 1861 there were more males to females in the townland. From 1871 to 1911 this balance changed from 1 per cent more to 5 per cent less in each decade.[69] The evidence shows that emigration of entire families continued until 1871. The number of houses declined from thirty-four in 1841 to twenty-two in 1871.

64 Ibid.   65 *Tuam Herald*, 30 January 1915, Letter from 'A Tuam Soldier at the Front'. 66 Catholic birth register, parish of Tuam, 1799–1900.   67 Catholic marriage register, parish of Tuam, 1799–1900.   68 *Tuam Herald*, market reports, analysis of monthly returns in the years, 1850, 1870, 1880.   69 *Census of Ireland*, 1871–1901.

During the last thirty years of the nineteenth century the population stabilised and appeared to have reached its level of economic survival. The number of inhabitants remained static at 104 for the next fifty years. However, the economic depression of the 1880s ensured that the community was still under pressure, as by 1901 the number of houses declined to eighteen, which left a house density of almost six once more.[71]

The birth and marriage records reveal an even more dramatic change in the kinship structure. New surnames begin to appear in the townland between 1850 and 1901. Thomas Donnellan from Carantanlas, a townland about eight miles from Cloonfush, married into the farm of Kate Shaughnessy. John Fleming married in to Bridget Bermingham's land. John Nicholson from Lissavelley, a few miles away, married into Ellen Bermingham's family.[72] Other new surnames were Staunton, Murray, Devine, Quinn and Judge. Michael Kelly married Luke Foley's daughter, Rose, and inherited the plots 13abcd, marked on the valuation map in Appendix 1.[73]

Another interesting pattern is revealed through a study of surnames and family Christian names associated with Cloonfush in the parish. There is very little evidence of outside marriages. For example, when Michael Connor (or O'Connor) and his wife Mary Ford registered the birth of their son on 20 December 1823, they built their house in the adjoining townland of Kilmore, where rents were low. Sabina Crisham, a daughter of one of the longest established core families of Cloonfush, married Thomas Gilligan of Kilmore, where they reared a family of eight children. The first born was registered in 1850.[74] There are a small number of other possible connections, yet intermarriage between these two adjoining townlands is not as prevalent as would be expected. The community, with a few exceptions, remained cohesive and when they had to leave they left as families.

However, after 1871, the pattern of emigration changed. The evidence indicates that most of the young men emigrated, to the point where 50 per cent of the farms were left without a male heir. There is only one example of a widow listed in the revision books as the rated occupier, being replaced by her son, who returned from the coalfields of Wigan. The young girls also left for the 'brighter lights', except from a house where no marriageable son remained. Then she became a 'woman of substance' where the matchmaker was concerned, and this probably accounts for young men being married into the locality.[75]

However, this slow erosion of this closed community based on kinship was not at all times an easy transformation and this opening of the community did not always improve the quality of life in Cloonfush. The land tenure was so interlinked that friction between at least one young man that married in led to

70 *Census of Ireland*, 1841–71.   **71** VO, Cancellation books, Cloonfush, 1856–86. **72** Catholic marriage register, parish of Tuam, 1799–1900.   **73** Catholic marriage register, parish of Tuam, 1799–1900.   **74** Catholic birth register, parish of Tuam, 1799–1900.   **75** James Donnellan and others, Cloonfush, Co. Galway, in conversation with author, 15 October 1994.

a feud that split the community for generations.[76] Neither faction ever brought their case outside the townland, nor do the police files contain a record of any disturbance. Yet the card games were played in different sides of the village for many years. The community spirit was beginning to decline.

When Mr D. Williamson and his team of surveyors revisited Cloonfush on 1 January 1843, they discovered a long established and complex system of land use and tenure.[77] This survey, which took seven months to complete, included the amount and value of each category of soil and the area of each category, with a number allotted to each of the eighteen types. A map was also compiled in conjunction with a valuation map, which identified each occupier, the land he farmed, and even included numbers from the category table which denoted the quality.[78] The houses, out-houses and gardens were also surveyed and the information on habitations from these House Books, which subsequently became the basis of Griffith's *Valuation*, paint a very clear picture of this townland's version of a partnership system of agriculture.[79]

The area of the townland totals 398 acres, on which, in 1843, stood a village cluster of thirty-four occupied houses. The total valuation of the land was £148 11s. Of this, 117 acres were farmed by a herd named Patrick Ryan. His house was valued at 15s. and the land at £66. The category of soil in this farm was listed as class ten, eleven, twelve, seventeen and eighteen. For example, class ten was 'arable, shallow, but stony and cold soil' worth 6s. per acre. Category seventeen was listed as 'good flat meadow liable to floods', while class eighteen was 'good pasture and arable, which was also liable to be covered by water'. This farm was described as suitable for meadow and sheep. The graveyard and ruins stood at the end of the road on this farm, which was never leased to any tenants by the Marshall Day family.[80] This area was certainly not the best land in Cloonfush and it is possible to understand John Marshall Day's frustration with the Drainage Commissioners and valuers who admitted they overvalued this townland.[81] This was obviously a sheep-grazing farm and, as Griffith's map and the revised maps show, there were no internal fences, except the road which ran past the children's burial ground and on to the river Clare.[82]

The 'village' of thirty-four houses is shown situated on high ground near the centre of the townland. A note included on the margin of the Primary Valuation manuscript notebook 'that no house on this townland is worth £3 a year' was signed on 4 July 1843.[83] In fact only three houses were worth 15s. Fourteen occupied houses had no value whatsoever. The total valuation of all buildings in the townland was £11. 2s.

---

76 James Donnellan and others, Cloonfush, Co. Galway, in conversation with author, 15 October 1994.   **77** NA, Field book, Cloonfush, Co. Galway, dated January–July 1843. **78** VO, Field book, Cloonfush, Co. Galway, signed by D. Williamson, July 1843.   **79** NA, House books, Cloonfush, D. Williamson, July 1843.   **80** VO, Field book, Cloonfush, Co. Galway, 1843.   **81** *Tuam Herald*, 14 July 1855.   **82** VO, map, no. 43. Co. Galway. 1854. **83** VO, Field book, Cloonfush, Co. Galway, 1843.

To become a Tuam Town Commissioner in 1843, a property qualification of £20 was necessary.[84] The view of the valuers on habitations in Cloonfush confirm the descriptions given by travel writers. The 282 acres of the tenanted area was divided into a patchwork of strips running at right angles to the central road (see Appendix 1). There were twenty holdings averaging about fifteen acres. These holdings were not consolidated but were subdivided into plots in different parts of the townland, so that each shared the different categories of land. Each holding usually contained four types of soil: poor tillage, good tillage, bottom pasture and bog. There were also two types of commonage shared by the inhabitants. These were plot 18a, which was deep bog used for turf and manure by the tenants and bottom meadows and callow liable to flood, shared in common by named occupiers. There were forty-nine occupiers of land in Cloonfush in 1843 who shared these twenty holdings.[85]

The 'village' itself was divided into four distinct sections within the one cluster. To illustrate the complex situation that had evolved, one of these sections, plot 16, had a total area of eight acres one rood and seventeen perches, which was sub-divided, in all probability by the original family. This area corresponds to the smallest ancient division, called a 'gneeve', which was noted by the enumerators of the 1821 census.[86] By 1843 eleven related families shared seventy-two parts of plot 16, on which each had a house and a garden. The subdivisions were even by that date, no longer in sequence (see Valuation Lists, in Appendix 2). Plot 16a was occupied by Jeremiah Shaughnessy, with a share of $^6/_{72}$ parts. John Shaughnessy on 16b occupied the same amount. William Shaughnessy on plot 16c had $^4/_{72}$ parts. Patrick Reilly on 16d held $^3/_{72}$ parts. Jeremiah Forde, Mary Forde, Patrick Forde and Honoria Ford, held twenty parts between them. John Thornton, Matthew Higgins and Thomas Higgins held the remaining twenty two parts. The subdivisions actually add up to more than seventy two, which would suggest that even more subdivisions had occurred. Each occupier had about a tenth of an acre.[87] Most of the tenanted area was not fenced. The divisions shown on the map were 'green fences', which meant that a green strip of grass divided the arable strips, marked the boundary and ensured that no land was lost under fences. The road through the 'village' was fenced by stone walls as was the herdman's grazing farm and the commonage.[88]

Evidence from the Devon Commission confirmed that in the Tuam hinterland the large farms were generally in grazing but the smallholdings and cottier were almost exclusively in tillage.[89] A dairy inspector's report of 1904 reveals that there were only four cows in Cloonfush in that year.[90] It was a custom in this townland

---

84 Tuam Town Hall, Minutes Tuam Town Commissioners, vol. i, 1843. **85** Griffith, *Valuation*, Co. Galway, Barony of Clare, Union of Tuam. **86** Introduction to general topographical index of *Census of Ireland*, 1901. **87** Griffith, *Valuation*, Co. Galway. Barony of Clare, Union of Tuam. **88** James Donnellan and others, in conversation with author, 15 Oct. 1994. **89** Devon Commission, Minutes of evidence Pt 11 H.C.[416] 1845, Tuam 1845. p. 526. **90** Tuam Library, Dairy Inspectors Report, 1904, Cloonfush, Co. Galway, Tuam Library.

to drink 'whitewater' made from grain. The weekly prices and toll accounts in the Tuam markets show a consistent trade for grain, particularly oatmeal, potatoes, meat, wool, eggs, fish and fowl.[91] Also the earliest photographs from the Lawrence Collection show the Tuam market and its turf sellers.[92] Baskets of turf on a donkey were a common sight. However, tillage was very labour intensive and in Cloonfush this involved the entire family unit.

A comparative study of the 1901 and 1911 censuses confirms the emigration trends already identified but also raises many questions. Every person in Cloonfush was Roman Catholic. Everyone was born in county Galway. The head of family in every house was listed as a farmer. Other members of the household were either housekeepers (18), general labourers (3), domestic servants (2), while the remainder were described as farmers' sons or daughters or as scholars.[93] In 1901 there were eighteen houses and 104 inhabitants. The houses were built of stone and all were whitewashed and thatched. No house had more than two rooms. Most houses were graded in class three and measured about 18 feet by 12 feet. The condition of the houses had improved dramatically since 1843, but the townland only had to support half the 1841 population. However, large family units still existed. Figure 1 shows the population of Clonfush from 1841–1911.

Figure 1   Cloonfush population 1841–1911

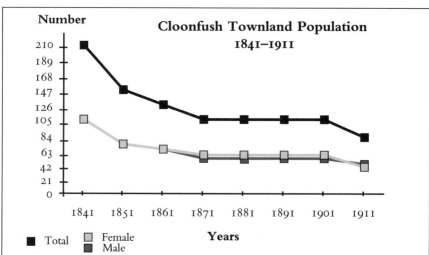

By 1911 the population was reduced to seventy-nine people living in eighteen houses, which left the number of people per house at its 1871 level. The increased valuation and obvious improvement in living standards, was contributed to in no

91 Market reports, *Tuam Herald*. Analysis for month of August in the years 1900–4. **92** NLI, Lawrence Collection, Catalogue nos. 6758, 6759, 6639, 6754, 6757. Tuam Square, *c*.1900.   **93** NA, *Census of Ireland*, 1901. Also, *Census of Ireland*, 1911.

small way by the 'parcel' from America that contained clothes wrapped around a few dollars. This invisible income and visible change of fashion, helped change the townland's economy.[94]

Another factor that contributed to change in Cloonfush, in stark contrast with comparative townlands, is that of a great emphasis placed on education. Half the adult population and all the children between the ages of five and seventeen could read and write and were described as scholars, and all could speak both Irish and English.[95] There was no education available in the townland but the Presentation, Mercy Sisters and the Christian Brothers schools in Tuam were the destination of the barefooted children.[96] Only six households had children over seventeen years in either the 1901 or 1911 census. This tells its tale of emigration and its effect on the townland's economy. However, even more surprising is the evidence that only three households had grandparents. It appears that the belief that the elderly were well cared for in an extended family is a myth, as very few seemed to survive to what is considered old age today. The age profile shows the head of the house as being between fifty and sixty years of age. Wives were generally ten or fifteen years younger than their husbands, yet widows were not numerous in this townland. Families were large, with ten children being common. An intriguing observation of ages of the children is that a two year gap divides the births.[97] A 1901 profile of one particular family lists the father as fifty, the mother as thirty-eight, and the ages of the children as eighteen, fifteen, thirteen, nine, seven, five and two.[98] It was also noticeable that infants' Christian names were not repeated. Most children lived to adulthood by 1901, and this improvement coincided with the rise in the standard of living. This improvement in infant mortality statistics is also reflected in neighbouring townlands, including one townland where the birth pattern was generally a three-year interval.[99] The stated ages of adults in Cloonfush, in the early returns, must be treated with caution, as it is quite possible that in 1901 they were not actually sure of their age or were not specific enough. In many cases, a definite discrepancy exists between the stated age in 1901 and 1911. This would raise a question as to whether the granting of the old age pensions was responsible for a woman of forty-five in 1901 being sixty-five by 1911, while her sixty-year-old husband of 1901 is seventy-seven by 1911![100] Time passed quickly for some in Cloonfush.

The pattern of large families had continued but the population remained static at 104 between 1871 and 1901. The partnership system of agriculture, as it existed in 1843, remained almost unchanged in 1911. The evidence from the valuation revision books show that in 1854, fifty-four inhabitants owned eighteen fragmented farms. By 1871 the number of occupiers was fifty. By 1903 the number

94 Photographs from Cloonfush, 1912 (private collection). **95** NA, Census of Ireland, 1901–11. **96** Related to author in programme filmed in Cloonfush, Co. Galway, 'Memories of Cloonfush', September 1993. **97** NA, Census of Ireland, 1901–11. **98** NA, Census of Ireland, 1901 (Corcoran family, Cloonfush, Co. Galway). **99** *Census of Ireland*, 1901. **100** NA, Census of Ireland, 1901–11 (age profile of Family X Cloonfush, Co. Galway).

of occupiers was thirty-nine.[101] After the purchase of the estate in 1915 by the Congested Districts Board, attempts at consolidation were made by transplanting the herdsman and five smallholders to farms outside the townland.[102] The available land was then distributed among the remaining occupiers. However, in 1920 the number of owners still numbered thirty-eight. The number of holdings were in fact extended to twenty-five when the Day property of 116 acres was divided. Plot 25 was on that date still owned by eleven people.[103] The extracts from the resale register of the Land Commission, showing the resale position on 10 December 1980, shows that forty-eight people still owned land in Cloonfush. Most of the 1980 surnames of families resident in the townland in that year can be proved to be direct descendants of the 1843 occupants. Consolidation of the townland and relocation of its inhabitants proved to be impossible.[104] A descendent of the O'Shaughnessy family, James Donnellan, still farms his fragmented twenty-four acre farm, of tillage, meadow, callow and bog.

Life was difficult for the inhabitants of Cloonfush, yet an insight into their world gives the impression of a very happy people, despite the apparent economic hardship that they endured until at least the end of the nineteenth century. They worked exceptionally hard at turf, and use of the donkey and his turf baskets survived into this century. Market gardening, selling cabbage plants, growing and harvesting oats for their own use also continued. Oat meal porridge was a major part of the diet, while white water from steeped oats was used for man and beast. They possessed exceptional skills at eel fishing. They knew exactly the weather conditions when the eel would run for the sea, on the darkest moon on a windy wet night. They used a bobbin of hemp on set lines that caught the eels by the hundredweight. Every house kept a pig – but only for sale. They burned their own lime to whitewash and disinfected their thatched houses. Every man was a craftsman, depending on the job that had to be done. A special occasion demanded a goose or a pig's head and during Lent fish was boiled. No money was spent, except on school fees, as they did not have any. They were totally self sufficient except for tea and sugar. They made their own clothes and were experts at spinning and carding. They traded turf for kelp, which was burned seaweed used to fertilize the land.[105]

It is difficult for people living in today's modern, highly mobile society to comprehend that such a community, based on blood, place and mind, could exist. The shared experience of this territorial group of people over many generations may now be just a memory but it is not a myth.

Everything was shared and everything was celebrated together. They were a deeply religious people and lived by very high standards of morality. The Rosary

101 NA, ILC, Survey Branch, Resale Progress Register, vol. v, p. 138, Day Estate, CDB record no. 9927, SB 3327.   **102** VO, Cancellation book, 1900–20, Parish of Tuam, Cloonfush, Co. Galway.   **103** VO, Cancellation book, 1910–20, Parish of Tuam, Cloonfush, Co. Galway.   **104** NA, ILC, Survey Branch, Resale Progress Register, vol. v, p. 138, Day Estate, CDB record no. 9927, SB 3327.   **105** James Donnellan, Cloonfush, Co. Galway, in conversation with author, 15 Oct. 1994.

was said every night and this always marked the end of the card games. About nine thirty, the murmur of prayers in Irish rose in unison from every house and even when the language changed this tradition did not die. These people did not need a church, only a rosary beads by the open fire. Their living, their dead and their emigrants were still part of the community and were prayed for every night. When a couple married, only the couple went to the church. The witnesses register confirms this. The rest of the family did not have the finery necessary for such an occasion. The festivities began on their return to the townland. They never went outside the village for entertainment. They went to certain houses every night. They played for a goose, they danced in the kitchen to the music of a melodeon. Their ancient airs were unique to this townland and some can still be remembered. They told ghost stories. They were experts at predicting the signs of the weather. When the swallow flew low, it meant that the flies were low and that wet weather was ahead.[106] The new moon on its back meant bad weather. A ring around the moon was a warning of a storm. They were keen observers of their environment.

The range of topics covered in the townland's folklore include stories of hidden treasure, fate and marriage, old cures and spite. These stories had a purpose. Spite folklore avoided direct violence, fate helped them to accept their lot while the 'pot of gold' kept their gave them hope. An infinite variety of puzzles kept their minds sharp. Stories of the 'banshee' kept young people in at night. Folklore dictated their behaviour.[107]

Politics never bothered them. However, while praising the education they received from the Christian Brothers, they remarked on the strict discipline of the teachers, which was admired in Cloonfush. They also remarked on the fact that the brothers hated England and landlords. This bias did not affect these inhabitants to any great extent as they looked to Britain or America to support their children. As for landlords, 'they were fine people', and letters from Stephen O'Shaughnessy of Cloonfush from the Irish Guards on the Western Front, are remarkable for their lack of political opinion.[108]

However, the long haemorrhage of emigration slowly eroded this community. The social cohesion, that stamped its inhabitants identity, character and sense of place, was still in evidence in 1915. But a townland without its youth has nothing to pass on. A new age, long delayed, had at last arrived.

James Donnellan lives alone and sits in front of his open fire. He still farms the tiny fragmented farm as his mother's people, the Shaughnessy's did for countless generations. He well understands why no one will continue his way of life, nor would he want them to go back to 'hard times'. However he is intensely proud of his heritage. This former county councillor will also tell you, with pride, who he is. He is not just a Donnellan. He is James Donnellan from Cloonfush, a man in his place.

106 *Tuam Herald*, 30 January 1915, Letter from a soldier at the Western Front.
107 Transcript of schools manuscripts, Department of Irish Folklore, Galway Library.
108 *Tuam Herald*, 30 January 1915.

APPENDIX I

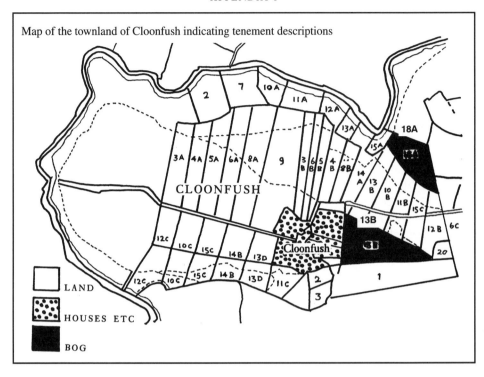

Map of the townland of Cloonfush indicating tenement descriptions

Griffith valuation map of the town of Cloonfush including tenement valuations

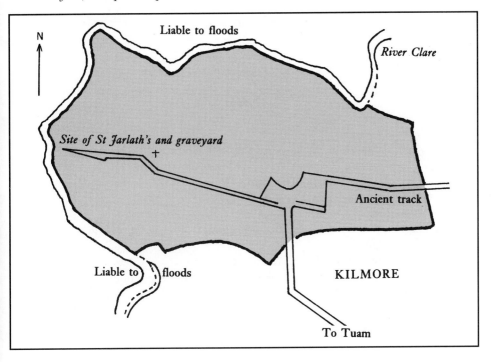

Cloonfush, county Galway, 1838, 398 acres

APPENDIX 2

CLOONFUSH LANDOWNERS LISTED IN THE
CANCELLATION BOOKS, 1903

No.	Occupier
1	William Quinn
2	Michael Staunton, Denis Forde (gone), Thomas Murray (gone), Peter Higgins (gone), Thomas Devine, Catherine Forde (gone), Thomas Murray, Peter Higgins, William Thornton, Thomas Murray, Luke Forde (gone), Peter Corcoran (gone).
3	Luke Forde
4	Thomas Murray, William Thornton (gone), Thomas Murray (gone), Peter Higgins (gone)
5	Michael Staunton, Thomas Murray (gone)
6	Thomas Devine, Peter Corcoran (gone), Luke Forde (gone)
7	Peter Corcoran, Patrick Higgins (gone), Mary Higgins (gone), Laurence Shaughnessy (gone), Catherine Hanley
8	Michael Roche, Mary Higgins (gone)
9	Laurence Shaughnessy (gone), Michael Kelly
10	John Fleming, John Nicholson (gone)
11	Peter Crisham
12	Peter Higgins
13	Laurence Shaughnessy
14	Patrick Higgins, Patrick Higgins, Luke Forde
15	(gone)
16	Margaret Shaughnessy
17	Denis Forde, Mary Forde (gone), Catherine Hanley (gone), Thomas Fleming (gone), John Bermingham (gone),
18	William Thornton, Patrick Higgins (gone), Luke Forde (gone)
19	John Nicholson
20	Patrick Ryan & tenants of townland
21	Ellen Loftus, Luke Forde, Thomas Murray, Mike Staunton, Thomas Devane, Patrick Corcoran
22	Laurence Shaughnessy, Margaret Shaughnessy, Patrick Shaughnessy, Patrick Higgins, Denis Forde, William Thornton.

Note.   The word 'gone' indicates a previous occupier.

APPENDIX 3

CLOONFUSH 1911 CENSUS — HOUSEHOLDS

No.	Name	Age	No.	Name	Age
1	Michael Staunton (Head)	77	7	Mathias Higgins (Head)	38
	Bridget (Wife)	65		Honor (Wife)	40
	Kate	26		Peter	5
				Nora	4
2	Thomas Devine (Head)	67		Mary	1
	Katie (Wife)	62		Peter Higgins (Grandfather)	81
	Michael	21			
			8	William Thornton (Head)	69
3	Peter Corcoran (Head)	61		Mary (Wife)	47
	Margaret (Wife)	49		Thomas	23
	John	18		Patrick	21
	Patrick	16		William	16
	Teresa	15		Bridget	13
	Josephine	13		Ellen	10
	Crissy	8		Sabina	7
	Michael	6		Michael	4
	Anthony	4			
			9	Denis Forde (Head)	68
4	Catherine Crisham (Head)	72		Bridget (Sister)	72
	Patrick	38			
	Michael	32	10	Michael (Head)	37
				Mary	43
5	Michael Roche (Head)	50			
	Bridget (Wife)	53	11	Thomas Murray (Head)	47
	John	23		Ellen (Wife)	49
				Mary	25
6	Michael Kelly (Head)	68		John	21
	Rose (Wife)	58		Patrick	14
	Luke	23		Kathleen	12
	Katie	19		Ellen	10
	John	17			
	Rose	14	12	Thomas Donlon (Head)	40
	Nora	12		Kate (Wife)	33
				Bridget Shaughnessy (sister-in-law)	34

No.	Name	Age	No.	Name	Age
13	Laurence Shaughnessy (Head)	70	16	John Nicholson (Head)	39
	Ellen (Wife)	60		Ellen (Wife)	40
	Patrick	24		Thomas	14
	Bridget	15		Mary	10
				Stephen	8
14	Patrick Conway (Head)	60		Jarlath	3
	Mary (Wife)	48			
	Patrick	14	17	Unoccupied	
	Michael	12			
	Mary	7			
	Edward	4			
15	John Fleming (Head)	65			
	Bridget (Wife)	50			
	Thomas	22			
	Patrick	20			
	Nora	16			
	Katie	10			

Drumcavan, county Clare

BRIAN Ó DÁLAIGH*

On the morning of 10 May 1318 Conchobhar Ó Deá, loyal vassal of O'Brien of Thomond, laid a careful ambush at the ford of Ballycullinan. The Anglo-Norman lord, Richard de Clare, advancing with his host, observed a small group of Irishmen ostensibly in the act of driving the last of the cattle herd towards the river-crossing. Instead of defending the ford, O'Dea deliberately retreated into the townland of Drumcavan where the main body of his men were concealed. Impetuously de Clare charged forward. Without warning O'Dea's force rose up and charged into the fray; one group going to kill the Norman baron and his retinue while the larger force sealed the ford to prevent the rest of the de Clare's army coming to his rescue. In the early fourteenth century the mounted knight in armour was no longer invincible and de Clare and his men were quickly dispatched. The killing of de Clare was the prelude to the battle of Dysert O'Dea, where the Anglo-Normans were decisively defeated by Muircheartach Ó Briain, king of Thomond and his allies O'Dea, O'Hehir and O'Connor.[1] The battle resulted in the permanent expulsion of the Normans from Thomond and ensured that the Gaelic way of life continued to flourish undisturbed in county Clare for another three centuries.

I

Drumcavan enjoys a high profile among Clare's 2,255 townlands; not just because of its association with the battle of Dysert O'Dea but because of its strategic location.[2] The townland straddles the main arterial route from Ennis, the county's capital, into north Clare. Roads, as we shall see, were to have a major impact on the history of this townland, affecting population levels, settlement patterns and the calibre of tenant attracted to farm the land. As if to emphasise its strategic location, the townland lies at the meeting point of three parishes in the barony of Inchiquin: it is located on the western boundary of the parish of Ruan, just where it joins the parishes of Dysert and Rath.[3] Indeed in the

* I am indebted to the Hanrahan and Hehir families of Drumcavan for their kind hospitality and the information which they shared so generously with me.   1 Katherine Simms, 'The Battle of Dysert O'Dea and the Gaelic Resurgence in Thomond' in *Dál gCais*, v (1979), pp. 59–65.   2 William Reeves, 'The townland distribution of Ireland' in *PRIA*, vii (1861), p. 484.   3 OS, six-inch map, county Clare, sheet 25, edition of 1920.

sixteenth and seventeenth centuries Drumcavan was counted among the townlands of the parish of Dysert but by the early nineteenth century had been moved
into the parish of Ruan.[4]

The name Drumcavan (*Droim Chaomhain*) signifies Kavan's hill or ridge.[5] The
ridge referred to is the long low drumlin that runs from east to west along the
southern boundary and is the most significant physical feature of the townland.
The ridge, rising to a height of 178 feet, is crowned by Drumcavan ringfort, a
large single rampart fort, whose steep banks, though much overgrown, still
impress. From the summit a perfect view of the townland may be had: the land
slopes away gently to the north-west where layers of limestone rock project
above the covering of soil. The soil, laid down during the last ice age, is the
shallow brown earth derived from limestone, which is typical of the grasslands
of central Clare. The earth is a mature, well drained, mineral soil, good for tillage
and with proper management produces a rich pasture.[6] Forming the western
boundary are three lakes: Drumcavan Lough, which is more swamp than lake,
and floods intermittently in winter; Shanvalley Lough, a deep, pot-shaped lake,
feared by locals for its dreadful springs; and Ballycullinan Lake, the largest of the
three, out of which flows Ballycullinan stream, the water course that forms the
south-western boundary of the townland. Only portion of Ballycullinan lake
belongs to Drumcavan townland. The northern boundary, rising on steeper
ground, is defined by the Ruan Corofin road, for many years the main routeway from Ennis into north Clare. No natural feature defines the eastern boundary;
it is formed instead by a series of broad, irregular hedges and ditches, which
separate Drumcavan from the adjoining town land of Cloonfeaghra. The total
area of Drumcavan is 231.7 acres, which includes 21.56 acres of water.[7]

4 Gearoid Mac Niocaill, 'Seven Irish Documents from the Inchiquin Archive' in *Analecta
Hibernica*, xxvi (1971), pp. 50–1; *Books of Survey and Distribution, county Clare 1636–1703*,
ed. R.C. Simington, IMC (Dublin, 1967), p. 544; *A census of Ireland circa 1659 with supple-
mentary material from the poll money ordinances (1660–61)*, ed. Seamus Pender, IMC (Dublin,
1939), p. 176; NA, TAB, parish of Dysert, county Clare, 5/25, f. 212; OS, field name
books, Dysert parish, county Clare, bk. 3, p. 27 (NLI, microfilm pos. 1017).   **5** Cavan,
cabhán means a hollow, as in the town and county of that name; or as in Cavanalough,
Cabhán an locha, hollow of the lake, county Fermanagh; Drumcavan, *Droim chabháin*,
therefore would mean ridge of the hollow, a name that would suit the topography.
However, in a conveyance of the townland, 1592, the name is rendered *Droma Caomhain*:
cf. Mac Niocail, 'Inchiquin Archive' in *Analecta Hibernica*, xxvi (1971), p. 51; and again in
1839 John O'Donovan gives *Droim Chaomhain*, meaning Kavan's ridge: cf. field name
books, Dysert parish, bk. 3, p. 27.   **6** T.F. Finch, *Soils of county Clare*, Soil Survey Bulletin
no. 23. An Foras Taluntais (Dublin, 1971), pp. 7, 12–3.   **7** *Alphabetical Index to the
Townlands, Towns etc. of Ireland 1851* (Dublin, 1861, reprint Baltimore, USA 1992), p. 402.

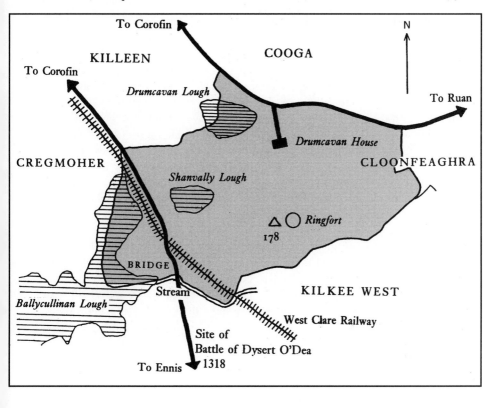

Drumcavan, county Clare, 1917, 232 acres

II

Over the centuries the ownership of this piece of earth has passed through many hands. In 1543 the overlordship of O'Brien was recognised by Henry VIII when Murchadh Ó Briain, first earl of Thomond, was created baron of Inchiquin.[8] During the composition of Connacht in 1585 the overlord's traditional exactions of cattle and food and lodgings for his soldiers were transmuted to cash when O'Brien was granted a yearly rent charge of five shillings out of every townland in the barony of Inchiquin.[9] Notwithstanding the overlord's dues, mortgage deeds of the late sixteenth century indicate that the O'Hogans, an old ecclesiastical family of the district, were in possession of Drumcavan. In a deed drawn up in Irish by Ualgharg Mac Bruaideadha and dated 15 March 1592 the townland was conveyed from one O'Hogan to another:

> I, Conchobhar Óg Ó hÓgáin son of Conchobhar Ó hÓgáin, acknowledge that I have given Drumcavan in mortgage for the amount of chattels specified hereafter, viz. 20 milch cows and 20 heifers which had fourteen female calves and 20 dry cows of next May and 11 horses and a palfrey and a brass cauldron and a piece of silver and a flock of sheep totalling six and five score sheep to Aodh son of Giollapadraig son of Aodh Ó hÓgáin; and the said Drumcavan is thus situated: it is in the parish of Dysert ... bordering Kilkee on the south and Ballycullinan on the west and Drumfinglas on the north and Cooga on the east; and I, the said Conchobhar Ó hÓgáin give Drumcavan ... to Aodh son of Giollapadraig Ó hÓgáin ... with wood and marsh and turf and water and earth and every profit of which the said Drumcavan is possessed.[10]

Clearly Conchobhar Ó hÓgáin's hold on Drumcavan was insecure. Originally he mortgaged the townland to Daniell Neylon, bishop of Kildare, in 1587.[11] Under the above agreement the property is re-mortgaged to Aodh Ó hÓgáin, presumably to prevent the townland falling into the possession of an individual outside his own kin group. Conchobhar Ó hÓgáin can only hope to redeem the property in the unlikely event that he can furnish the requisite number of animals and goods. The property over time is likely to fall to the possession of his kinsman Aodh Ó hÓgáin. Despite being written in Irish, both parties are concerned that the agreement be 'put into the legal form of the sovereign of England'; evidently there was a keen awareness of the changed legal requirements in county Clare under the newly established English law.

---

8 Ivar O'Brien, *O'Brien of Thomond* (Chichester, 1986), pp. 14–6.   **9** *The compossicion book of Conought*, ed. A.M. Freeman, IMC (Dublin, 1936), pp. 22–3.   **10** Mac Niocail, 'Inchiquin Archive' in *Analecta Hibernica*, 1971, pp. 51–4.   **11** John Ainsworth (ed.), *The Inchiquin Manuscripts*, IMC (Dublin, 1963), no. 905, pp. 282–3.

Drumcavan was obviously a well defined entity in the sixteenth century. The townlands that surround it are the same today except that Cloonfeaghra rather than Cooga borders it on the east and Drumfinglas is now called Killeen in the parish Rath.[12] The adjoining townland of Kilkee was the residence the McBrodys, one of the great literary families of Thomond. Such was their standing that on the completion of the *Annals of the Four Masters* in 1636 the approbation of Conchobhar Mac Bruaideadha of Kilkee was sought as an endorsement for that great work.[13] As the above document illustrates family members also functioned as clerks and public notaries. More general points, however, can be made: in the 1590s the rural economy clearly functioned without the use of money. Animals rather than precious metal represents the main form of transportable wealth. There is no evidence of tillage in the document; pastoralism, the raising of cattle, sheep and horses appears to be the principal farming activity.

A feature peculiar by it absence from the townland is the castle or tower house, a feature common on the lowlands of central Clare. There is no castle in Drumcavan while the adjoining townlands of Kilkee and Cregmoher each boast of one. Why did the transition from ringfort to castle fail to occur in Drumcavan? It is all the more unusual considering the strategic location of the townland. There are a number of possible solutions to this problem. In county Clare castles were built, not primarily as places of strategic defence, but rather, as the modern term 'tower house' implies, as places of domestic residence. Castles were status symbols as much as anything else and a family had to be financially secure before it could afford to build one. The O'Hogans provided the hereditary clergy to the neighbouring parish of Rath, they were a church family of relatively low standing, and unlikely to be in a position to accumulate the resources necessary to construct a castle.[14] More important than these considerations was the insecurity of tenure. Drumcavan, as we have seen, was heavily mortgaged and O'Hogan, even if he had the means, was unlikely to invest in a property over which he had so tenuous a hold. The form of land tenure then and the availability of resources, more than strategic considerations, determined whether or not a castle was built in a particular townland.

III

How did Drumcavan fare in the turmoil of the seventeenth century? Up until the Cromwellian upheaval of the 1650s the Hogans continued to hold the townland. In 1641 Patrick Hogan was in possession of the quarter of Drumcavan consisting of 154 acres of arable and pasture and 19 acres of rough pasture.[15]

12 *Book of Survey and Distribution, Clare,* p. 531.   **13** Brendan Jennings, *Michael Ó Cléirigh and his Associates* (Dublin, 1936), pp. 154–6.   **14** Michael MacMahon, *A History of the parish of Rath* (Ennis, 1979), pp. 29–33.   **15** *Book of Survey and Distribution, Clare,* p. 531.

Hogan also held the neighbouring denominations of Cuggie (*Cuigiú*, a fifth) and Cuggie Mounterhuire (*Cuigiú Mhuintir hIomhair*, the fifth of the Howard family); both are now subsumed in the modern townland of Cooga. Over the next century or so both townlands (Drumcavan and Cooga) were held in common as the lands passed through a succession of tenants. Under the census of 1659 John Comyne was recorded as the principal tenant; we do not know who Comyne was, except to suggest that he may have been one of the luckless Catholic landowners transplanted under the Cromwellian dictum 'to hell or to Connacht'.[16] In any event his association with the townland was shortlived, because at the restoration of Charles II in 1660 the infamous Murrough 'the Burner' O'Brien, having been elevated in the peerage to earl of Inchiquin, was restored to all his property in county Clare.[17] Under Inchiquin Patrick Hogan continued to occupy Cooga but by 1664 he had lost Drumcavan to John Addie.[18] As a result of the Cromwellian land settlement the old proprietors lost, not only a portion of their former lands, but also their freehold status and in many instances became the tenants of the new landowners. Notwithstanding the reduced status of Patrick Hogan, it is likely that little changed for the majority of the inhabitants of the townland. Three quarters of the Irish population was landless and was largely unaffected by changes in land ownership. According to the census of 1659 twelve people resided in Drumcavan, eight in Cooga and nine each in the townlands of Kilkee and Cregmoher.[19] Such was the demand for labour to work the land in the more settled conditions of the 1660s that the standard of living of many of these people may actually have improved. In 1669 Inchiquin leased Drumcavan and Cooga to Henry Ievers Esq. for a term of ninety-six years.[20] Ievers, an English Protestant, had come to Ireland before 1641 as a mere clerk, yet through speculation in confiscated lands, he became one of the wealthiest landowners in county Clare. His income was estimated at £2,600 per annum in 1680, an enormous sum for those days.[21] In consideration of a large entry fee, Inchiquin leased the townlands for a rent of just £9 per annum.[22] This lease was to govern the property until 1766. Ievers in turn sublet the lands to Pierce Butler, the son of a transplanted settler.[23] Butler is an interesting individual; he was married to Honora Hogan, the daughter of the old proprietor, and resided at Cooga. Butler actively set about trying to reestablish the old freehold title of the confiscated Hogan lands. He refused to pay Ievers the annual rent for Cooga and Drumcavan. He even attempted to repossess the ancient church lands of the Hogans in the parish of Kilnamona, at that stage, the

---

16 Pender, *Census of Ireland c.1659*, p. 176.   **17** O'Brien, *O'Brien of Thomond*, pp. 93–5; John O'Donoghue, *Historical Memoir of the O'Briens* (Dublin, 1860), pp. 300, 531. **18** James Frost, *The History and Topography of County Clare* (Dublin, 1893), p. 489. **19** *Census of Ireland c.1659*, ed. Pender, p. 176.   **20** NLI, Inchiquin Mss., Ms. 14,815, no. 26.   **21** Ciarán Ó Murchadha, 'The Scapegoat and the Opportunist' in *The Other Clare*, x (1986), p. 21.   **22** NLI, Ms. 14,815, no. 26.   **23** Ainsworth (ed.), *Inchiquin Mss.*, no. 1541, p. 546.

legal property of the Protestant bishop of Killaloe. The case, which made legal history, was heard before the Committee of Privileges in the Irish House of Lords in 1709. Butler, not surprisingly, was eventually imprisoned and spent six years in the common jail of Ennis until his contempt was purged.[24]

There were now two interests operating in the townland: that of the middle-man Henry Ievers and that of the occupier Pierce Butler. The Ievers' interest was sold to Samuel Lucas of the city of Dublin by 1720.[25] In the Inchiquin rental of the same year Lucas paid a mere £4 6s. 6d. rent for Drumcavan and Cooga, while the real annual value of the property was recorded as £72 2s. 0d.[26] The difference gives a good indication of the large profits that accrued to middle men. The straitened circumstances of Pierce Butler after his years in jail, on the other hand, compelled his family to vacate Cooga and Drumcavan. However, the Butlers insured that the Hogan connection continued by selling their interest on to Edmund Hogan.[27] The new occupier, though, was not Hogan but John Lucas. It was almost certainly through his relative Samuel Lucas (who had bought the leasehold from Ievers) that John Lucas came to occupy Drumcavan. Lucas was a descendant of Colonel Benjamin Lucas, a Cromwellian army officer, who settled on the lands of Corofin in the 1650s.[28] The Lucas family were to have a long association with Drumcavan. John Lucas was married to Mary Davenport of Ennis and had three sons and three daughters.[29] His eldest son, whose name unfortunately is not recorded and who appears not to have been a legitimate offspring of the marriage, kept a detailed diary of the farming activities for the period May 1740 to October of 1741.[30] By good fortune a copy of the diary survives and through it we get a clear picture of the kind of agriculture that was practised in Drumcavan in the eighteenth century.

IV

John Lucas farmed both Drumcavan and Cooga, but unlike the previous occupiers, resided at Drumcavan. He also held a large tract of land in Balingaddy East about seventeen miles to the west near the village of Liscannor and some smaller tracts in the vicinity of Corofin, which he held on short leases.[31] In all

24 J. Falvey, 'Pierce Butler of Coogy' in *The Other Clare*, xviii (1994), pp. 33–9. **25** RD, 28/234/17436; NLI, Ms. 14,371, Rental of the 4th earl of Inchiquin, 1720. **26** NLI, Ms. 14,371, no. 27. **27** RD, 72/4/49424. Edmund Hogan was the son of William Hogan Esq. of Ennis, cf. G.O., Ms. 141, f.25. **28** *Census of Ireland c.1659*, ed. Pender, p. 175; G.O., Ms.812 (24), Draft pedigree of Lucas 1350–1886. **29** GO, 529, no. 22, Will of Thomas Davenport of Ennis, 1748; NLI, Ms. 14,101, Diary of Farmer Lucas, 1740–1, *passim*. **30** NLI, Ms. 14,101. **31** NLI, Ms. 14,101, 1 January 1741. Lurgo is a sub-denomination of the townland of Balingaddy East. Mounroe, near Corofin, was leased from the Earl of Thomond, 24 May and 1 June 1741. Mounroe does not now name any townland in the barony of Inchiquin.

he had between seven and eight hundred acres of land available to him.[32] How did he farm this large acreage? Some of the more distant lands he sublet to tenant farmers; the greater portion, however, he farmed himself through the employment of large numbers of farm labourers. There was no shortage of labourers. Some resided at the western end of the townland near the lake at Shanvalley (*Sean Bhaile*, Old Town); others came from the neighbouring town-lands of Kilkee and Killeen. Lucas was the collector of tithe for Kilkee and many labourers worked a set number of days in lieu of payment of tithes.[33] Others he hired for longer periods, like his manual servant John Welsh[34] or the ploughman James Flanagan,[35] both of whom he employed at the rate of ten shillings per quarter year. For his more permanent workers he provided a house and vegetable garden for which they paid a heavy rent. In June of 1741 he engaged Philip Rhyne and his brother in law Michael McBrody as labourers for a year at Cooga. They were have a house rent free but were to pay £1 4s. for the grass each of their three cows.[36] Lucas was to supply them with a garden in spring for which they were then to pay rent. Little money changed hands in these trans-actions; the debt was paid in labour at the rate of 3d. per day, in this instance, 288 days labour for the grass of three cows.

At busy periods of the year, when sowing or harvesting was in progress, up to twenty labourers might be employed. These day labourers worked for a notional 3d. per day; they were not paid with money, however, but with bushels of oats; in the economy of the townland oats rather than money was the principal medium of exchange. Oaten meal clearly formed the staple diet of farm labourers. In the famine year of 1741 Lucas charged 2s. per bushel of oats in January[37] and this had risen to 4s. per bushel by April.[38] At the same time because workers were so plentiful he was able to bargain down the price of labour from 3d. to 2d. per day.[39] The wages of landless labourers were so low it is difficult to see how they could have participated in the money economy. In April Lucas turned off Donough Hickey and William Keefe, two workers he had employed to thrash corn; he dismissed them with the revealing phrase: 'I gave them in cash for their roguery.'[40] Clearly men preferred to be paid in food rather than money. Women were also employed as farm workers at particular times of the year, generally to winnow corn or bind barley, for which they received two sheaves per day.[41]

Animal husbandry formed the principal part of his farming activity. Lucas raised large numbers of livestock. At Drumcavan he kept sixteen three-year-old bullocks, fourteen cows, twelve calves, ten two-year-old heifers, five mares, a

---

32 Drumcavan comprising of 230 acres, Cooga 290 acres: cf. *Townland Index of Ireland 1851*, pp. 402, 282; Lurgo 170 acres: cf., R.D., 6/272/2124 (calculated at 1.62 statute acres per Irish acre); Mounroe 100 acres (estimate).   **33** NLI, Ms. 14,101, 8 June 1741.   **34** NLI, Ms. 14,101, 6 July 1741.   **35** NLI, Ms. 14,101, 8 February 1741.   **36** NLI, Ms. 14,101, 1 June 1741.   **37** NLI, Ms. 14,101, 27 January 1741.   **38** NLI, Ms. 14,101, 20 April 1741.   **39** NLI, Ms. 14,101, 30 July 1741.   **40** NLI, Ms. 14,101, 14 April 1741.   **41** NLI, Ms. 14,101, 14 July 1741.

three-year-old filly and one horse. On Cooga he kept 121 two year old bullocks, thirty-six hoggets and fourteen ewes; and at Balingaddy, twenty-seven two-year-old heifers, three mares, four colts and two foals.[42] In all he owned 202 head of cattle, fifty sheep and sixteen horses. Animals required constant care and herdsmen were employed to feed and water them and conduct them to fresh pastures. Lucas entered into formal agreements with his herdsmen. In May 1741 he agreed with John Higgins that he should herd his cattle at Balingaddy. Higgins had to save the hay of the meadows with the help of only six men, although Lucas was obliged to provide him with horses. Higgins was to keep the bounds in good order and to convey the cattle in his care forwards and backwards to fairs and markets; for this he was to enjoy land rent free and receive a specified amount of corn.[43] Lucas penalised herdsmen severely for neglect of duty. A herdsman, John Joyce, through carelessness allowed a two-year-old bullock, worth 30s., to drown in Drumcavan lake. Lucas proceeded with the bailiff to Shanvalley where Joyce lived, confiscated his cow and only released it on the agreement that Joyce would serve him until the debt was paid.[44]

Herdsmen had the arduous task of walking animals to and from fairs. Lucas frequented fairs in about a fifteen-mile radius of his farm. The market for live stock was clearly depressed in 1741 and many fairs were attended before animals were sold. In June Lucas brought his sheep to the fairs of Spancilhill and Tubber but failed to sell a single one.[45] In June and again in October he sent twenty bullocks by his herdsmen to the fair of Quin, a round trip for man and beast of over thirty miles, and had to returned on both occasions without the sale of a single animal.[46] At Clonroad fair in July he had more luck selling thirty bullocks at £1 13s. 9d. each to Mr Morgan Trumble[47] and again in September at Tubber he sold 20 two-year-old bullocks to Mr Matthew Phibbs at the reduced price of £1 8s.0d. per animal.[48] He earned a total of £78 12s. 6d. for his cattle in 1741.

V

Apart from the raising of livestock, tillage was his other main farming activity. With a ready supply of cheap labour Lucas engaged in extensive cultivation of crops. His principal cash crops were barley, oats and flax. To maximise his yields, he experimented with different varieties of barley. The chief variety was bere, a type of barley suitable for brewing, but he also grew Dutch barley, English barley and small barley. The corn was conveyed by car the eight miles to Ennis where it was sold to the malt house owners of the town at £1 3s. per barrel.[49] In March of 1741 Lucas sold thirty three barrels of barley for which he received

42 NLI, Ms. 14,101, 1 January 1741.   **43** NLI, Ms. 14,101, 1 May 1741.   **44** NLI, Ms. 14,101, 2 February 1741.   **45** NLI, Ms. 14,101, 14 and 22 June 1741.   **46** NLI, Ms. 14,101, 27 June and 17 October 1741.   **47** NLI, Ms. 14,101, 21 July 1741.   **48** NLI, Ms. 14,101, 9 September 1741.   **49** NLI, Ms. 14,101, 7 and 15 March, and 9 April 1741.

£37 19s. On receipt of payment Lucas purchased clothes and implements for the farm and reduced the accounts he kept with the shopkeepers of the town. Oats he grew in extensive quantities both as a commodity of barter and as a livestock feed. Flax was grown in smaller quantities and when ready was sold at the Limerick rather than the Ennis market, because a linen industry had yet to develop in county Clare. In 1741 it accounted for just £7 3s. 6d. of Lucas's income.[50] Beans and peas were intensively cultivated and were clearly important in the townland diet.[51] Potatoes too were becoming important but they still did not dominate. In April fifteen labourers were employed for two days sowing fields of potatoes.[52] Considering the suitability of the land for pasture, dairying formed a surprisingly small part of the farming activity in Drumcavan; this was probably because of the distance of the townland from suitable markets. Only fourteen cows were kept, principally to provide dairy products for the household. Nonetheless milk was churned and firkins of butter when filled were brought for sale to the Ennis market.[53]

When in funds Lucas was careful to pay his rent. In relation to his income the rent he paid was extremely onerous. The half yearly rent for 1741 amounted to £51 0s. 2d. which he paid to Edmund Hogan.[54] Hogan was the man who had bought the previous occupier's interest in Drumcavan in 1722; he had clearly risen in the world because by 1741 he was also in possession of the leasehold on the property; through him the Hogan interest in Drumcavan was maintained.[55] Hogan was evidently a man of ability. He had become a Protestant and engaged in extensive property dealings.[56] His expertise in property titles was such that he was appointed a land agent of Henry, earl of Thomond;[57] and at the Clare election of 1745 it was he who assessed the titles of the forty shilling freeholders before they voted.[58] Lucas cultivated his goodwill. He sent his servants to herd and brand his cattle and invited him to be the godfather of his youngest son.[59] Lucas hoped to profit by his friendship with Hogan by being granted land falling out of lease.[60]

What use did Lucas make of the adjacent urban centres? The village of Ruan, two miles from Drumcavan, was the social centre of the parish; Lucas went there on Sunday afternoons to watch hurling matches and spent the evenings drinking in the village alehouses.[61] For church services he travelled the three miles to

50 NLI, Ms. 14,101, 14 January and 9 June 1741.   51 NLI, Ms. 14,101, 1, 7 and 9 April, and 11, 19 and 20 August.   52 NLI, Ms. 14,101, 16 and 24 April 1741.   53 NLI, Ms. 14,101, 18 February, 7 March and 3 July 1741.   54 NLI, Ms. 14,101, 15 and 24 March 1741.   55 RD, 72/4/49424.   56 Edmund Hogan was the son of William Hogan Esq. of Ennis, see note 27 above. William Hogan converted to the Established Church in 1710:cf. *The Convert Rolls*, ed. Eileen O'Byrne, IMC (Dublin, 1981), p. 136; Edmund Hogan served as provost of Ennis in 1734: cf. *Corporation Book of Ennis*, ed. Brian Ó Dálaigh (Dublin, 1990), p. 124.   57 Petworth House Archive, Ms. Catalogue, vol. 1, ff. 296–300 (NLI, microfilm pos. 4767).   58 TCD, Ms. 2059, Poll book of the the Clare Election 1745, nos. 13 and 277.   59 NLI, Ms. 14,101, 22 January, 5 February, 2 and 3 July 1741.   60 NLI, Ms. 14,101, 20 October 1741.   61 NLI, Ms. 14,101, 23 August and 6 September 1741.

Corofin where the Protestant minister Ambrose Upton presided.[62] The manor court of Inchiquin also convened at Corofin, and local disputes when they arose, were settled there; like, for instance, the case Lucas prosecuted against Thomas Sheeghan in July 1741, for allowing cattle to trespass on a field of his oats.[63] However, for conducting his main business affairs, Lucas journeyed the eight miles on horseback into Ennis. Despite their social standing the family did not possess a carriage. Lucas's aged mother travelled on the same horse as her servant to Ennis because of the condition of the roads.[64] Ennis was the commercial centre of the county; there the farm produce was sold, goods were purchased and services availed of; the family interacted with the town approximately once a week. Occasionally Lucas travelled further afield. In June he journeyed to Limerick to collect money owing to him for his flax. Leaving Drumcavan at ten in the morning he completed the thirty mile journey on horseback in seven hours. While in Limerick he purchased those exotic goods unavailable in the urban centres nearer home: a fancy hat for his sister Doll, a quarter of stone blue, a pound of brown sugar and a quarter ounce of dwarf cabbage seed.[65]

Socially and economically Lucas towered above everybody in his townland; one cannot speak of a social structure in Drumcavan, as such, the community was too small for that. Nevertheless at the lower end of the scale some distinctions can be made: those who held land in lieu of labour, for instance, were clearly better off than those who laboured for 3d. a day or those who were employed as servants by the quarter year. There was little social interaction between Lucas and the labouring mass, separated as he was from them, not just by social class, but by religion, language and culture. For social entertainment the Lucas family mixed with members of their own class. On Sunday afternoons they visited with the land owning families of neighbouring townlands: the Bloods of Craugaunboy, for instance, to whom they were related by marriage[66] or the family of Ambrose Upton the Protestant minister.[67] Occasionally important visitors were entertained at the house. In September 1741 David Bindon, MP for Ennis, and his brother Nicholas called on the family. The Bindons, a family of extensive landed interests in Clare and Limerick, were heartily entertained and partook of refreshments and wine at a cost of 6s. 11d.[68] Notwithstanding his connections with the ascendancy, Lucas could not be counted among the county gentry. No Lucas, for example, was appointed a justice of the peace or served on the Clare grand jury for the whole of the eighteenth century,[69] indicating that while the family

62 NLI, Ms. 14,101, 1 March, 16 August 1741. **63** NLI, Ms. 14,101, 21 June and 22 July 1741. **64** NLI, Ms. 14,101, 3 July 1741. **65** NLI, Ms. 14,101, 9 June 1741. **66** NLI, Ms. 14,101, 5 February 28 August 1741; NLI, microfilm pos. 5074, Pedigree of Blood family of England and county Clare. Mathew Blood of Craugaunboy was married to Elizabeth Lucas a sister of John Lucas of Drumcavan. **67** NLI, Ms. 14,101, 5 and 10 September 1741. **68** NLI, Ms. 14,101, 27 September 1741. **69** Frost, *History of Clare*, pp. 615–18, 624–5, 626–8.

were above strong farmer level, they were not quite of county gentry status. Edmund Hogan, on the other hand, the man who held the lease on Drumcavan, rose to the highest office in Clare by being appointed county sheriff in 1759.[70] His tenure in that office was short lived, however, as Hogan died in June of the following year at Bushy Park near Ennis.[71] The lease he held on Drumcavan had just six years to run.

VI

With the death of Edmund Hogan the long connection of the Hogan family with Drumcavan ceased. Lucas was clearly not in a position to purchase the leasehold of the townland and by 1762 the lease of Drumcavan was in the hands of John Arthur, Esq., a merchant of Ennis.[72] The Arthurs were one of the many Catholic families of Limerick transported to Ennis in the 1650s[73] because under the Cromwellian code Catholic merchants were not permitted to trade in walled towns. In the unwalled town of Ennis the Arthurs prospered and eventually became Protestant.[74] Evidently the earl of Inchiquin renewed the lease of Drumcavan with John Arthur in 1766, because the Arthurs were to retain possession of Drumcavan townland down until the first decade of the present century, only selling out to the tenants following the Wyndham land act of 1903.[75] Initially, at least, Lucas continued as principal tenant; he may even have been granted a lease, which expired in 1796. In any event, the Lucas tenure of Drumcavan was coming to an end. The last record of their occupation of Drumcavan is August 1796.[76] There is still at Drumcavan today an inscribed stone with the initials J.L. and the date 27 July 1796.[77] It almost certainly refers to the date that John Lucas had to leave Drumcavan after his family occupying the property for three generations. That he went to the trouble of inscribing a stone indicates that his departure from Drumcavan had been signalled well in advance. John Lucas died in 1809 at the advanced age of 86.[78] His son, another John Lucas, became a coroner in the town of Kilrush.[79]

Why did Arthur refuse to renew the lease of John Lucas? The reasons are obvious enough. Arthur was no longer prepared to let his property by the townland; he wished to break up the large single holding and set the land in

---

70 *Faulkner's Dublin Journal,* 17–21 June 1760.   **71** *Faulkner's Dublin Journal,* 10 June 1760.   **72** RD, 887/380/587380.   **73** Molyneux Survey, TCD Ms. 883/1, f.227. **74** John Arthur made freeman of Ennis 1749; urban freemen were obliged to take the oath of supremacy on admission: cf. *Corporation. book of Ennis,* ed. Ó Dálaigh, p. 157. **75** VO, Cancellation books, parish of Ruan, county Clare.   **76** GO, Ms. 443, printed list of freeholders of county Clare, 1829.   **77** The stone was found in the farmyard during demolition work and is retained at Drumcavan House by the owner, John Hehir. **78** *Ennis Chronicle,* 20 May 1809.   **79** Pigot and Co., *City of Dublin and Hibernian provincial directory* (Dublin, 1824), pp. 277–8.

smaller lots to maximise his rental income. Lucas, as we have seen, had already sublet portions to tenant farmers. Arthur wished to remove Lucas, who in effect had become another middle man, so that tenants could then rent directly from him. The new tenant of Drumcavan house was Constance Curtin, appointed parish priest of Ruan and Dysert in 1803.[80] Fr Curtin held just fifty-four acres of the townland. Why did Fr Curtin choose Drumcavan as his place of abode? Drumcavan was situated on the boundary midway between Ruan and Dysert and so was the most convenient location for the priest to minister to his congregation. The site of a stone bench where the priest married the young couples of the district is still pointed out at Drumcavan house.[81]

VII

In the Grand Jury map of county Clare, drawn up in 1787, the road from Ennis to Ruan and Corofin is depicted passing east west through Drumcavan townland.[82] Between then and the publication of the first edition of the Ordnance Survey maps in 1840, a new road was built connecting Ennis with Corofin and north Clare.[83] This road again illustrates the strategic location of Drumcavan; the road, moving from south to north, skirted the western edge of the townland; it crossed the ford of Ballycullinan before passing through the narrow stretch of ground between Ballycullinan Lake and Shanvalley Lough; the same narrow ground defended by Conchobhar Ó Deá against Richard de Clare at the battle of Dysert O'Dea five centuries previously. This new road was to have a profound effect on Drumcavan: by making Corofin more accessible it changed the whole orientation of the townland. People now tended to go to Corofin rather than Ruan for their shopping and entertainment. Corofin prospered at the expense of the older centre. The road also influenced the settlement pattern as new houses began to be built along the road frontage. John O'Donovan refers to the two roads of Drumcavan in his description of the townland for the Ordnance Survey in 1839:

> Drumcavan is in Ruan parish, bounded on the north by Cooga; west by Rath parish; east by Cloonfeighra and Kilkee West; and south by Cloonagh, Ballycullinan and Ballycullinan Lough. The townland is the property of Thomas Arthur Esq. About 50 acres of this townland is uncultivated rough pasture, the remainder under tillage and pasture. There are two roads in the townland, in its east and the other near its west side. There is a lough in

---

80 Ignatius Murphy, *The Diocese of Killaloe 1800–1850* (Dublin, 1992), p. 426.   **81** Personal communication with John Hehir, Drumcavan.   **82** Henry Pelham, *Map of County Clare, 1787* (reprint Dublin, 1989).   **83** OS, six-inch map of county Clare, sheet 25, edition of 1840.

the townland called Drumcavan lough, and a fort called Drumcavan fort and a neat cottage called Drumcavan house, the residence of the Revd Constance Curtin.[84]

This is the most complete description of the townland recorded. The Revd Curtin, a man who had been educated at Trinity College, Dublin and had studied theology in Portugal, died in February 1845 at the age of 86, after ministering in Ruan and Dysert for forty-three years.[85] We have no knowledge of the other tenants of the townland until the tithe applottment survey of the 1830s. Tithe was a tax levied on land for the maintenance of the clergy of the Church of Ireland. A full account of the tenants, the size of holdings and valuation of land was recorded in the applottment books. The tithe applottment survey corresponds quite accurately with the Griffith *Valuation* survey of 1855. The advantage of both surveys is the view they provide of the townland before and after the great famine of 1845–48. They are illustrated in Tables 1 & 2.

Table 1   Tithe Applottment Survey of Drumcavan 1830s[86]

Tenants	*Size of Holding*[87]		*Valuation*
Murty Holahan	70	acres	£33 4s. 6d.
Revd C. Curtin	54	acres	£28 7s. 6d.
Thomas Curtis	36	acres	£19 10s. 0d.
John McDonell	16	acres	£ 5 4s. 0d.
Mich Macken	15	acres	£ 5 11s. 6d.
Michael Kelliher	3	acres	£ 1 10s. 0d.
Water	32	acres	
Roads	1	acre	
Total	**227**	**acres**	**£93 3s. 6d.**
Proprietor	Major Arthur		

Here for the first time we see how the Arthurs redistributed the land following the departure of John Lucas in 1796. The townland is no longer let as a single unit but has been broken up into six separate holdings. The holdings are quite large only one being less than five acres. It is quite possible that some of the labourers, who rented from Lucas continued on as tenants under Arthur. For instance, at Drumcavan the ruins of labourers' cottages are still pointed out of whom it is said 'they could not be paid in money so they were given land

---

84 OS, Field name books, Dysert parish, county Clare, bk., 3, p. 27.   **85** Murphy, *Diocese of Killaloe 1800–50*, p. 426.   **86** NA, TAB, parish of Dysert, county Clare, 5/25, f. 212. **87** Original acreage in Tithe Applotment Survey is in Irish plantation measure; here calculated at the rate of 1.62 statute acres per Irish acre and rounded off to the nearest acre.

instead'.[88] The bridge over the ford of Ballycullinan today is called Macken bridge presumably after Mick Macken who held fifteen acres in the townland in the 1830s.

Table 2   Griffith *Valuation* Survey of Drumcavan 1855[89]

Tenants	Size of Holding		Valuation		
Martin Taafe	93	acres	£54	0s.	0d.
Thomas Hanrahan	75	acres	£27	5s.	0d.
John Mc Donnell	21	acres	£ 8	10s.	0d.
Revd J. Vaughan	13	acres	£ 8	0s.	0d.
Laurence Hayes	1	acre	£ 0	2s.	0d.
Unoccupied House			£ 0	5s.	0d.
Water	22	acres			
Total	**230**	**acres**	**£98**	**12s.**	**0d.**
Proprietor	Col. Thomas Arthur				

The great famine, clearly, had a major impact on the townland. Arthur, it appears, took advantage of it to clear out the old tenants and effect a complete redistribution of land. The number of holdings was reduced from six to five. Murty Holahan, Thomas Curtis, Mich Macken and Michael Kelliher disappear from the townland and new tenants, Martin Taafe and Thomas Hanrahan, are introduced. The only old tenant to survive was John McDonnell whose holding was increased from 16 to 21 acres. The parish priest, Fr Constance Curtin, who died in 1845, was replaced by Fr James Vaughan. The priest's holding was reduced from 54 to 13 acres; he no longer resided in Drumcavan but at Laurel Vale in the adjoining townland of Kilkee West. Martin Taafe, a man who appears to have come from outside the county, became the principal tenant and he resided at Drumcavan house. Taafe also held 130 acres in the townland of Cooga so in a real sense he became the successor of John Lucas

What motivated Arthur in effecting so many changes? Clearly the famine provided him with the opportunity of enlarging and consolidating the holdings within the townland. The old tenants may not necessarily have been evicted or have died of starvation; generally tenants with five acres or more were cushioned from the worst effects of famine. But the threat of starvation and the great hardships endured in the terrible years 1845–8 induced many to emigrate; and emigration, as we shall see, was to become the dominant factor in townland life in the century that followed. By enlarging the holdings Arthur was facilitating

---

88 Personal communication with John Hehir, Drumcavan.   **89** Griffith, *Valuation*, union of Corofin, county of Clare, (Dublin, 1855), p. 52.

the widespread changes that were occurring in Irish agriculture, especially the switch from tillage to the grazing of cattle, and at the same time securing his own rental income. By the second half of the nineteenth century the Arthurs had become thoroughly Anglicised; they resided in England and generally held commissions in the British army.[90] They had little contact with their tenants. It was a point of honour among Clare landowners not to deal directly with their tenants. The Studderts of Cregmoher, one of the few remaining Protestant families in the district, acted as land agents for the Arthurs.[91] Consequently the only relationship that existed between landlord and tenants was that of receiver of rent through a third party.

VIII

The famine set in motion a trend whereby generation after generation left the countryside in search of better lives in the New World and beyond. The population fell with monotonous regularity for the remaining decades of the century. Table 3 uses the census figures and shows how deeply famine and emigration impacted on the townlands.

Table 3   Population of Drumcavan and Adjoining Townlands, 1841–1911[92]

	Drumcavan	Cregmoher	Cooga	Cloonfeaghra	Kilkee West	Total
1841	51	114	72	29	56	322
1851	44	49	58	26	54	231
1861	32	49	50	13	33	177
1871	26	31	34	5	37	133
1881	28	38	34	9	37	126
1891	30	20	17	10	30	107
1901	31	16	11	6	22	86
1911	27	21	10	4	17	79

90 The landowner in 1832 was Thomas Arthur, Esq., Lieutenant of his Majesty's third regiment of Dragoons, (RD, 887/380/587380); in 1871 Col. Thomas Arthur of Manor House, Desborough, Market Harborough, Leicestershire was the owner of 2,672 acres in county Clare (*Land Owners in Ireland: Return of owners of land of one acre and upwards ...* (London 1876); in 1893 Capt. Henry H. Arthur, Beecham Grange, Kilworth, Leicester was owner in title of Drumcavan (VO, cancellation books, parish of Ruan, county Clare). **91** Personal communication with John Hehir and Agnes Hanrahan, Drumcavan. **92** *Census of Ireland*, 1841–1911, province of Munster.

Figure 1   Drumcavan Townland Population 1841–1911

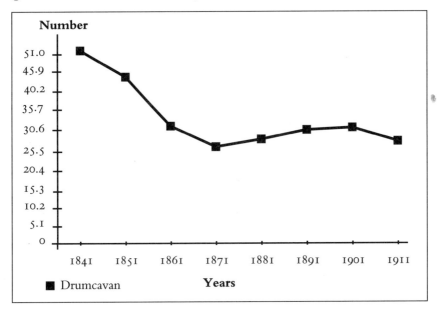

In 1841 Drumcavan, when compared with its neighbours, had the lowest density of population: one person to every 4.51 acres. Cregmoher with a density of one person per 2.96 acres was about to experience the worst ravages of the famine; Kilkee had the highest population density with one person per 2.48 acres. The low population level of Drumcavan in 1841 can be best explained by the active intervention of the landlord, who had recently reset the townland in large units and who ensured that no subdivision of holdings occurred. The population, nevertheless, fell from a high of 51 in 1841 to 27 in 1911. However, when compared-with the townlands of the locality Drumcavan experienced the lowest rate of population decline. Between 1841 and 1911 Drumcavan's population fell by just 47 per cent, Kilkee West fell by 70 per cent, Cregmoher by 82 per cent, Cooga by 86 per cent and Cloonfeaghra by a whopping 95 per cent. By 1911 Drumcavan had in fact the largest population of the five townlands. This untypical demographic experience can be best appreciated in Figure 2 when Drumcavan is compared with the population trends of the parish and the county.

Figure 2   Population of Townland, Parish and County expressed as a percentage
of the 1841 census[93]

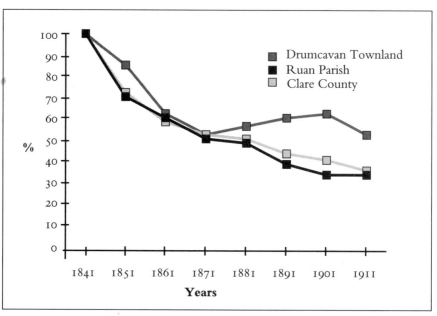

The population of the parish of Ruan fell steadily in the second half of the
nineteenth century; by 1911 it was just a third of what it had been in 1841 and
was below the average population decline of the county. The population of
Drumcavan by contrast had fallen by less than a half and was well above the
county average. What special factors operated in Drumcavan? The townland was
not endowed with any particular resources; its soil, for instance, was not necessarily
more fertile than that of other townlands in the parish. However, the relatively
large size of its farms made agriculture more economically viable. Additionally
the road network facilitated communication with the adjacent urban centres and
made the area more attractive as a place of residence. Furthermore in the latter
part of the century a new element was introduced that increased the population
level and boosted economic activity. In 1880s the first strips of land were
acquired for the laying down of the tracks of the West Clare Railway.

IX

Railway surveyors as early as 1870 choose Drumcavan as the most direct route
into north Clare for the Ennis and West Clare Railway.[94] Eventually in 1886 the

93 *Census of Ireland,* 1841–1911, province of Munster.   **94** Patrick Taylor, *The West Clare Railway* (Brighton, 1994), pp. 12–3.

ground for the rail track, '160 line perches', was purchased from John Hanrahan.[95]
The narrow gauge railway followed a familiar route, crossing the stream of
Ballycullinan, it entered the townland from the south east; it intersected the
Ennis to Corofin road, where a railway crossing was built; it then ran parallel
with the road, proceeding through the gap between Ballycullinan Lake and
Shanvalley Lough and continued on to Corofin. The line opened in July 1887;
three trains ran back and forth each day to Miltown Malbay.[96] The railway
introduced a new family to the townland. James Murphy, a railway section boss,
and his family resided in the new gatekeeper's cottage at the railway crossing.
The Murphys made an important contribution to the population. In the 1901
census nine people were enumerated in the Murphy household, accounting for
nearly a third of the townland's population.[97] Although the trains of the West
Clare trundled through the townland daily, the railway made surprisingly little
impact. Parcels and poultry were brought by train from Ennis and were collected
at the Ruan or Corofin stations. In the summer people travelled on excursions
to the seaside at Lehinch or Kilkee. But apart from turf, little freight was carried.
Cattle, for instance, were still walked to the fairs of Miltown Malbay and Ennis.[98]
The railway never really prospered. The introduction of the motor car reduced
passenger traffic and lorries were found to be more convenient for the transport
of turf and cattle. When, after seventy-four years in operation, it was finally
decided to close the railway, the service was hardly missed. The last train of the
West Clare Railway passed through Drumcavan gates on 31 January 1961.[99] The
rail tracks were quickly pulled up and the ground sold back to the local farmers
for far less than the original cost. An ambitious enterprise in the history of the
townland had come to an end.

X

The general transfer in land ownership, that occurred as a result of the Land Acts
in the closing decades of the last century, afforded security of occupation to
tenants in a way unthinkable in pre-famine times. The triumph of the Land
League under Davitt and Parnell ensured that the basic stock of tenants, laid
down after the famine, remained essentially the same. The present occupiers have
enjoyed the longest period of undisturbed tenure in Drumcavan since the
O'Hogans of the sixteenth century. Family names have changed, but not because
land has been sold to outsiders, but rather because land has passed from one
generation to another by way of marriage. There are now essentially four
holdings in the townland. The holding of John McDonnell, recorded in the tithe

95 VO, cancellation books, parish of Ruan, county Clare.   **96** Taylor, *West Clare Railway*, p. 22.   **97** NA, Census of Ireland, 1901, county of Clare, parish of Ruan, Drumcavan, 20/19.   **98** Personal communication with John Hehir and Agnes Hanrahan, Drumcavan.   **99** Taylor, *West Clare Railway*, pp. 197–8.

applottment books of the 1830s, passed by way of marriage to Daniel Dillion in 1865 and again by marriage to Peter McMahon in 1955.[100] Similarly, with the largest holding in the townland, Martin Taafe was drowned in 1870, while attempting to pull a cow out of Errinagh Lake.[101] His daughter, Helena Taafe, married John Hehir and the property, after five generations, still remains in the ownership of the Hehir family.[102] The holding of Thomas Hanrahan is also retained by his descendants only recently the name changing, again by way of marriage, to O'Brien.[103] The only holding to have had a succession of owners was that held by Fr Jeremiah Vaughan in 1855. For most of the last century it was held by Patrick Mackey passing to Michael O'Brien in 1902 and to William Ballinger in 1960.[104] The landlord's interest was bought out under the land purchase act in the 1920s so that today all property in the townland is held in freehold.[105] The legacy of the landlord system, however, can still be discerned; a yearly 'rent' continues to be paid to the Irish Land Commission; the land agents, the Studderts of Cregmoher, are still spoken of, but the Arthurs are now just a vague memory.[106]

Today, unlike the eighteenth and nineteenth centuries, tillage is completely absent from the townland and grazing dominates. With the introduction of milk quotas, dairying, which provided the main source of farming income for many decades, is declining and suckler cows are becoming the norm. The cleavage between Corofin and Ruan remains. Families on the western end of the townland attend school and church at Corofin, those on the east go to Ruan. Although all continue to bury their dead in the old churchyard of Ruan. In recent years the suburban spill-over from Ennis has reached Drumcavan with ribbon development taking place on the Ennis Corofin road. Three new bungalows have been built overlooking Ballycullinan Lake and the old railway cottage has become a holiday home. Indeed the bulk of the population is now formed by these new landless commuter families. Whatever about Drumcavan's history, the future of the townland is going to be very different from its past.

---

100 VO, cancellation books, parish of Ruan, county Clare. 101 Personal communication with John Hehir, Drumcavan. 102 Personal communication with John Hehir, Drumcavan. 103 Personal communication with Agnes Hanrahan, Drumcavan. 104 VO, cancellation books, parish of Ruan, county Clare. 105 VO, cancellation books, parish of Ruan, county Clare. 106 Personal communication with Agnes Hanrahan and John Hehir, Drumcavan.

PAUL CONNELL*

I

The townland of Dysart is situated in the barony of Moyashel and Magheradernan, five miles southwest by south of Mullingar in the County of Westmeath. The village of Dysart is located on the western fringes of the townland but outside its boundary. The village contains the Roman Catholic church and school and is the centre of the civil parish. The main road between Mullingar and Castletown-Geoghegan cuts through the townland emerging just east of the village of Dysart. A further road cuts off to the south in the direction of Kilbeggan. The townland is situated on the western shore of Lough Ennell and contains a number of small islands, the largest of which is called Dysart Island. The total area of the townland is given in Griffith's *Valuation* of 1854 as 1,827 acres including the islands in Lough Ennell.[1]

A first glance at the 1837 and modern Ordnance Survey maps shows clear evidence of ancient activity and settlement. The Westmeath Archaeological Survey lists no less than twenty-eight sites. Along with a monastic site, graveyard and earth works, there are remains of a castle, two crannogs, a site containing old field systems and habitations, a holy well, along with a mound, eight earthworks and no less than thirteen ringforts. A cursory walk of part of the townland area has revealed further evidence of ancient settlement which is not marked on the survey map.

Father Paul Walsh gives the following description of the origin of Dysart:

> The name in Irish is *Díseart*, a word derived from the Latin *desertum*, and hence meaning 'a lonely place', 'hermitage', 'waste', or the like. It occurs frequently in different parts of the country, and to distinguish a particular *diseart* from others, a saint's or hermit's name is commonly added. The full name of the present parish is *Díseart Maeltuile*.[2]

Father Anthony Cogan in his description of the abbeys of Westmeath in the third volume of his *History of the Diocese of Meath* tells us that:

* I would like to dedicate this essay to my father Thomas Connell and his family the Connells and Mahons, natives of Dysart, Co. Westmeath.   **1** Griffith, *Valuation*, Co. Westmeath, Barony of Moyashel and Magherdernon, Union of Mullingar, Parish of Dysart.   **2** Revd Paul Walsh, *Placenames of Westmeath* (Dublin, 1957), pp. 203–4.

A religious house was founded here, called *Díseart Maeltuile*, i.e., 'St Maeltuile's desert or wilderness', on the west of Lough Ennell, in the present barony of Moyashel and Magheradernan, by St Maeltuile. The festival of St Maeltuile Mac Mochuire, founder of this place is set down in the *Martyrology of Tallaght* at the 30th of July, and his holy well, called Tobar Multilly, is still pointed out, near the old churchyard of Dysart.[3]

We read in the Four Masters that in 1033: '*Díseart Maeltuile* was plundered by Murchadh O'Melaghlin.' In the table of the *Martyrology of Donegal*, at the 29th of May, the following entry is inserted: 'There is a *Cill Maoltuile*, a parish church in *Disert-Midhe*, in the diocese of Meath. His baculus works miracles on perjurers before they go out of the church. His well, and his yellow bell, and his baculus and his statue, are still there.[4]

Archdall says that St Colman built an abbey at Dysart and that a monastery for Conventual Franciscans was afterwards founded.[5] The remains of a church can still be seen today along with the holy well which is still called Multilly's Well. Cogan tells us in his description of Dysart parish that the church measured seventy-three feet by twenty feet and three inches.

Perhaps the most interesting evidence of the ancient importance of this area are the two sites known as *Cró Inis*, and *Dún na Sciath* (Fort of the Shields). *Dún na Sciath* is a conspicuous mound which Professor Macalister described as a Norman moat which may cover the site of an earlier structure.[6] When Tara was forsaken in the sixth century, the high kings of Ireland established their palace at *Dún na Sciath*. The Four Masters state that Dún na Sciath was the seat of King Malachy the Great and that it had several concentric entrenchments, two of which are still visible today. He came to the throne late in the tenth century and was later deposed by Brian Boru. After Brian was killed at Clontarf he reigned again. *Cró Inis* is an island in Lough Ennell which lies opposite *Dún na Sciath*, about three hundred yards from the shore. Here in 1022, King Malachy died aged seventy-three having just defeated the Danes decisively at Athboy in county Meath. The Four Masters called him the 'pillar of the dignity and nobility of the Western World'. The archbishop of Armagh and other high ecclesiastics were present on *Cró-Inis* at the time, along with many of the 'seniors of Ireland'.[7] O'Donovan's Ordnance Survey Letters describes both of these sites in detail.[8]

Hugh de Lacy retained in his own hand 'the lake and vill of dissert and one knight's fee around the said vill'.[9] It may be that he reserved it as a residence for

3 Revd Anthony Cogan, *The diocese of Meath, ancient and modern* (3 vols, Dublin, 1867; reprinted, Dublin, 1992), iii, 559.   4 Ibid.   5 Mervyn A.M. Archdall, *Monasticum Hibernicum or the history of the abbeys, priories and other religious houses in Ireland* (Dublin, 1786), p. 710.   6 Laurence Geoghegan, 'Topographical Survey of Westmeath', October 1942, Unpublished manuscript in the Westmeath County Library, p. 3.   7 Ibid.   8 Revd Michael O'Flanagan (ed.), *Letters containing information relative to the antiquities of Co. Westmeath, collected during the progress of the Ordnance Survey in 1837* (2 vols, Bray, 1931), i, pp. 10 and 11.   9 G.H. Orpen, *Ireland under the Normans* (2 vols, Oxford, 1968), ii, 82.

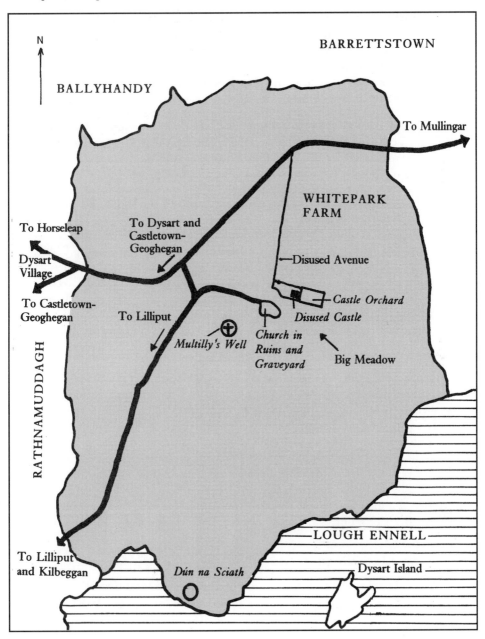

Dysart, county Westmeath, 1837, 1827 acres

the particular O'Melaghlin favoured at the time by him. The parish church of Dysart was bestowed on the Norman abbey of St Thomas, Dublin, before 1202. William Pipard, who died around 1227, held the lands of Dysart from Walter de Lacy and this fief remained in the hands of the Pipard family until 1301, when it was surrendered to the Crown. An extent of the manor was taken in 1303 and it stated that the lands were 'totally in the march of warlike land', and that

> the manor aforesaid is so contiguous to the Irish of Leinster and Meath that no English or peaceful man remains among them, and that the manor will not answer to the Lord for any profit unless the Lord shall apply a custody there.[10]

On 22 July 1304 the custody of the land was granted by the king to Richard de Burgh, earl of Ulster.[11]

A genealogical outline of the Nugent family of county Westmeath tells us that the estate of Dysart came into the family when James the son of Richard Nugent, tenth Baron Delvin, married Elizabeth, the eldest daughter and heiress of Robert Hollywood of Artane in county Dublin.[12] The Dysart estate had been purchased by her father from the heirs of Sir Thomas de Verdon, who had married the eldest daughter of Sir William de Lacy. While there would appear to be some discrepancy between the accounts given by Walsh and Lyons, it is certain that from the 1450s onwards the estate remained in the hands of the Nugent family until the beginning of this century.

In 1600 during the Nine Years War, the county of Westmeath was in the charge of Christopher Nugent, fourteenth Baron Delvin. Delvin kept a safe distance from Tyrone, not venturing to come nearer to him than Mullingar and Dysart. His son Richard, fifteenth Baron Delvin, was knighted in 1603 but implicated in a plot against the government in 1607. He was pardoned in 1608 along with his cousin Sir Robert Nugent of Dysart. Sir Robert was granted the lands of Dysart townland by James I in 1611. His brother and heir Andrew was confirmed in possession by Charles I in 1638. In the 1641 rebellion Dysart Island was garrisoned and used as a magazine by the Army of the Confederation. It was taken twice by the Parliamentary forces and subsequently held by them until the Restoration.[13]

The Nugents were dispossessed by the Cromwellians in the aftermath of the 1641 rebellion. However following the restoration of Charles II in 1660 they applied to the Court of Claims to have their lands restored. In a claim heard on 26 March 1663, Lavallin Nugent, the son of Andrew, and his mother Katherine were declared by the court to be innocent papists and were restored to their lands.[14]

---

10 Revd Paul Walsh, *Irish Chiefs and Leaders*, ed. Colm O'Lochlainn (Dublin, 1960), pp. 235–7. 11 Ibid. 12 John Charles Lyons, *The Grand Juries of Westmeath – from the year 1727 to the year 1853, with an historical appendix* (2 vols, Ledestown, 1853), i, pp. 217–19. 13 Samuel Lewis, *Topographical dictionary of Ireland, with historical and statistical descriptions* (2 vols, London, 1837), i, 592. 14 NA, ILC, Nugent Estate, Co. Westmeath, EC 2448, Box No. 3611, Copy of Decree of Innocence, Court of Claims, 26 March 1663 made by the Record Office Custom House, Dublin, 2 November 1846.

Lavallin did not seem to have had any difficulties during the 1690 rebellion as he died in 1701 still in possession of Dysart townland and estate. His great-grandson John, the governor of Tortola in the West Indies, died in 1812, leaving the Dysart estate to his grandnephew Andrew Savage of Portaferry in county Down, on condition that he took the surname of Nugent.[15] This he did and the estate remained in the hands of the Savage-Nugents of Portaferry, county Down until his grandson John Vesey Nugent sold the estate to the Land Commission in 1909.

II

The first indication of population levels in the townland appears in a census of 1659.[16] It states that the total number of persons living in the townland was sixty-nine, of whom sixty-six were Irish and three were English. A Mr Lucas and Roger Mounrag are the names listed as the holders. This census records only males as heads of households and unmarried females over eighteen. If this census figure is multiplied by three, it provides an estimate of 207 persons in the townland in 1659. Population figures for the townland are not available again until 1841. Table 1 shows the figures given in each of the census years from 1841 to 1911.[17]

Table 1. Dysart Townland Population 1841–1911

Year	Male	Female	Total %	Drop	Co % Drop
1841	184	145	329		
1851	148	122	270	18.0 %	21.5 %
1861	123	125	248	8.0 %	18.4 %
1871	119	103	222	10.5 %	13.7 %
1881	94	95	189	15.0 %	8.5 %
1891	86	72	158	16.5 %	9.3 %
1901	77	53	130	18.0 %	5.3 %
1911	66	45	111	14.6 %	2.7 %

These figures show a continuous decline in population throughout the century. The 1851 figure represents a drop of 18 *per cent* on 1841. This no doubt reflects the effects of the famine. Up to 1881 the drop in population in the townland is less percentage wise than in the county, but is far steeper than the county after that. The 1911 population when compared to the 1841 population represents a significant drop in population of 66 *per cent* or two thirds.

15 NA, ILC, Nugent Estate, Co. Westmeath, EC 2448, Box No. 3611, Testament of Wills. Will of John Nugent of Dysart, Lieutenant Governor of Tortola and Leeward and Caribee Islands 1801, with codicil 1811.   **16** Seamus Pender (ed.), *A Census of Ireland circa 1659* (Dublin, 1939), p. 514.   **17** *Census of Ireland*, 1841–1911.

Figures 1 and 2 shows these population trends.

Figure 1. Dysart Townland Population 1841–1911.

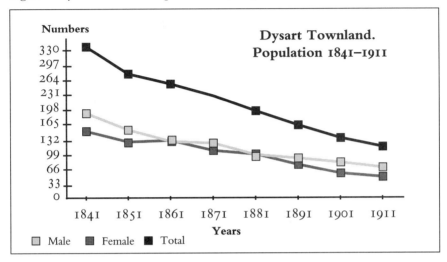

Figure 2. Dysart Townland – % Drop in population 1841–1911 *Townland v. County*

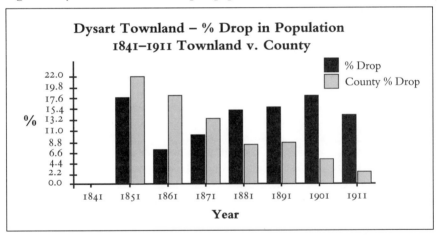

Throughout the century, as with the population figures, the housing stock diminished considerably. In 1841 there were fifty-four inhabited houses. This dropped dramatically to thirty-nine in 1851, another indication of the severity of the famine. By 1901 the figure was thirty-three inhabited houses. With the decreasing population however, came a better ratio of inhabitants to houses. In 1841 a population of 329 lived in fifty-four houses. This represents a an average of six persons per house. By 1901 the equivalent ratio was a little over three persons per house.

In order to give a somewhat wider picture than that of the townland it is possible to look at the parish records. Unfortunately they do not record the townland nor indeed any address. However, figure 3 gives a good indication of the pattern of baptisms and marriages in Dysart parish (as distinct from the townland) from the 1820s to the early 1900s. It should be borne in mind that the townland population figure as a percentage of the parish population figure was about thirty four *per cent* from the 1850s onwards. What is striking is the dramatic drop in marriages and baptisms in the aftermath of the famine.

Figure 3. Dysart Parish – Baptisms and Marriages 1837–1901

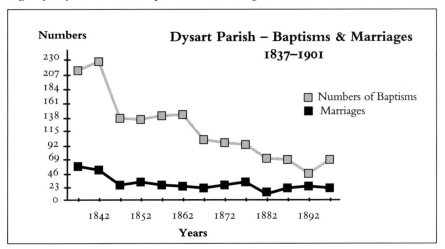

III

The population structure of the townland can be looked at in great detail using the 1901 census. From the enumeration forms for this census it is clear that the 130 persons were divided into thirty-three households. Two of these persons are listed as tinsmiths and have no identifiable abode, and so were probably members of the travelling community. There were in fact thirty-five houses in the townland but two were unoccupied. Three other persons were visitors on the night and should not really be included in the regular population.[18]

The 130 persons are divided into seventy-seven males and fifty-three females. All of them were Roman Catholics and there were no Irish speakers among them. The vast majority of them (119) were born in county Westmeath. A study of the parish registers, and inquiries among the present inhabitants would

18 NA, Enumeration forms for the 1901 & 1911 Census for the parish of Dysart, District Electoral Division of Mullingar, Co. Westmeath. 1901, 64/9, 1911, 64/5.

indicate that the townland was quite closed, with marriage partners coming from the townland itself or from the neighbouring townlands. Of the remaining eleven persons listed, five were the family of an agricultural labourer, all of whom were born in county Offaly. Two others were a retired RIC man and his wife from county Longford. One was an agricultural labourer from Co. Longford and the other was a woman from county Meath who had married an agricultural labourer. Finally there were the two travellers. In total there were thirty four persons under the age of eighteen. Of the other ninety six, twelve could not read or write, while a further four could read but not write.[19]

Figure 4, 5 and 6 look at the age structure in the townland in the 1901 census and compare it with the 1911 census age structure.

Figure 4. Dysart Townland – Age Structure 1901 v 1911 Census

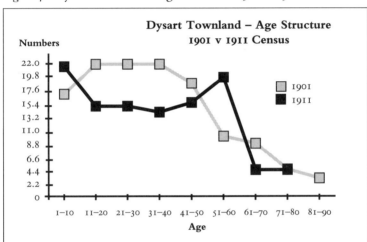

Figure 5. Dysart Townland – 1901 Census by Age

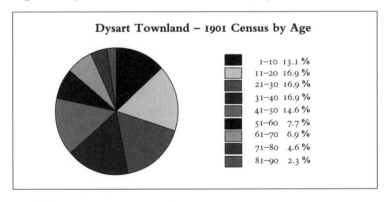

19 Ibid.

Figure 6. Dysart Townland – 1911 Census by Age

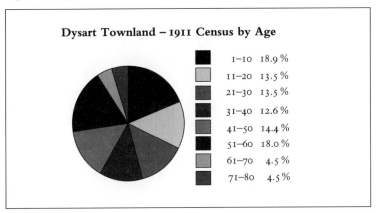

Dysart Townland – 1911 Census by Age

1–10	18.9 %
11–20	13.5 %
21–30	13.5 %
31–40	12.6 %
41–50	14.4 %
51–60	18.0 %
61–70	4.5 %
71–80	4.5 %

Tables 2 and 3 indicate the quality of housing stock and the number of persons per family, excluding the visitors and agricultural labourers living with families.[20]

Table 2. Dysart Townland – 1901 Census

No. of Rooms per household					
Rooms per house	2 Rooms	3 Rooms	4 Rooms	5 Rooms	Over 5
Number	10	8	10	3	2

Of the two houses with more than five rooms, one had nine rooms and the other had ten. All of the houses had two or more windows in front, while eight houses had five or more windows in front.[21]

Table 3. Dysart Townland – 1901 Census

No. of persons per family						
Persons per family	1	2	3	4	5	6	7
Number	6	8	7	5	2	1	4

20 Ibid. **21** Ibid.

As the townland was entirely rural and contained no village it is not surprising that the vast majority of occupations were farm related. Twenty-one persons are listed as farmers and heads of households. There were thirty-two agricultural labourers. Of these, eight were heads of households while a further eight were farmers' sons. Nine women are described as housekeepers but three of these were farmers' wives. The other occupations were: one domestic servant, one postman, one stone mason, one carpenter and one tin smith. Three persons were retired, one was a retired farmer, one a retired herdsman and the other an RIC pensioner. All of these were over eighty years of age.[22]

IV

The loss of the enumeration forms for the census material before 1901 prevents an equally detailed study of settlement for the nineteenth century. However, a clear enough pattern emerges from the use of other sources that are available. The most important of these from the point of view of landholding is Griffith's *Valuation* along with the perambulation and field books.[23] All of these were completed by the mid 1850's. The perambulation book for Dysart gives some idea of the soil type in the townland. It was described as gravely soil, a mixture of pasture and arable. Some of the townland was poorly drained with the better quality land to the west of the main Mullingar to Castletown–Geoghegan road. There were a number of islands in the lake situated in the western part of the townland. The field book gives the first detailed account of landholding and valuation.

From the printed Griffith's *Valuation* it is clear that there were some forty-six occupiers in the townland in 1854. These ranged in size from a holding of some 236 acres held by Thomas Murray, a non-resident occupier, to the hovel of no value occupied by Margaret Warren. The total acreage was almost 1828 acres. There were four large holdings in particular. A farm of 236 acres was held by Richard Wade. Mary Killian had a holding of some 206 acres while Thomas Loorame held 104 acres. These were all residents of the townland. Thomas Murray was not, however; he lived in a large house in the adjoining townland of Barretstown. In total he had four holdings in Dysart townland, amounting to some 577 acres. The large holdings were all situated to the west of the main road from Mullingar to Castletown–Geoghegan.

The field book is more enlightening about the conditions of tenancy. Of the thirty-seven main holdings, thirty-one were held at will, while six had leases. Thomas Murray held three of his holdings, some 570 acres in total, on a lease for one life or twenty-one years. His remaining portion of seven acres was held

22 Ibid.   **23** Griffith, *Valuation*, Co. Westmeath, Barony of Moyashel & Magherdernon, Union of Mullingar, Parish of Dysart; VO, First valuation, perambulation & field books for Co. Westmeath, Barony of Moyashel & Magherdernon, Union of Mullingar, Parish of Dysart.

at will. Mary Killian and Richard Wade had similar leases. One other holding had a lease. This was one of twenty-six acres held by Patrick Meehan on a lease of two lives or thirty-one years. Leaving out those holdings which were merely houses and gardens, all the other holdings held at will ranged from five acres to eighty-seven acres. Figure 7 looks at the pattern in the size of holdings.

Figure 7. Dysart Townland – Griffith's Valuation. Size of Holding

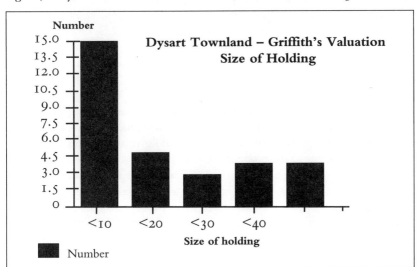

Using the cancellation books, an update of Griffith's *Valuation*, it is possible to trace the land occupancy in the townland down to the census of 1901 and beyond.[24] A study of these cancellation books for Dysart indicates a clear pattern of closure. Holdings changed automatically from father to son in most cases. Thus for example, Mary Carey's holding of thirty-seven acres passed to her son John in 1878. Thomas Clarke's holding of six acres went to his son John in 1865 and then to his wife Anne in 1889. Christopher Dignum had a holding of sixty-four acres which he passed on to his son-in-law, Michael Ballesty, in 1901. Interestingly enough, a study of the parish registers show that he had five children, of whom his daughter Ann Ballesty was the youngest. It appears that emigration or death took the others. Thomas Molloy held some nine acres of land, which included the garden and orchard of the old Nugent castle and residence. His nephew Thomas Lestrange took it over on his death in 1864 and his great-grandchildren are still there today. There was only one holding which changed hands completely. Richard Wade's holding was taken over in 1880 by Richard White, and he in turn was replaced by John Cleary in 1885.

24 VO, First valuation, cancellation books for Co. Westmeath, Barony of Moyashel & Magherdernon, Union of Mullingar, Parish of Dysart.

Apart from using the Valuation Office material it is possible in the case of Dysart townland to make a closer examination of land holding patterns by looking at the estate papers. The fact that the entire townland constituted one estate is very helpful. Rentals and correspondence for the estate survive in the Savage Nugent papers in the Public Record Office of Northern Ireland.[25] The correspondence shows that by 1839 the Savage Nugents were considering selling the estate, and they received an offer of 50,000 guineas in that year.[26] The value of the estate was estimated to be £57,500, based on a twenty five years multiple of the annual rental of £2300. In December 1843 a valuation of the estate was made by Lockhart Remage.[27] He placed a valuation of £1800 on it, which compares favourably with Griffith's valuation of £1400.[28] By the end of 1843, however, all thoughts of sale seem to have been put aside. In a long letter to Thomas Webb, the estate agent, John Nugent showed clearly his intention of improving rather than selling the estate. He accepted that some of the rentals were too high, considering the state of the land. However, he refused to reduce rents, as this would be counterproductive. Instead, he decided he would give abatements of rent for any improvements made to the properties, especially for drainage. In an interesting development, he told the agent to proceed with evictions but instructed him to give the evicted tenants two or three acres and a new cabin. He concludes:

> I should prefer keeping the old tenants on the property, and try what a new system of giving them employment will do, as they had not much of that before.[29]

Much of the subsequent estate correspondence deals with the granting of abatements of rent to some of the tenants for various improvements. On 21 January 1861 Thomas Molloy, one of the tenants who rented the old castle orchard, wrote to the landlord asking for some pear, plum and cherry trees:

> I do humbly flatter myself that I hav puntualy met my engagements that your honor may in your kindnys have me provided with some five dosen of thes threes.[30]

While there is a huge volume of correspondence existing for most of the century, there are two unfortunate gaps. The papers for the famine years and for the Land League years are missing. This makes a full and detailed examination of landlord tenant relations difficult. The general impression from the correspondence and from local folklore however, is that relations were generally good and there were few evictions. An interesting address was made on behalf of the tenants to General Nugent by Richard White and James Killian on the occasion of a visit he made to the estate on 4 of August 1886:

25 PRONI, Savage Nugent Papers, D 552. **26** PRONI, D 552/A/9/12/4. **27** PRONI, D 552/B/3/3/104. **28** PRONI, D 552/14/9/12/13. **29** PRONI, D 552/14/9/12/20. **30** PRONI, D 552/A/13.

For the many acts of kindness that have characterised your dealings with us, we cannot find sufficient words with which to express our gratitude ... the leaseholder and the yearly tenant being treated with equal consideration ... Your own generous acts, which when the historian comes to write the pages of history, wherin shall be recorded the relationship for some years past subsisting between landlords and tenants in Ireland, shall stand forth as almost the only bright spot upon that dark and dismal record.[31]

V

Estate rentals exist for most of the nineteenth century. Using these it is possible to study the presence of certain families in the townland throughout the course of the century. The rentals however only give the name of the main tenant, and so there is no way of establishing the numbers of agricultural labourers or cottiers before 1855. Looking in detail at rentals for 1824, 1846 and 1905 and linking them with Griffith's *Valuation* provides interesting data.[32]

There are twenty-eight tenants listed in 1824 and they paid a total of £2436 in rent. Arrears listed for the year to November 1824 amount to some £4595 which perhaps indicates why the Nugents considered selling the property. In practice, all of this money would not have been arrears, as typically tenants on many estates were allowed to be behind a certain amount in payments. Also, this figure included the second moiety due for the second half of 1824. Still, it is clear from the evidence that the estate was behind in rental collection.

By contrast the 1846 rental, which is just at the beginning of the famine shows a total of thirty seven tenancies. A total of £1918 was collected in 1846 and arrears to 1 November 1846 amounted to some £1220. The rental lists the arrears due up to 1 November 1844 and 1845 and in both cases the figure is also around £1220. A comparison of the 1824 and 1846 rentals shows that nine new tenancies were created during this period. Of twenty-six family names on the 1824 rental only four do not appear on the 1846 rental.

When the 1824 rental is compared to Griffith's Valuation it becomes apparent that some changes occurred in the intervening period.[33] Firstly, six family names no longer appear. Secondly, some families seem to have smaller holdings, while others have larger ones. Three families, the Carneys, the Mahons and the Nestors have smaller holdings. The Carneys have gone from twenty-six acres to eight, the Mahons from forty one acres to just a cottage, and the Nestors from thirty three acres to fifteen. Unfortunately, without estate maps it is not possible to pinpoint these locations exactly. On the other hand, the Killians have gone from thirty-eight acres to 206, the Loorams from sixty-seven acres to 104 and of course

31 PRONI, D 552/A/15/ 1–4. **32** PRONI, Estate Rental 1824, D 552/B/3/2/188; Estate Rental 1846, D552/B/3/2/190; NA, ILC, Nugent Estate, Co. Westmeath, EC 2448, Box No. 3611, Estate Rental 1905. **33** Griffith, *Valuation* Co. Westmeath, Barony of Moyashel & Magherdernon, Union of Mullingar, Parish of Dysart.

the Murrays from 91 acres to 577. In the case of the Murrays, they simply took over two large holdings which had been held by a family called Finnegan. Of all of these, the only family to lose out during the famine period were the Mahons.

Overall a total of forty-eight family names appear in the rentals and Griffith's *Valuation* from 1824 to 1905. Of these, fifteen survive from 1824 to 1905. A total of thirty-two family names appear in Griffith's Valuation. Of these, twenty-seven are still in the townland in 1905. All this reinforces the impression that occupancy within the townland remained very closed throughout the nineteenth century. While the population continued to drop, the holdings were passed on from one family member to another. While it is hard to gauge with any accuracy it is clear from talking to present residents that there was a good deal of emigration from the 1840s onwards. Much of this seemed to be directed towards the United States. A number of the Lestrange family went there for example.[34]

One of the Meehan families had a history of emigrating to Scotland. James and Ann Meehan married in the 1870s. They held a tenancy of thirty seven acres which James took over from his father James in 1881. They had eight children, two of whom had died by 1911. Patrick and Katherine emigrated to Scotland. After many years Patrick returned and was known locally as 'Paddy the Scot'. Thomas attempted to go, but got cold feet when he saw the boat in Dun Laoghaire and henceforth he was known as the Clyde Meehan. Christopher and John made a living locally as agricultural labourers. In all there were four different Meehan families in the townland.[35]

Some estimate of emigration levels can be arrived at by comparing the 1901 and 1911 census figures for the townland. By 1911 the townland's population has dropped from 130 to 111. Taking out those of ten years or younger we get a figure of 90. Comparing the names in both the 1901 and 1911 census and not counting new persons moving into the townland it is clear that there are fifty-seven people missing. Thirteen people from the townland died during this period and were buried in the local graveyard.[36] This leaves a total of forty-four persons unaccounted for. Some of course may have married or settled in other townlands. A few certainly went to work in Dublin. Nevertheless there is implied in this figure a substantial number of people who must have emigrated.

VI

As has been mentioned already, the only type of employment available in the townland was agricultural. The inhabitants were either farmers themselves or

---

34 Rose & Seamus Lestrange, Dysart, Co. Westmeath, in conversation with author October 1995.   35 John Molloy, Dysart, Co. Westmeath, in conversation with author March 1996.   36 Register of Burials in the burial ground of Dysart in the Union of Mullingar, Electoral Division of Dysart, Dispensary District of Castletown-Geoghegan, 1872–1953. (copy in St Finian's College, Mullingar, Archives).

they worked for farmers as labourers or herds. With regard to the type of farming carried on, the evidence points to a mixture of tillage and pasture. An early indication is provided by the Tithe Applotment Books.[37] The tithe was basically a land tax for the upkeep and support of the Anglican church and its ministers. Supposedly a tenth of all crop valuation, the actual amounts collected varied enormously from place to place. Up to the reform of the tithe in 1825 pasture land was not titheable.

A comparison of the Tithe Applotment Book of 1825 and Griffith's *Valuation* shows that of the main occupiers in Dysart townland in 1855, nineteen are mentioned in the tithe applotment book. The total area titheable in 1825 was 820 acres which represented forty five per cent of the total townland acreage of 1,826 acres. The amount of tithe payable was £42 which represented only 1.7 per cent of the 1824 estate rental. The tithe figures give therefore some idea of the extent of tillage in the townland. An interesting point is that of the nineteen occupiers who are mentioned both in the 1824 rental and the tithe applotment book, ten are listed as having the same acreage in both. A comparison of the tithe and the rents they paid show that the tithe represented between two and three percent of their rents.

The 1843 valuation of the estate completed by Lockhart Remage provides further evidence with regard to farming type. He pointed out that many of the farms were 'reduced to great poverty by bad management'.[38] In particular, he singled out the con acre system for special criticism. This was the subletting of land by the tenants to labourers and others for the purpose of growing crops. The system was a lucrative one for the tenant as usually he could more than pay for his rent from the proceeds. Forty acres of a 135-acre holding was set by Simon Kiernan in February 1815 at a rate of £7. 10s. per con acre. Remage was adamant that many of the holdings on the estate, including the two largest, were totally exhausted by the con acre system which 'ought never to be allowed on any farm'.[39] One holding was so badly damaged that 'I really believe a goat per acre would hardly live on it for some years to come'.[40] The picture he paints of the smaller farmers is interesting. Some of them were 'too poor to effect any improvements', and he frequently refers to tenants who were 'deficient of both knowledge and capital'. On the other hand, some tenants like the Nallys

> appear to be more industrious than the other small tenants, particularly Matthew, who has his land well stocked with cattle and is managing his little so well I think him deserving of encouragement.[41]

From 1847 national statistics were published on agricultural outputs.[42] Initially they were done by electoral divisions within a county. The 1847 figures for Dysart

37 NA, TAB, County Westmeath, Parish of Churchtown, 30/43. Film No 106. **38** PRONI, D 552/A/15/1–4. **39** Ibid. **40** Ibid. **41** Ibid. **42** *Return of number of agricultural holdings in Ireland in 1841, 1851, 1861 and 1867. Extent of arable land, extent of land under tillage, under meadowing and clover; number of livestock*, HC 1867–68(287) lv 631, and subsequent years.

electoral division, an area much wider than the townland, show that of nearly 1900 acres under crops, there were 1116 acres of oats, only eleven acres of wheat, 120 acres of turnips and twelve acres of potatoes. For the rest of the century the agricultural statistics are based on the barony or Poor Law Union. In the Poor Law Union of Mullingar as a whole there is a gradual decline in tillage production and a move towards pasture from the 1850s onwards. As regards stock numbers, between 1855 and 1895 in Mullingar Poor Law Union horse numbers remained steady, sheep, pigs and goats declined by a quarter and cattle and poultry numbers grew by a third.

Throughout the century there was a decline in the levels of rent paid by the tenants. Rents were at their highest during the Napoleonic wars at the beginning of the century. An 1815 rental, while difficult to compare with later rentals, seems to indicate that the rental income from the estate was in the region of £3,500. By 1824 this had dropped to £2,436. The rent collected in 1846 was in the region of £1,900 and by 1905 the Land Commission records show a rental of roughly £1,500. The estate was not unaffected by the various land acts. By 1905 most of the tenants were judicial tenants and they had on a number of occasions sought reductions of rent through the land courts. They met with varying degrees of success. Kate Nally was threatened with ejectment from her nineteen acre holding in December 1898. On 18 January 1899 her rent was reduced by the land court from £16 to £13. Michael Ballesty had a holding of sixty-four acres and sought a reduction in his rent from the court in July 1898. His rent of about £47 was reduced by only a shilling. One family, the 'Sailor Meehans', were evicted in 1877 but they seem to have been provided with a cottage.

VII

As already mentioned, the Nugents were offered 50,000 guineas for the estate in 1838. They considered the possibility of selling the property again in 1872. William Evans, the land agent, drew up a report for General Andrew Nugent in May of that year. He estimated the value of the property at £48,600, on the basis of twenty-five years rental of £1944. He suggested selling the estate in four lots, in order to maximise the price. Once again, the Nugents changed their minds and decided not to sell.[43] In 1903 however, like many other landlords they made the decision to sell the estate to the Land Commission. The sale was held up by the death of General Nugent in 1905. However, it was sold in one large and one small lot by his brother and heir John Vesey Nugent in 1909 and 1910 for a total of £32,717. He also received rental income to July 1909, a total of £1328. In common with other estates there were a number of debts to be paid off. The Representative Church Body had a mortgage on the estate of £15,000 and a total of £3,667 was due to family members under various trusts. John

43 PRONI, D 552/B/3/3/110.

Vesey Nugent ended his centuries long family connection with the Dysart townland in 1910, receiving a total of £15,378 clear of debts.[44] He had no heirs and his Portaferry estate passed to a cousin in 1926 after his death.

The sale of the property did not proceed without some controversy. Two farms were bought by two Dysart tenants despite the opposition of the local branch of the United Irish League. They wanted one of the holdings, a large grazing farm of 200 acres called 'Whitepark', divided up among some of the local agricultural labourers. This was part of a general campaign being conducted by the League throughout the county against the sale of grazing farms. The situation was further complicated by the fact that the other holding called the 'Big Meadow' was without a sitting tenant since the death of the estate agent, William Evans. He had rented it from the landlord after the then sitting tenant, Edward Gavagan, was evicted from it in 1882. The locals wanted his relatives to have first option on the property.

When the neighbouring tenant, Patrick Lestrange, bought this holding from the Land Commissioners he was told by the League to give it up. When he refused to do this, a cattle drive occurred on 22 January, 1909. As a result, twenty-six local men were arrested and sent to Tullamore and Mountjoy jails after refusing bail. The result was total uproar in the district and enormous pressure was put on Lestrange to give up possession of the land in question. This he did on 28 January following a visit from a local deputation led by the parish priest Fr. James Kelly. One cannot but have sympathy for Lestrange as the twelve acres in dispute adjoined his property and would merely have doubled his land holding. After seeing what happened to Lestrange, the new tenant of Whitepark, also gave up possession.[45] The whole episode is an interesting example of local interaction and tension within the townland. The Gavagan family took possession of the 'Big Meadow' but despite all the agitation, Whitepark eventually ended up in the possession of one of the largest farmers in the area.

It is clear, both from the archaeological remains that still exist, and from its links with the high kings of Ireland that Dysart has very ancient roots. That one Catholic family, the Nugents, kept possession of the townland, as an entire estate, from the 1450s to the early 1900s, makes it an especially interesting study. This fact alone perhaps explains the generally good relations that existed between landlord and tenants on the estate, even during the Land War. This stability of ownership was also mirrored in the tenantry. Even today, the majority of the landowners are their direct descendants. The townland was not immune to outside influences however, and it suffered the same tribulation of famine and emigration as the rest of the country. Just as the various land acts from 1870 onwards saw the demise of landlordism in the country as a whole, so it proved

44 NA, ILC, Nugent Estate, Co. Westmeath, EC 2448, Box No. 3611. **45** *Westmeath Examiner*, 10 Oct. 1908, 12 Dec. 1908, 19 Dec. 1908, 26 Dec. 1908, 16 Jan. 1909, 30 Jan. 1909, 6 Feb. 1909, 13 Feb. 1909. See also *Midland Reporter and Westmeath Nationalist*, 28 Jan. 1909, 4 Feb. 1909.

in Dysart. This in turn led to increased tension among the tenants themselves over the sale and distribution of the holdings. What emerges from this study is a limited insight into the life of an Irish townland in the nineteenth century. It should be possible to gauge the extent to which Dysart townland was unique, or similar to other townlands, locally or in the rest of the country, when other studies are undertaken.

APPENDIX I

DYSART TOWNLAND — 1901 CENSUS

No.	Name	Relationship to Head	Occupation	Age
1	Michael Jones	Head	Farmer	50
	Maggie	Wife		40
	Julia	Sister		
	Mary	Daughter		
	Teresa	Daughter		
	Bridget	Daughter		
	John	Son		
2	James Fallon	Head	Farmer	47
	Mary	Wife		4
	James	Son		4
	John	Son		2
	Patrick	Son		1
	Kate Looram	Visitor		21
	Patrick Looram	Visitor		9
3	Brian Looram	Head	Farmer	90
4	John Gouran	Head	Farmer	51
	James	Brother		42
	Annie	Sister		38
	Marcella	Sister		36
	John Gaynor	Servant		36
	Patrick Costello	Servant		60
5	James Carr	Head	Farmer	56
6	John Killian	Head	Farmer	33
	Fannie Bruton	Boarder	Housekeeper	40
	Annie Mahon	Servant		18
	Christopher Keenan	Servant		30
	Patrick Rock	Servant		33
	John Brennan	Visitor		40

No.	Name	Relationship to Head	Occupation	Age
7	John Cleary	Head	Farmer	42
	Kate	Wife		32
	Mary Philomena	Daughter		6
	Kate Dillon	Servant		21
	Patrick Finn	Servant		19
8	Uninhabited			
9	Anthony Brennan	Head	Labourer	49
	Kate	Wife		50
	Anthony	Son		15
	Joseph	Son		11
	Katie	Daughter		10
10	Thomas Claffey	Head	Stone Mason	60
11	Anne Looram	Head	Farmer	50
	James	Son		19
	Hester	Daughter		12
12	Thomas Mahon	Head	Labourer	70
	Catherine	Wife		48
	James	Son	Labourer	15
	Thomas	Son	Labourer	15
	Matthew	Son	Labourer	13
	Joseph	Son		6
	Michael	Son		4
13	James McDonagh	Head	Retired RIC	83
	Eliza	Wife		76
	Robert	Son	Labourer	41
	Mary Anne	Daughter	Housekeeper	39
14	Patrick Brennan	Head	Labourer	80
	Julia	Wife		67
	Margaret Byrne	Daughter	Housekeeper	37
	Lizzie Byrne	Grandaughter		14
	Patrick Byrne	Grandson		13
	Michael Fullam	Brother-in-law	Labourer	59
15	Uninhabited			

No.	Name	Relationship to Head	Occupation	Age
16	Anne Meehan	Head	Farmer	61
	Annie	Daughter		32
	Patrick	Son		30
	Delia	Daughter		18
17	Rose Lestrange	Head	Housekeeper	66
	Patrick	Son	Farmer	44
	Ellen	Daughter		32
	Katie	Daughter		22
	Michael Nally	Servant		25
	Thomas Conlan	Servant		23
18	Joseph O'Brien	Head	Herd	53
	Patrick	Son		13
	John	Son		11
	Annie	Daughter		15
	Nicholas Killian	Father-in-law	Retired Herd	75
19	Thomas Nally	Head	Farmer	38
	Kate	Wife		26
20	James Meehan	Head	Farmer	44
	Anne	Wife		44
	Thomas	Son		21
	Catherine	Daughter		18
	Christopher	Son		16
	Michael	Son		14
	John	Son		12
21	James Tuite	Head	Farmer	35
	Elizabeth	Wife		42
22	Michael Ballesty	Head	Farmer	45
	Anne	Wife		46
	Bridget	Daughter		13
	Eugene	Son		12
	Patrick	Son		10
	John	Son		9
	Michael	Son		8
23	James Killian	Head	Labourer	55
	Mary	Wife		52
	Patrick Heniffy	Brother-in-law	Labourer	53

No.	Name	Relationship to Head	Occupation	Age
24	Patrick Seery	Head	Farmer	80
	Ellen	Wife		72
	Ellen	Daughter		45
	James	Son		40
25	John Carey	Head	Farmer	47
	Anne	Sister		48
	Kate	Sister		30
26	John Fallon	Head	Farmer	67
	Bridget	Daughter		30
27	John Nally	Head	Farmer	77
	Matt	Son		40
	Bridget Nally	Daughter		37
28	Michael Tuite	Head	Farmer	33
	Bridget	Wife		29
	Michael	Son		1
	Peter	Son		
29	Thomas Rock	Head	Farmer	28
	Mary	Sister		30
30	Anne Clarke	Head	Farmer	64
	Michael	Son	Postman	28
	Daniel	Son	Farmer	25
	Annie	Daughter		22
31	James Meehan	Head	Farmer	60
	James	Son		35
	Bridget	Daughter		31
32	Christopher Rock	Head	Labourer	68
	Mary	Wife		65
	Michael	Son	Labourer	25
33	Thomas Brennan	Head	Retired	88
	Bridget	Sister	Housekeeper	70
34	Patrick Meehan	Head	Labourer	36

No.	Name	Relationship to Head	Occupation	Age
35	Christopher Rock	Head	Labourer	30
	Anne	Wife		21
Road	James Sheppard	Head	Tin Smith	24
	Ellen	Wife		30

APPENDIX II

OCCUPIERS OF DYSART TOWNLAND BASED ON VALUATION
OFFICE CANCELLATION BOOKS

Griffith Valuation Holding No.	Acreage A–R–P	Occupier	Year of Occupation
1	6–2–4	Thomas Murray	1860
		William Murray	1885
2	236–1–38	Thomas Murray	1860
		Caroline Murray	1873
		William Evans	1884
2a	Ho & garden	Nicholas Killian	1879
		Vacant	1884
		James Killian	1892
2b	Ho & garden	Joseph O'Brien	1892
2b	Ho & garden	Michael Fullam	1892
3	185–0–6	Thomas Murray	1860
		William Murray	1879
4	149–2–8	Thomas Murray	1860
		William Murray	1879
5	37–2–38	Mary Carey	1860
		Patrick Carey	1865
		John Carey	1878
6	64–2–27	Christopher Dignam	1860
		Michael Ballesty	1901

Griffith Valuation Holding No.	Acreage A–R–P	Occupier	Year of Occupation
7	33–3–10	Patrick Seery	1860
		Ellen Seery	1905
8	2–0–14	Christopher Innis	1860
		Patrick Tuite	1899
		James Tuite	1901
9	5–0–17	Thomas Molloy	1860
		Thomas Lestrange	1864
		Patrick Lestrange	1895
10	4–1–20	Thomas Molloy	1860
		Thomas Lestrange	1864
		Patrick Lestrange	1895
11	37–3–20	James Meehan	1860
		James Meehan Jnr	1881
12	8–3–11	Catherine Carney	1860
		John Fallon	1886
		John Clarke	1906
13	10–2–18	John Nally	1860
		Matthew Nally	1908
14	14–0–22	John Nally	1860
		Matthew Nally	1908
15	6–3–0	Thomas Clarke	1860
		John Clarke	1865
		Anne Clarke	1889
		John Clarke	1909
16	7–2–30	Elizabeth Kilmurray	1860
		James Rock	1862
		Thomas Rock	1899
17	5–1–8	Bryan Looram	1860
		Michael Tuite	1896

Griffith Valuation Holding No.	Acreage A–R–P	Occupier	Year of Occupation
18	19–1–10	Catherine Nally	1860
		John Nally Snr	1861
		Catherine Nally	1881
		Thomas Nally	1886
19	87–3–7	Michael Kiernan	1860
		James Kiernan	1861
		Catherine Kiernan	1872
		James Kiernan	1892
20	26–2–17	Patrick Meehan	1860
		Anne Meehan	1892
21a	32–0–30	Patrick Meehan	1860
		James Meehan Jnr	1865
		James Meehan Snr	1892
21b	Ho & garden	Marcella Wise	1860
		Patrick Wise	1861
		Unoccupied	1898
22	40–3–3	Michael Leavy	1860
		James Meehan Jnr	1861
		James Meehan Snr	1874
		Bridget Meehan	1921
23	43–3–10	Elizabeth Jones	1860
		Christopher Jones	1861
		Michael Jones	1887
		John Jones	1920
23 B	Ho	Michael Molloy	1906
24	15–1–14	Bartholomew Nestor	1860
		Christopher Nestor	1865
		Mary Nestor	1876
		James Nestor	1878
		Mary Nestor	1881
		John Clarke	1916

Griffith Valuation Holding No.	Acreage A–R–P	Occupier	Year of Occupation
25	15–1–30	James Fallon	1860
		James Fallon Jnr	1907
26a	206–0–39	Mary Killian	1860
		James Killian	1861
		John Killian	1894
		Thomas Killian	1908
		John Killian	1922
26b	Ho & garden	Patrick Gavin	1860
		Eliza Gavin	1886
		John Killian	1894
		Thomas Killian	1908
26c	Ho & garden	Patrick Rock	1860
		Bryan Rock	1861
		Christopher Rock	1877
		Michael Rock	1910
		Thomas Killian	1912
26d	Ho	James Conway	1860
		Michael Kelly	1861
		John Byrne	1871
		Edward Finn	1878
		Christopher Finn	1893
		Christopher Thompson	1894
		Rose Mahon	1895
		Thomas Brennan	1901
		Thomas Killian	1907
26e	Ho & garden	Patrick Corsely	1860
		Michael Kelly	1871
27a	2–2–10	Thomas Meehan	1860
27b	Ho & garden	Patrick Mooney	1860
		Mary Mooney	1886
		Julia Wyer	1888
		Edward Finn	1889
		Christopher Rock	1902
		Edward Meehan	1906
		Pat Keenan	1918

Griffith Valuation Holding No.	*Acreage A–R–P*	*Occupier*	*Year of Occupation*
28	4–1–30	Bryan Looram	1860
		John Killian	1903
		Thomas Killian	1908
		John Killian	1922
28b	Ho	Ann Fagan	1907
		Thomas Killian	1908
		John Killian	1922
29a	Graveyard		
29b	Ho & garden	Patrick O'Brien	1860
		Anne O'Brien	1866
		House knocked	1871
30	23–0–39	Thomas Newman	1860
		Michael Newman	1861
		Daniel Fagan	1869
		Michael Fagan	1886
		Anne Fagan	1888
		James Kiernan	1899
30a	Hovel of no value	Margaret Warren	1860
		Margaret Fullam	1866
		Michael Fullam	1880
		Patrick Brennan	1894
		Julia Brennan	1904
		Joseph Kelly	1922
30b	Ho	Anne O'Brien	1861
		Vacant	1888
31A	46–2–8	Patrick Gavacan	1860
		Reps of above	1865
		Thomas Casey	1885
		William Casey	1901
31a	Ho	James Mc Donagh	1886
		Robert Mc Donagh	1899
		John Casey	1909

Griffith Valuation Holding No.	Acreage A–R–P	Occupier	Year of Occupation
31b	Ho	Mary Mahon	1860
		Thomas Mahon	1868
		Catherine Mahon	1909
		James Mahon	1909
32	19–2–20	Patrick Gavacan Snr	1860
		Edward Gavacan	1876
		evicted	1884
		William Evans	1889
		Julia Gavacan	1925
33	104–1–9	Thomas Looram	1860
		Mary Looram	1861
		James Looram	1874
33A	Ho	Ann Looram	1902
		James Looram	1906
33B	Ho	John Gaynor	1904
34	7–0–7	Peter Looram	1860
		Thomas Looram	1881
		John Gouran	1883
		James Looram	1913
35	36–3–11	Michael Meehan	1860
		James Meehan	1862
		Patrick Meehan	1870
		George Wade	1878
		Richard White	1880
		John Cleary	1891
35a	Ho	Anthony Brennan	1902
		John Daly	1906
36	41–0–28	Michael Claffey	1860
		James Claffey	1873
		Ellen Claffey	1876
		Bridget Claffey	1880

Griffith Valuation Holding No.	Acreage A–R–P	Occupier	Year of Occupation
37	233–2–16	Richard Wade	1860
		Reps of above	1863
		Richard White	1880
		John Cleary	1885
38	1–3–30	Michael Carr	1860
		Bridget Carr	1879
		James Carr	1886

Eskerbaun, county Roscommon

WILLIAM GACQUIN

I

The townland of Eskerbaun in county Roscommon contains 460 acres. Up until 1896 it contained 490 acres 3 roods 1 perches but in that year 27 acres 2 roods 27 perches were transferred to the neighbouring townland of Derryglad. It lies on the south eastern side of the parish of Cam, barony of Athlone, county Roscommon, about nine miles from Athlone to the north eastern side of the road from Athlone to Tuam. The townland has a roughly rectangular shape and is divided by the road linking the villages of Brideswell and Curraghboy.

The name of the townland, written 'Iskerbane' by John O'Donovan in the Ordnance Survey Namebook for county Roscommon in 1837, derives from the Irish *Eiscir Bán*, meaning the white esker.[1] The name gives some indication of the type of terrain in the townland. The western part of the townland rises gently to form what could be a low esker in an area where some fine examples of eskers are to be found, as, for example, the esker running through Derryglad townland to Lough Funshinagh in Cam parish. The eastern part of the townland forms part of the low plain through which the Cross river flows. This river, formerly known as the Crannagh river, is the only substantial tributary of the Shannon from south Roscommon. This river forms the boundary of the townland with the neighbouring townlands of Curraghboy and Derryglad which like Eskerbaun have some good agricultural land and some marginal land. The source of this river is about one mile to the north west of Eskerbaun. In his long poem on the Shannon and its tributaries Micheál Ó Braonáin writing in Irish in 1794 has the following lines:

> An Chrannach chéanna, Tobar Bríde
> i gceartlár Mhaine tús a scríbe,
> sruth phoill Sheáin is Fuarán Mháire
> treisíonn a thrill le hiar na nárda,
> Trí eangaigh bhoga Cheathrú an Tobair is na hEiscreach Báine leanann a hobair.
>
> (The same Crannagh, Brideswell in the centre of Mainigh is the beginning of her course, the stream of Poll Sheáin and Fuarán Mháire strengthen her course by the land of the heights, Through the soft marshes of the Well quarter and Eskerbaun her work continues.

---

1 OS Namebook, county Roscommon 1837, typescript copy, Roscommon County Library.

Poill Sheáin is known locally as Poll Sheoin and is a large pool which adds to the flow of the river.[2]

There is a small ring fort in the north of the townland. There is also a sweat-house in the townland set into the rising ground, about twenty metres from the road. It is partly collapsed. None of the present residents saw it in use, but an oral tradition of it being used to cure colds and pleurisy survives. According to the oral tradition it was used at the start of the present century. The dividing line between the good agricultural land and the marginal land corresponds to the 200 ft. contour. Until the early nineteenth century the land below this line was very marginal. It has been improved greatly by drainage in the twentieth century and as early as the 1820s work on improving this land had begun.[3] The descriptions of this land in the Valuation Office field book dated 1839 is mostly of moory or bad moory pasture on shallow clay soils.[4] However some of it was described as 'moory pasture or meadow well drained'. From the Field Book also it is clear that access to some of this land was difficult. The land above the 200 ft. contour on the other hand is described generally in the Valuation Office field book as 'arable' on either 'dry gravelly soil' or 'shallow black dry soil with open subsoil'. This land is valued at from 9s. to 14s. per acre and the moory soil is valued at from 4s. 6d. to 6s. per acre. The settlement of houses in the townland follows the line of the road from Brideswell village through the townland towards the neighbouring townland of Cam, which is almost concurrent with the 200 ft. contour and just below it.

The farming carried on in the townland today is exclusively pastoral, with all farms having sheep and cattle. This system has evolved from the more common practice of mixed farming when all farms had tillage as well as animals. Tillage is now reduced to vegetable growing for domestic purposes. A feature of this townland was that a number of its farmers were also involved in dealing in animals, particularly sheep. This has formed part of the life of the townland for at least three generations but has left only an oral record which suggests that the 'dealing' was established in the townland by the end of the nineteenth century.

As Micheál O Braonáin's poem says, Eskerbaun was located in Uí Maine or Hy-Many. This was a Gaelic territorial division which once covered most of south Roscommon and east Galway. Uí Maine was an O'Kelly territory while the area about Cam parish was called Clann Uadach and the immediate chiefs of the area were the O'Fallons. The O'Fallons were allied to the O'Connors, so Eskerbaun and its parish became part of Elphin diocese while most of Uí Maine became part of Clonfert diocese.[5] The surnames of the two principal families of Uí Maine and Clann Uadach are to be found in the townland of Eskerbaun from the mid eighteenth century onward and were probably there much earlier.

2 Micheal Ó Braonáin, *Príomhshruth Éireann* (Limerick, 1994), p. 47. 3 Thomas Bermingham, *The Home Colonies of Castlesampson and Iskerbane* (Dublin, 1835), copy in RIA Haliday Pamphlets, vol. 1624 (3), pp. 140–54. 4 NA, VO Field book, OL 4. 1590. 5 John O'Donovan, *Tribes and Customs of Hy-Many* (reprint Cork, 1976), pp. 1–21.

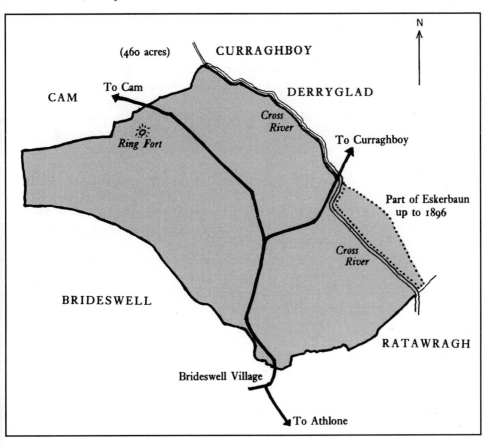

Eskerbaun, county Roscommon, 1838, 490 acres

II

It is not until the seventeenth century that there is any record of the ownership of the townland. In 1617 Sir Charles Coote surveyed the lands of the barony of Athlone and listed Robert Dillon of Cloonbrictan, county Galway, as the owner of the quarter of Eskerbaun as well as other adjoining lands.[6] By 1629 a dispute had arisen between his son Richard Dillon and Philip Dowell over the ownership of the lands at Eskerbaun.[7] From a series of questions prepared for witnesses for a case before the courts it appears that Philip Dowell's father Walter McDowell sold the lands of Eskerbaun to Thomas Dillon, chief justice of Connacht and grandfather of Richard Dillon. This document also gives an older name for the townland, as the lands in dispute are referred to as follows 'the quarter of Iskerbane alias Kyllivilly'. The first part of this name 'Kyll' may be the Irish word *coill* or wood, but the rest is uncertain. It would appear that the Dillons were successful in holding onto the lands of Eskerbaun, as the Book of Survey and Distribution for county Roscommon shows Richard Dillon as the owner in 1641 of the quarter of Eskerbaun, comprising 127 plantation acres profitable.[8] However, Philip Dowell is shown as the owner of the quarter of Tobberbreedy, later known as Brideswell, adjacent to Eskerbaun in 1641.

The Dillons remained in ownership throughout the seventeenth century and were mentioned in a number of leases and mortgages involving the townland in the eighteenth century and up to the second quarter of the nineteenth century. In 1725 Robert Dillon of Clonbrock, county Galway, raised a mortgage of £700 on Eskerbaun from Richard Sherlock of Dublin.[9] This was transferred by order of the court of exchequer to Thomas Gleatowe, also of Dublin, in 1745.[10] By 1750 this mortgage was assigned to Major General Thomas Bligh who in that year advanced more money to Luke Dillon on this land and other lands in county Galway.[11] In 1731 Robert Dillon leased 120 plantation acres of Eskerbaun to Bartholomew Hughes of Carrick, county Roscommon, for thirty-one years at a yearly rent of £39 stg.[12] A house and stables were to be built at the expense of the lessor. Bartholomew Hughes died on 28 June 1736, aged forty-seven, and was buried in Cam cemetery where a tombstone was erected to his memory by his son Terrence.[13] According to the Religious Census of Elphin of 1749 Terrence was living at Farneykelly (part of Carrick townland).[14] From the returns in the census of 1749 Terrence Hughs and two others of the same surname were Catholic. This lease of 1731 was given to James Stanley of Dublin by Luke Dillon in 1748, but the terms were changed to three lives and thirty-one years after the

6 NLI, Mss. 14 F 10–12, microfilm pos. 5363. 7 NLI, Reports on Private Collections No. 4, Dillon Papers, vol. 1, p. 59. 8 R.C. Simington (ed.), *Books of Survey and Distribution, county Roscommon* (Dublin 1949), p. 100. 9 RD, 44/296/29313. 10 RD, 123/4/82433. 11 RD, 143/107/95825. 12 RD, 67/534/47070. 13 William Gacquin, *Tombstone Inscriptions Cam Old Cemetery* (1992), p. 24. 14 NA, Religious census of the Diocese of Elphin, M 2466.

last life.[15] In 1769 John Glass and his wife, Jane, the heiress of James Stanley, leased 276 acres of Eskerbaun, together with some bog, to Daniel Fallon of Cam, George Fitzgerald of Gortacoosan and Mary McEntire of Lisdalon 'as the present tenants' at the yearly rent of £158. 4s.[16] The term of the lease was thirty-one years. Daniel Fallon was living in Cam in 1749[17] and still living in 1781 when he erected a tombstone for himself and his wife, Catherine Fitzgerald, that year in Cam cemetery.[18] Their only child, a daughter, Mary Fallon, married Laurence Keogh of Corkip, Taughmaconnell in 1767.[19] However, in 1789 Catherine Hewelson of Athlone, a widow and one of the daughters of James Stanley named in the 1748 lease, sold her one undivided moiety of Eskerbaun to Courcey Ireland of county Mayo.[20]

While I can find no record of a lease or mortgage from the Dillons to Matthew Lyster of New Park, Lyster made a lease from 1 May 1794 of seventy-two acres of arable pasture in Eskerbaun to seven named tenants for a term of twenty-nine years or the life of Arthur Stanley, whichever was the longer, at a yearly rent of £40 stg.[21] Another record shows that this lease returned to the head landlord, Lord Clonbrock, in 1824–5 when the twenty-nine years had elapsed.[22] The Lysters also listed Eskerbaun along with a number of other townlands put in trust on the marriage of Elizabeth Lyster, daughter of Matthew to Ralf Smyth in 1808.[23]

A deed memorial dated 1830 put the land of Eskerbaun in trust on the marriage of Robert Lord Clonbrock to Caroline Spencer.[24] This deed empowered Lord Clonbrock to sell the Roscommon estates for the purposes stated in the trust, which he did some years later. In 1838, despite extensive improvements carried out on the Eskerbaun estate which will be discussed later, the townland, consisting of 187 acres Irish plantation measure was sold along with the nearby townland of Cornageeha to George King of Milltown (Derryglad townland), county Roscommon.[25] Almost immediately, George King and his wife Ann Byrne mortgaged the two townlands and lands in county Longford to W.G. Scott in county Down.[26] In July 1838 George King leased 18 acres 2 roods Irish measure of Eskerbaun from Lord Clonbrock which was adjacent to King's land and house at Milltown.[27] In August that year George King granted an annuity of £204 2s. 4d. to his wife out of the lands of Eskerbaun and Cornageeha and set up a trust for ninety nine years for that purpose.[28] George King raised another mortgage of £2000 on the same lands as in 1838 from James Biron of Dublin, and at the same time Biron was assigned the Scott mortgage.[29] James Biron bought all the lands mentioned in these mortgages, including Eskerbaun, from the Encumbered Estates Court in 1854.[30] The area of Eskerbaun was given as just over 456 acres.

15 RD, 164/50/108796. **16** RD, 276/523/179453. **17** NA, Religious census of Elphin, M 2466. **18** Gacquin, *Tombstone Inscriptions*, p. 13. **19** RD, 264/633/174361. **20** RD, 410/360/269030. **21** RD, 563/522/380435. **22** Bermingham, *Home Colonies*, p. 141. **23** RD, 598/396/410548. **24** RD, 816/317/574317. **25** RD, 1838/15/151. **26** RD, 1838/15/152. **27** RD, 1838/15/154. **28** RD, 1838/15/156. **29** RD, 1844/11/16. **30** RD, 1854/13/26.

Between 1861 and 1875 Revd Edward Biron, son and heir of James Biron, who lived in Kent in England, raised mortgages of almost £10,000 on his estates in Ireland, including Eskerbaun, Cornageeha and Pollalaher in Cam parish. Revd Edward Biron died intestate on 25 January 1877 and was succeeded by his eldest son, Robert, who obtained two further mortgages of £1000 each on the same lands in 1877 and 1878.[31] In 1880 Robert Biron applied to the Commissioners of Public Works for £250 to improve Eskerbaun, monies to be charged on the lands.[32] This was also the year he tried unsuccessfully to have the lands of Eskerbaun sold in the Encumbered Estates Court, as they had become severely indebted.[33] At that time the rental income from Eskerbaun was £226 4s. per annum. By 1907 the lands of Eskerbaun were owned by the Land Commission, and the area of Eskerbaun was given as just over 460 acres.[34]

III

It is clear that none of the Dillon or Biron families who owned the townland from the seventeenth to the twentieth centuries ever lived there. It is not known if any of those to whom leases were made lived there either. The evidence there is on Bartholomew Hughes, who took a lease in 1731, or Daniel Fallon, whose lease is dated 1769, indicates they did not live there. This leads to the question of who or how many people occupied the townland over that three-hundred-year period. The first indication of a settlement of people in Eskerbaun comes from the census of Ireland of 1659.[35] This shows there were seventeen persons all of the Irish race living in Eskerbaun. Here it must be assumed that the area described as Eskerbaun in 1659 is the same as that area which became the clearly defined townland when the first Ordnance Survey map was published for county Roscommon in 1838.

The figure for population in 1659 cannot be accepted at face value as the 1659 returns records only males as heads of houses and unmarried females over eighteen. It would be reasonable therefore to use a multiplier of three on the 1659 returns to give a population figure of fifty-one for Eskerbaun. No evidence is available as to the population of Eskerbaun for ninety years until the Religious Census of Elphin in 1749. This gives a very interesting snapshot of the mid eighteenth century community. There were eighteen households in the townland and using a multiplier of 4.33, derived from figures for a number of parishes, a population of seventy-eight is obtained for Eskerbaun.[36] This is an increase of 52.9 per cent in ninety years. Population figures for individual townlands are not available in the nineteenth century until 1841. However, in the case of Eskerbaun a population figure for the period 1824–8 is available from a report on the state

31 RD, 1877/27/94. **32** RD, 1880/27/132. **33** NA, Landed Estates Court Rentals vol. 139, no 7. **34** RD, 1907/4/10. **35** Seamus Pender (ed.), *Census of Ireland c.1659* (Dublin, 1939), p. 591. **36** William Gacquin, *Roscommon before the Famine: Parishes of Kiltoom and Cam 1749–1845* (Dublin, 1996), p. 13.

of the townland before the landlord carried out an improvement.[37] This report gives a population figure of 370 individuals in sixty-two families. This gives a household size of almost six. After some thirty-five families had left Eskerbaun for another townland or had emigrated by 1828 there were 162 people in twenty seven families living in Eskerbaun. The average household size remained the same at six. The population figures for the townland are given in Table 1 and population movements are illustrated in Fig. 1.[38]

Table 1   Population of Eskerbaun, 1659–1911

Year	Population
1659	51
1749	78
1824	370
1828	162
1841	183
1851	159
1861	147
1871	94
1881	106
1891	90
1901	85
1911	72

Figure 1   Eskerbaun Population, 1659–1911

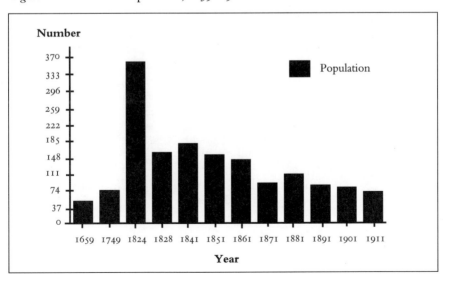

37 Bermingham, *Home Colonies*, p.141.   **38** *Census of Ireland* 1841–1911.

While the population of Eskerbaun rose again from 1828 to 1841 as seven new houses were added to the townland the average annual increase in population was only 1 per cent compared with an average annual increase of 2.1 per cent from 1749 to 1824. The decline in population from 183 in 1841 to eighty-five in 1901 represents a decline of 53.6 per cent over the sixty years. By 1911 the population was down to seventy-two or a 60.7 per cent decline in seventy years. From Fig 1 it can be seen that there was only one decade after the famine when there was an increase in population (from 1871 to 1881). This was short lived, as in the following decade there was a decrease of 15 per cent in the population. A comparison of the male female population balance from 1841 onward shows that the number of females was less than the number of males except in 1901. The trend of decline in population was present in the figures for both sexes (see Fig. 2). Over the period covered by the census figures from 1841 to 1911 the average household size varied from 4.9 to 5.5, but it never reached the level of the 1820s, a possible indication of later marriage and smaller family size.

Figure 2 Population in Eskerbaun 1841–1911

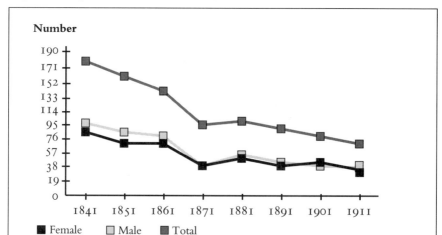

From the Religious Census of Elphin of 1749 it is possible to examine in some detail the community of Eskerbaun. As already said the population can be estimated at seventy-eight persons. These lived in eighteen households for which the census gives the names of the head of household in each case (see Table 2). An analysis of the surnames shows that there were six Kellys, three Dowllans (Dolans), two Gurhys, two Fallons and one each of the following families; Keaugh'n, Dillon, Grier, Kein and Doyle. All of these families were Catholic and this was also the case from the 1901 census returns. Eskerbaun was not unique in this regard, as only 0.97 per cent of the population of Cam parish was Protestant in 1749. The 1749 census gives the number of children per family. In the case of Eskerbaun, two of the eighteen houses there had no children, and a total of forty three children are returned for the remaining sixteen houses, of whom thirty-two were under fourteen and eleven were over fourteen. Table 3 shows the number of children per family.

Table 2 Iskerbane from the Religious Census of Elphin, 1749

Name	Occupation	Religion	Children <14	Children >14
Teady Dowllan	Tenant	Papist	3	1
Thomas Dowllan	Tenant	Papist		
Bryan Keaugh'n	Tenant	Papist	1	2
Patt Gurhy	Tenant	Papist	3	
Roger Dowlan	Tenant	Papist		
Thomas Gurhy	Labourer	Papist	3	
Thomas Dillon	Labourer	Papist	4	
Peter Grier	Labourer	Papist	2	
Bryan Kelly	Tenant	Papist	2	2
Teady Kein	Labourer	Papist		4
Robert Kelly	Labourer	Papist	2	
Teady Kelly	Labourer	Papist	1	
Patt Kelly	Labourer	Papist	2	
Dan Kelly	Labourer	Papist	1	
Will Fallon	Labourer	Papist	4	
James Doyle	Labourer	Papist	2	
Patt Kelly	Wigmaker	Papist	2	
John Fallon	Ale-seller	Papist		2

Table 3 Number of children per family in Eskerbaun, 1749

No. of children per family	No. of families
0	2
1	2
2	6
3	3
4	5

Only five families had four children and the other eleven had three children or less. The most common family size was two. These figures are similar to the figures for the parish of Cam as a whole. This small family size was probably as a result of the decrease in population following the famines of 1741–4, which were known to be severe in county Roscommon.[39] When the forty-three children are deducted from the total population thirty-five adults remain, which

39 Síle Ní Chinnéide (ed.), 'Dhá leabhar notaí le Séarlas Ó Conchubhair' in *Galvia*, i (1954), p. 38.

suggests that at least one house was occupied by one individual, either that of Roger Dowlan or Thomas Dowlan, for whom no children are recorded. An analysis of the occupations listed in 1749 shows there were ten labourers, six tenants, one wig maker and one ale seller. There is no evidence as to from whom the six tenants had leases, it may have been the head landlord or someone to whom he had made a lease. The great majority of the households are returned as labourers. While the census gives no indication how much land was held by each household it would seem likely that those listed as labourers held some land.

This category of person represented 51 per cent of the households in Kiltoom and Cam parishes and this proportion is too great to have been supported by the few large farms in those parishes.[40] It is likely that the only distinction between those listed as labourers and tenants in Eskerbaun was that the latter held a lease, which would have given them a greater sense of security. The remaining two households had less common occupations; one, Patt Kelly, was a wig maker and the other, John Fallon, was an ale seller. These two households may have been in the south western end of the townland which is adjacent to the village of Brideswell. The 1749 census shows another ale seller in Brideswell (called Corrantober in 1749). Apart from the lease in 1794 from Matthew Lyster to the seven named tenants, no other evidence survives from the eighteenth century. The seven tenants were: Mathias Fallon, Daniel Fallon, William Watson, Bryan Kelly, Frank Kelly, Patt Kelly and Thomas Gurhy. With the exception of Watson the other names represent names which were numerous some forty-five years earlier and some no doubt are the direct descendants, probably sons or sons in law of the 1749 occupants.

IV

It has not been possible from the evidence of the eighteenth century to examine how the townland was divided between the families. Thomas Bermingham, writing a pamphlet on the improvement scheme carried out by the landlord, Lord Clonbrock, states that the division was similar to that in operation at that time in many parts of Ireland, particularly in the west.[41] The townland had originally been divided in four divisions according to Bermingham and this is borne out by the fact that in the Tithe Applotment Book for Cam parish, dated 1828, only four occupiers names appear.[42] Each was allocated seventy two acres. From these original four occupiers the townland was occupied by sixty two families by 1824. This had resulted from subdivision as sons and daughters married and the population rose from the second half of the eighteenth century on. The village or partnership system of settlement left many families with small portions of the different quality of land available. This distribution of the plots was carried out according to the various regulations made by the heads of the

40 Gacquin, *Roscommon before the Famine*, p. 21.   41 Bermingham, *Home Colonies*, p. 140.
42 NA, TAB, county Roscommon, Parish of Cam, 25/52.

village, probably four in the case of Eskerbaun. The tillage land of one person one year was allocated to another the next and the grazing land in the same way. As the subdivision continued from one generation to the next the portion being worked by a particular family could become a very small fraction of the original plot. In the case of Eskerbaun it must be remembered that about 50 per cent of the land was in need of drainage in the eighteenth century and that if the total acreage of the townland was divided between all sixty-two families each would have less than eight acres. Sixteen of the families in Eskerbaun in 1749 had children and if each was to halve their farm between two children and allowing thirty years to a generation there would have been thirty-two families by the 1780s. Assuming the same rate of division in the next generation one could expect to find sixty-four families in the townland by 1820. We know that the actual figure in 1824–25 when the lease expired and the head landlord took possession of the estate was sixty-two families, consisting of 370 individuals. These sixty-two families in Eskerbaun had between them thirty cows and eight horses.[43] These figures mean that there was less than one cow for every two families. This small number of cows must have led to shortages of milk from time to time and a great need for co-operation between the families if all were to survive.

From two early nineteenth-century maps it is possible to examine how these families were arranged in the townland. The first of these maps, a Grand Jury map dated 1817, shows approximately thirty houses arranged in five clusters of from four to eight houses per cluster.[44] This pattern of clusters is confirmed by an Ordnance Survey Boundary Department sketch map dated 1835.[45] On this map there are four main clusters of houses arranged randomly and suggesting a clachan type arrangement. Both these maps show a road leading from Brideswell to Curraghboy through Eskerbaun but do not show any road northwards from this road to Cam townland, as appears on the first Ordnance Survey map for county Roscommon dated 1838. The two early nineteenth-century maps seem to represent the spatial arrangement of the houses in the townland prior to the improvements carried out in the 1824–8 period, except that the number of houses shown is too small to accommodate the sixty-two families unless many houses had two families living in them. The majority of the houses shown on these maps were not on the road from Brideswell to Curraghboy. One of the house clusters was on a raised site which was later completely abandoned. If there were approximately thirty houses in the townland in 1824 or thereabouts then the number of thirty cows would seem more reasonable but it would mean that there was an average of twelve people per house. This seems very high, as many of these houses were considered unfit for use a few years later.

To tackle the problems of subdivision and overpopulation the landlord selected twenty-seven of the 'most respectable and best conducted' families and reallocated the land of the townland between them.[46] Each family was given a

43 Bermingham, *Home Colonies*, p. 147. **44** Grand Jury map of county Roscommon 1817 (NLI, Mss 16. I. 12(1–2)). **45** NA, OS Boundary Dept. Map, OL 3.4155. **46** Bermingham, *Home Colonies*, pp. 140–54.

share of the different quality land in clearly defined divisions throughout the townland. Of the remaining families, five accepted aid of £5 each to help them emigrate and thirty families were relocated some two miles south of Eskerbaun in the townland of Castlesampson, where the landlord had property previously set to a grazier. As part of the resettlement of the townland, all of the marginal land was drained and brought into use and a road was constructed linking all the houses to the road which passed through the townland towards Cam townland. A total of fifteen new houses were constructed for the families who remained in the townland. These were built at the tenants' own expense but the landlord supplied the timber and the windows. These houses measured 34 ft. by 14 ft. by 9 ft. high and all had three windows to the front.

When the surplus tenants moved to Castlesampson they were employed in the construction of thirty new houses measuring 34 ft. by 14 ft. by 8 ft. high at the expense of the landlord. These houses had a kitchen and three rooms and cost £25 16s. to build. As a large part of Castlesampson was bog, a considerable amount of drainage work was carried out. As well as getting new houses the thirty families who moved to Castlesampson were encouraged to do so by being allowed to take the last year's crop from Eskerbaun and were given the first year's rent free. They were also allowed to burn the surface of the garden ground to the rear of their new abodes. By 1831 the twenty-seven families remaining on in Eskerbaun had thirty-five cows, sixteen horses and some heifers. Every house had a pig, about half of them had two pigs and some had three. This meant that families went from having an average of 0.48 cows each in 1824 to having an average of 1.3 cows per family in 1831. Those who were moved to Castlesampson had also increased their stock numbers greatly. If this increase in cow numbers, which must have been important for an increased supply of milk to combine with the potatoes (the staple food of rural Ireland), is taken in conjunction with the forty-five new houses, then they indicate a substantial increase in the standard of living for the sixty-two families who lived in Eskerbaun in the mid 1820s.

In 1824 the total rent to the head landlord from his Eskerbaun estate was £126. After the improvements were made this rose to £183 5s. 10d. The landlord expended in all £206 11s. 5d. on Eskerbaun itself but with the increase in rent this would have been recouped in four years. The expenditure on the Castlesampson estate to accommodate those who left Eskerbaun was much greater at £1005 5s. 5d. and would take much longer to recoup. However, according to Mr Bermingham, profit was not the only motive for the landlord. He was anxious to treat his tenants kindly and hoped that the peace of the country around would be secured. While there were no reports of agrarian outrages from the townland for the remainder of the nineteenth century a brutal murder and rape was reported by the police from Brideswell in 1835.[47] Lord Clonbrock sold the Eskerbaun estate to George King of Milltown in 1838. There seems to have been good relations between the tenants and the landlord

---

47 NA, Outrage Papers, county Roscommon 1835, 25/21.

at this time and there is no evidence of resistance to the resettlement. Because of this resettlement programme carried out in the period 1824–8 it is possible to examine the surnames of the occupiers at that time and to compare them with those of 1749. The map which accompanies the resettlement scheme shows in detail the plots allocated to the different families.

Table 4 Surnames in Eskerbaun, 1749 & 1828

Surname	No. of families in 1749 in Eskerbaun	No. of families in 1828 in Eskerbaun	No. of families in 1828 in Castlesampson
Kelly	6	7	6
Dolan	3	3	
Gurry	2	1	4
Fallon	2	2	1
Keaugh'n	1		
Dillon	1		
Grier	1		
Kein/Coin	1	1	1
Doyle	1		
Crean			1
Leonard			1
Grehan			1
Brien			1
Curley			1
Anigly			2
Fowly		1	1
Watch			2
Brennan			1
Egan			1
Logue			2
Faraher			1
Cumber			1
Harny			1
M'Nally			1
Murry			1
Hardiman			1
Corley		1	
Hamrog		2	
Glennon		1	
Duignan		2	
Cunningham		1	
Doorly		1	
Donnellan		1	
Kenny		1	
King		1	

As can be seen from Table 4 the surnames of the resettlement period are more varied than those of 1749. In that year there were nine surnames in the eighteen houses in Eskerbaun. However, when the listings of the newly settled families in Eskerbaun and their neighbours and relatives who moved to Castlesampson are examined, there are twenty-six names in Eskerbaun and not twenty-seven, as the Bermingham document suggests, as one of the divisions is allocated as a school and if it was occupied by a teacher his name was not given. Of those twenty-six, it is known that George King did not live in Eskerbaun but in Milltown. Bermingham lists thirty-three names in Castlesampson which he says came from Eskerbaun. This gives fifty-eight families, excluding King and the school (one more than one would expect if five emigrated) with thirty different surnames.

Of the thirty surnames listed in 1828, five are the same as those of 1749 and, of these, four (Kelly, Dolan, Fallon and Gurry) are the most numerous in both 1749 and 1828. These four names account for thirteen of the eighteen households in 1749 and twenty-four of the fifty-eight households in 1828. Of the other twenty-six surnames in 1828 all but five have a frequency of only one. It is not possible to determine the origin of these surnames accurately given that the parish register for the parish of Kiltoom and Cam does not commence until 1835 and those for most surrounding parishes begin later. It is possible to say that fourteen of the surnames listed in 1828 were to be found in Kiltoom and Cam parishes in 1749. If the surnames of the Eskerbaun tenants (those remaining and those in Castlesampson) of 1828 are compared with those in Kiltoom and Cam as a whole in the same year 66 per cent are to be found within the parish. This suggests that some of the new surnames which came to the townland between 1749 and 1828 may have come from within the immediate area. Of the households in Eskerbaun itself in 1828 56 per cent are of old families while of those who moved to Castlesampson only 41 per cent are of old families, which suggests it was predominantly newcomers to Eskerbaun who were selected to move to the new estate by the landlord. For example, William Watson was new to the townland in the 1794 lease, but his surname was not there in 1828. However, the Thomas Watch (an old form of Watson in south Roscommon) and Edward Watch listed in Castlesampson in 1828 were probably his sons. On the other hand two of the plots of 1828 in Eskerbaun are occupied by Thomas Degnan and Luke Degnan, a surname not there in 1749. But this family may have arrived in Eskerbaun shortly after 1749, as a tombstone in Cam cemetery shows that Luke Diegnan died on 21 March 1753 and was survived by his son Thady Diegnan, probably the father of Luke and Thomas of 1828.[48] Thomas was succeeded by his son John in 1855, giving four generations of this family in the townland.[49]

An examination of the eighteen marriages involving people from Eskerbaun from 1865 to 1900 where the parish register identifies the residence of the partners shows that all were to people from within Kiltoom and Cam parish.[50]

---

48 Gacquin, *Tombstone inscriptions*, p. 23.   **49** Griffith, *Valuation*, county Roscommon, Barony of Athlone, Union of Athlone, p. 57.   **50** Catholic parish registers, Kiltoom &

In the period 1835 to 1865 the marriage register does not identify the residence of marriage partners clearly but, using the baptismal register involving Eskerbaun families in this period and from oral tradition, it is possible to examine a further nineteen marriages. Of these, two involved marriages where both partners were from the townland itself, nine involved partners from within the parish, four involved partners from adjoining parishes and four were uncertain but were most likely to partners from within the parish. It can be seen therefore that of the marriages that can be examined from the parish register, 89 per cent involved marriage to partners from within the home parish. This figure does not take account of the marriages of people who emigrated, but it shows that of those who remained in Ireland the marriage horizon did not extend beyond the neighbouring parishes and was primarily confined to the parish of Kiltoom and Cam, with at least two marriages within the townland itself. Of the married couples in the townland in 1901, 50 per cent of them were of couples from within the parish and the other 50 per cent of couples where one partner was from a neighbouring parish.

From the 1828 list of occupiers in the townland itself, it is possible using various sources to follow the new holdings of land through the nineteenth century. The second most substantial listing of occupiers is supplied by Griffith's *Valuation* in 1855. When the estate was being sold under the Encumbered Estates Act in 1880 a rental and maps were prepared which gives a full list of occupiers. The map gives a very good breakdown of the farms and shows that the resettlement divisions were being strictly adhered to. The gaps between those lists are amply filled in by the records of the Valuation Office.[51] The fortunes of each plot are considered in Appendix 1.

Of the twenty-seven divisions made in 1828, seventeen are occupied by the same families in 1855. The school house may not have been occupied in 1828 and, if it was, the occupant was most likely Patrick Smith, who is listed as a teacher in Brideswell in 1826.[52] This is most likely the Brideswell school, as the part of Eskerbaun where the school was is adjacent to the village of Brideswell. Some of the changes in occupiers from 1828 may be the result of consolidation of farms as old occupiers died out. Thomas Fallon who takes possession of John Kelly's holding (109–112) joins with the other Fallon holding (88–92) in 1858. Patrick Donnellan who takes over Bartle Glennon's holding (82–87) is most likely the son of Thomas Donnellan of 1828. Thomas Higgins takes over three holdings from 1828 (32–42). He probably came from the neighbouring townland of Derryglad. His son, Patrick Higgins, who was in occupation in 1901 and 1911, gives his place of birth as America in the 1911 census (but not so in 1901) which suggests that Thomas lived for some time in America. From 1855 on only two new names appear in Eskerbaun with no obvious connection with the

Cam parish 1835–1900, Ms in possession of V. Revd C. Hayes, PP, Kiltoom. **51** VO, Cancellation books, Ballinamona DED, county Roscommon 1858–1900. **52** Appendix to *Second report of the Commissioners of Irish Education Inquiry*, HC 1826–7 (12), xii, p. 1282.

townland. Thomas Wall who takes over a Duignan holding in 1865, did not live in Eskerbaun but in Derryglad. The other new name is that of Hugh Rooney, who occupies a small holding in 1868 but his son, Roger Rooney, leaves Eskerbaun in 1885.

It can be seen from the continuous occupation of the land by the same families from 1828 to 1901 and the localised marriage horizon that the society of the townland was a relatively closed one. This close knit community had for generations existed under the partnership system which was replaced with the individual farm system in the 1824 to 1828 period. The Tithe Applotment Book of 1828 shows only four divisions of land in the townland, each of seventy-two Irish acres and the names of four head tenants: Bryan Kelly, Thomas Kelly, Frank Kelly and Dominick Corley. These four names correspond to the first four divisions in Griffith's *Valuation*, which does not identify separately the amount of land held by the individuals listed on plots 1, 2 or 3. It would seem also that the four named in the Tithe Applotment Book are representatives from the main house clusters that predated the resettlement of the 1820s. In the case of some families they can be seen to have been in the townland from 1749 through to 1901 and indeed throughout the twentieth century. One such family is the Gurry family. There were two representatives of that family in Eskerbaun in 1749, Patt Gurhy and Thomas Gurhy, both with three children. One of these children, Thos Gurhy, is named on a tombstone in Cam cemetery as having died on 19 May 1786 at the age of fifty-one, he had a brother James and a son Edmd.[53] The Thomas Gurhy named in the lease of 1794 is probably the son of James and he in turn is the father of William M'Gurry in 1828. This William had two sons, John Gurry and Michael Gurry. John's son, also John, was in occupation of a holding in Eskerbaun in 1901 and he was succeeded by his son Thomas and grandson John. In all there were eight generations of the one family over a 250-year period. The same is true for a number of the other families.

It has already been noted that there was a school in Eskerbaun in 1826, probably operated by Patrick Smith. A new national school was built in Brideswell[54] in 1858 and previous to that children from Eskerbaun attended the national school built in Curraghboy village (Carrick townland) in 1832 beside the recently constructed Catholic church.[55] The inhabitants of Eskerbaun usually travelled to Curraghboy by a mass path and not by road. An examination of the earliest Brideswell N. S. register, dated 1872, shows that a number of children from Eskerbaun are listed among its pupils. An entry for 1874 shows a child called Pat Leogue from Castlesampson attending the school, probably the grandson of one of the tenants who moved to Castlesampson in the 1820s. There is little evidence of literacy from the eighteenth century except that Mathias Fallon, one of the tenants named in the lease of 1794, was able to sign the lease. By 1835 there was a dispensary well established at Brideswell which served the people of

53 Gacquin, *Tombstone inscriptions*, p. 31.   **54** NA, National School Applications, ED 1/77/13.   **55** NA, National School Applications, ED 1/76/3.

the area.[56] This dispensary was visited twice a week by a doctor from Athlone. It was housed in a purpose built room and was well supplied with medicine. This dispensary was administered under the Grand Jury by a board of governors. George King of Milltown was governor, secretary and treasurer of the dispensary and he was both tenant and owner of Eskerbaun at different times.

From evidence taken by the Devon Commission in Athlone in 1844 from three people who lived in townlands in Cam parish a general picture of the condition of the people on the eve of the famine can be drawn.[57] Both Edward Byrne of Coolagarry and John Byrne of Lysterfield agreed that the condition of the poorer classes was not improving. The average rent per acre for land was from 22s. to 23s. per acre. The income of a labourer was 8d. per day in the summer and 6d. per day in winter if he could find work. Some people were able to get work on the Shannon Navigation scheme. Most of the Eskerbaun holdings were larger than those of the impoverished tenants of other parts of Cam parish, according to Edward Byrne. Potatoes and oats were the main crops grown. John Byrne noted in his evidence that Lord Clonbrock had helped his tenants with land drainage.

The population of Eskerbaun fell from 183 in 1841 to 159 in 1851, a decline of 13 per cent. This is much less than the decline for the civil parish of Cam which was 40 per cent. This could be an indication that the re-settlement carried out twenty years earlier had been a great help in reducing the worst effects of the famine on the townland. However, the pattern of population decline was set to continue for the remainder of the century and beyond. Little further sub-division took place after the famine period and the reduction in population was more the result of emigration. The oral tradition is the only source for an examination of this emigration and it suggests that America was the preferred choice of those emigrating, although some also went to England.

The occupiers of Eskerbaun had been Catholic from at least 1749 and probably longer, as the 1659 census says all the occupants were of the Irish race. As already mentioned a new Catholic church was built in Curraghboy village in 1830, to which the people of Eskerbaun travelled by a mass path. This church replaced a masshouse which had been built in Curraghboy in the early eighteenth century. The Report on the State of Popery in 1731 noted that large numbers of people assembled at a holy well in the parish at certain times of the year.[58] This was a reference to the pattern in honour of St Brigid, patroness of the parish, at Brideswell. The principal day of assembly was the last Sunday of July, known locally as Garland Sunday. This assembly took place within twenty meters of some of the Eskerbaun houses and was no doubt a very important aspect of their faith

---

56 *First report of the commission of inquiry into the state of the poorer classes in Ireland*, HC 1835 xxxii part 2, appendix B, p. 108. **57** *Commission of Inquiry into the state of the law and practice in respect to occupation of land in Ireland* [Devon Commission], Minutes of evidence, Pt.ii, HC 1845 (616) xx. 336–44. **58** 'Report on the state of Popery in Ireland 1731' in *Archivium Hibernicum*, iii (1914), p. 140.

down through the centuries. The pattern was discouraged by the clergy from 1829 or so onward because of the excesses of drinking, faction fighting and merrymaking associated with it.[59] However it continued to be held each year, even if on a reduced scale, and formed part of the traditional faith of the people.

VI

The 1901 census provides an opportunity to examine the townland from the viewpoint of the people and their houses. The houses provide a measure of the wealth of the community. Table 5 shows the quality of the houses and the number of out-offices attached to each. There were sixteen houses in all, twelve with three windows to the front and with two to four rooms. These houses are classed in the census as second class houses and were most likely the result of the building programme of the 1820s already discussed. Of the remaining four houses which are classed as third class houses, two had two windows to the front while the other two had only one window to the front and only one room each. The two one roomed houses were occupied by two elderly widows living alone; Mary Kelly and Catherine Burke. Both these houses were not returned in the 1911 census as their occupants of 1901 were probably dead. All of the houses in the townland had thatched roofs but there was one unoccupied building with a slate roof. This was a two storey building which had been a police barracks already abandoned by the time of Griffith's *Valuation*, if not before, in favour of a building in Brideswell village. All of the houses had some out-offices except the two one roomed houses.

Table 5   Houses in Eskerbaun, 1901

Rooms	Windows in front	Roof	Out-offices	Class	No. of houses
2–4	3	Thatch	2–4	2nd	12
2–4	2	Thatch	1–2	2nd	2
1	1	Thatch	0	3rd	2
				Total	**16**

The population of eighty-five in the townland in 1901 was made up of forty males and forty five females. A breakdown of the population can be seen in Figure 3. and in Table 6.

59 *Parliamentary Gazetteer of Ireland* (Dublin, 1844), i, 279.

Figure 3 Population in Eskerbaun, 1901

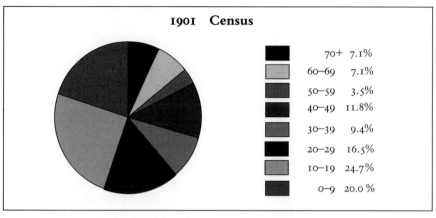

The number of males to females in the various age categories are relatively even, except in the over-seventy age group and in the two age groups under twenty, where females are in the majority. Table 6 also shows the state of literacy in the townland in 1901.

Table 6 1901 Population by Age/Sex and Literacy

Age Group	Male	Read/Write	Female	Read/Write
70+	2	2	4	2
60–69	3	2	3	1
50–59	2	2	1	1
40–49	6	5	4	3
30–39	4	4	4	4
20–29	7	7	7	7
10–19	8	8	13	13
0–9	8	–	9	–

If those in the 0–9 age group are ignored, then 93.75 per cent of the male population and 86 per cent of the female population were literate. The remaining 14 per cent of the females are accounted for by four individuals over sixty. Only three people from Eskerbaun were returned as being able to speak Irish in 1901, these were Thomas Fallon, aged eighty, Patrick Hamrock, aged seventy-five, both born in Eskerbaun, and Mary Kelly, a widow, also aged eighty, who was from the parish of Kiltoom and Cam and possibly from Eskerbaun. One further resident Bridget Hamrock, aged fifty in 1901, was returned as an Irish speaker in the 1911 census but not in 1901. She was a native of the nearby parish of Dysart, where Irish survived much longer. Eskerbaun had a lesser proportion of Irish speakers than many of the townlands in Cam parish adjacent to it.

Those Irish speakers who were natives of the townland were all born before 1830 which suggests that the decline in the use of the language may have been hastened by the break up of the partnership system in the townland and the considerable disruption to the social structure of the townland caused by the removal of 44 per cent of the population.

The census of 1901 shows that almost all of the occupants of Eskerbaun were engaged in farming. Only two of the households were occupied by people not described as farmers, these being two widows returned as housekeepers. Five of the households were headed by people over seventy, three of them women. In all of these houses there was a son who worked the land while the aged parent was given the place of honour as head of the household. With 45 per cent of its population, sixteen males and twenty two females under nineteen in 1901, and only fourteen farms and no alternative employment the townland of Eskerbaun was set to see further emigration as the twentieth century dawned.

VII

Throughout the eighteenth and early nineteenth centuries the townland of Eskerbaun was farmed under the partnership or village system. For all of that period the townland was owned by the Dillon family, who had been owners from the early seventeenth century. By 1749 there were eighteen houses in Eskerbaun. In most respects the townland exhibited no great difference from other townlands around it. One exception was that a greater proportion of its occupants were described as tenants rather than labourers in the Religious Census of Elphin. From 1749 to 1824 there was a tremendous growth in the population of the townland of 374 per cent which was in keeping with the general trend of population growth in Ireland at that time.[60]

Unlike any of its neighbouring townlands the landlord of Eskerbaun intervened in the period 1824–8, with no apparent resistance from the tenants to relieve the problems of over population and subdivision of holdings. This resulted in twenty-seven fixed holdings being assigned to selected tenants. These divisions were strictly adhered to up to 1901 and down to the present day. The best evidence of the benefit of this resettlement is that the townland was spared to some extent from the worst effects of the famine of the late 1840s in terms of population loss. The loss of population in Eskerbaun was 13 per cent from 1841 to 1851, while the loss for the civil parish of Cam over the same period was 40 per cent. There is no record of any agrarian unrest in the townland throughout the nineteenth century a situation which may have been helped by the resettlement of the 1820s.

With the population growth of the late eighteenth and early nineteenth century there was an influx of new surnames to the townland many of whom probably came from the surrounding townlands. This situation changed totally

---

60 K.H. Connell, *The population of Ireland 1750–1845* (Oxford, 1950), p. 1.

after 1828. From then on very few new names or families came to Eskerbaun. After 1855, for example, only one new family came to live in the townland and only for a short period from 1868 to 1885. The society of the townland became closed and marriage partners came from within the home parish or those close by. The pattern of population decline evident from 1841 on continued throughout the remainder of the century and on to 1911.

APPENDIX I

OCCUPIERS OF LAND IN ESKERBAUN, 1828–1901

The plots are listed in the order adopted by the Griffith *Valuation* with map references for 1828 and 1855 given in square brackets.

1828 John Kelly [109–112] to Thomas Fallon [1a] in 1855, still in occupation in 1901.

1828 Pat Dolan [105–108] to Michael Brien [1b] (he probably came from Cam townland where that surname was numerous) in 1855, still in occupation in 1880, to his widow in 1901.

1828 Bryan Dolan [101–104] joined to previous holding by 1855.

1828 William McGurry [97–100] to John Gurry [1c] in 1855, to his son John Gurry in 1901.

1828 Dominick Corley [93–98] to his son Matthew Corley [1d] in 1855, to his sons Thomas Corley and Dominick Corley in 1862, to Dominick Corley in 1881 (Thomas dead), still in occupation in 1901.

1828 John Fallon [88–92] to William Fallon [2a] in 1855, to Thomas Fallon [1a] in 1858, house down in 1867.

1828 Bartle Glennon [82–87] to Patrick Donnellan in 1855 [2b], to Michael Donnellan in 1862, to John Kelly in 1865, to his son Thomas Kelly in 1882, still in occupation in 1901.

1828 Thomas Donnellan [76–81] to William Caulfield [2c] (it seems his wife was Ann Dolan daughter of Patrick Dolan of Eskerbaun, according to the record of her marriage to Robert Reynolds of Kiltoom in 1891)[61] to John Bryan [2f] in 1855, Caulfield was still in possession in 1880, to Henry Hamrock in 1887, house probably occupied by Mary Kelly in 1901. John Bryan's house was down by 1865 but was reoccupied by Michael Gurry in 1880, to his son James Gurry in 1886 and to his widow in 1901.

1828 Luke Degnan [70–75] to John Hamrock [2–] in 1855, to Patrick Hamrock in 1865, to John Hamrock in 1874, still in occupation in 1901.

1828 Thomas Degnan [64–69] to John Duignan [2e] in 1855, to the landlord in 1863, to Thomas Wall in 1865, house down by 1873, to his son-in-law Michael Finneran in 1886, still in possession in 1901.

61 Catholic parish register, Kiltoom & Cam parish.

1828 Francis Kelly [58–63] to Peter Kelly [2d] in 1855, to Michael Gurry in 1863, to Thomas Dolan in 1871, house down in 1871, still in occupation 1901.

1828 Bryan Cunningham [53–57] to Owen Ford [3a] in 1855 (corrected to Fane in 1858, he married Catherine Cunningham, probably the daughter of Bryan Cunningham),[62] to the landlord in 1864, to Patrick Hamrock in 1865 who remains in possession in 1901. James Bryan[3b] has a house on this plot in 1855 only.

1828 Lackey Fowler [48–52] to Luke Fowly [3c] in 1855, to Jonathan Hamrock in 1858, to Patrick Hamrock in 1865, still in occupation in 1901.

1828 Daniel Dolan [43–47], divided in 1855 to (i) Daniel Dolan [3d], to Patrick Dolan in 1862, to Hugh Rooney in 1868, to Roger Rooney in 1870, to John Hamrock in 1855, house down 1886, still in occupation 1901 and (ii) Honoria Dolan [3e] to Patrick Dolan 1879, to John Hamrock in 1885, house down 1887, still in occupation in 1901.

1828 John Kenny [38–42] to Patrick Kenny [3f] in 1855, to landlord in 1863 and then joins next two holdings.

1828 Bryan Fallon [33–37] to Thomas Higgins in 1855, joins next holding.

1828 Thomas Kelly [28–32] to Thomas Higgins [3g] in 1855, to Patrick Higgins in 1876, still in occupation in 1901.

NOTE: all the houses 3a to 3g as plotted on the 1855 map do not correspond precisely to the pattern suggested by the 1828 map which suggests it may have been prepared as a plan rather than a map.

1828 Bryan Kelly [24–27], in occupation [4a] in 1855, to his son Bernard Kelly in 1865, to his widow Mary Kelly in 1901.

1828 John Kelly [20–23] to Michael Kelly [5a] in 1855, to his widow Margaret Kelly in 1864, to her second husband Patrick Burke in 1867, in occupation in 1901.

1828 John Hamrog [15–19] in occupation [6a] in 1855, to his son Henry Hamrock in 1865, to his widow Ann Hamrock in 1887, in occupation in 1901.

1828 William Kelly [11–14], to John Kelly [7a] in 1855, to Thomas Kelly in 1858, to Margaret Kelly in 1864, to her second husband Patrick Burke in 1867 to his stepson Francis Kelly in 1883, in occupation in 1901.

1828 Henry Hamrog [9–10] in occupation [10a] in 1855 house to William Fitzgibbon in 1861 to 1864, (William Fitzgibbon and his wife were teachers in Brideswell N.S.) land to James Hamrock in 1861, to Henry Hamrock (old) in 1880, to Ann Hamrock in 1887.

1828 Fardy Kelly [7–8] to Lawrence Dolan [9b] in 1855, house down 1861.

---

62 Catholic parish register, Kiltoom & Cam parish.

1828   Dominick Kean [4–6] to Michael Coyne (probably same name as Kane) [9d] in 1855, to Bridget Coyne in 1858, to James Hamrock in 1861, probably joined to next holding.

1828   John Doorly [2–3], to James Hamrock [9a] in 1855 to his son Henry Hamrock in 1882, in occupation in 1901.

1828   School [1], not mentioned in 1855 but probably joined to previous holding. In 1858 there is an extra house in this area, Eliza Brien [9e], to Catherine Burke in 1901.

1828   Mr King [113] to Bartholomew O'Brien in 1855, in occupation in 1901, but this plot was removed to Derryglad townland in 1896.

Kildoney Glebe, Kilbarron, county Donegal

FRANCIS HAYES

Kildoney is formed by the most south-westerly spur of the Donegal mountains. The townland overlooks the mouth of the river Erne and has half of its boundary formed by the Atlantic ocean. The spur divides the townland into a northern section with a long roll to the sea and a southern half which is more precipitous before flattening out into the neighbouring townland of Ballymacaward. Kildoney point is 105 feet high, while the highest part of the townland is 138 feet above sea level. Because of its low height Kildoney is not a headland but a promontory. The sea coast is regular without indentation with erosion happening evenly. Bunatroohan is the only bay in the townland A stream coming down the northern slope of the spur enters the sea at Bunatroohan, therefore the name, *Bun an tSruthdin*. Bunatroohan pier and slipway, built in the 1880s, are used for fishing and swimming.

The villages of Magherabui, Kildoney Upper and Lower are the main settlements, with smaller clusters of houses at Halifax, Coolcolly, Lugmore, Lough Mor and between the two Kildoneys. Magherabuí, Halifax and Kildoney Lower are spring line settlements, sited where the water table emerges at the bottom of the steeper slope in the northern roll. Kildoney Upper and Coolcolly are also sited beside wells. The prevailing winds are south-westerly so these three villages, Magherabui, Halifax and Kildoney Lower, or Oldtown, are sheltered in the lee of the spur. Coolcolly snuggles between two hills, while Kildoney Upper is very exposed. The Kildoney Upper houses are aligned mainly east-west with a gable into the prevailing south westerly winds, so as to gain maximum shelter.

The soil ranges from heavy clays to sandy arable soils.[1] Today the entire townland is given over to cattle grazing and a small number of sheep. A tiny amount of potatoes and oats are sown. The underlying rock is limestone, yet the rock outcrops on the Kildoney coast are sandstone. The durability and regular stratification of this sandstone made it suitable for building the present Bunatroohan pier and slip and also the slipway that preceded them. The former glebe house and its remaining outhouses and garden walls were all built from this coastal sandstone.[2]

---

1 NA, VO field book, Co. Donegal, Tirhugh Barony, Parish of Kilbarron, Kildoney Glebe, OL 4.0382, pp. 68–70. 2 W.S. Mason, *A Statistical account or parochial survey of Ireland* (Dublin, 1814), i, 425.

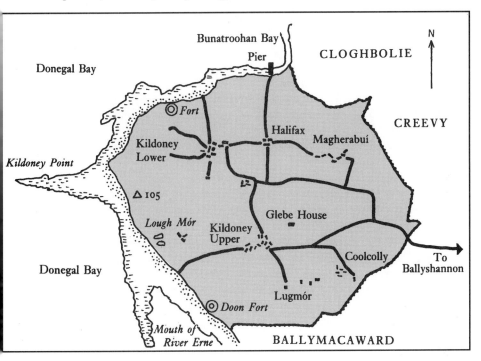

Kildoney Glebe, Kilbarron, county Donegal, 1837, 504 acres

KILDONEY CHURCH LANDS

Under the Irish Church act of 1869, the townland of Kildoney Glebe was offered for sale to the public. The abstract of title claimed that Kildoney was church land from time immemorial.[3] This referred back at least to 1626 when King James I installed a perpetual vicar in Kilbarron parish to attend the pastoral office.[4] Kildoney, with an area today of 500 acres, was given over as the main source of income for this newly created vicar of Kilbarron. From the seventh century Kildoney was connected with the early Christian church. Saint Maelduin established a monastic-church here in AD 620. Maelduin's successor, or coarb, was given the townland for the support of Kildoney church.[5] Earlier still, in 545, St Barron set up his church in nearby Kilbarron receiving four townlands as his support, one of which was Kildoney.[6] Maelduin may have been a son of Barron, and it is the latter who has given his name to the parish of Kilbarron of which Kildoney is part. Barron and Maelduin devoted their lives to prayer, so they set their lands to local families to farm it for them. Rent was made up in money, food and services. Support of the local clergy, along with repair and maintenance of churches, was the duty of these families, who were known as erenaghs. After Maelduin established himself in Kildoney the arrangement seems to have been that Kilbarron lands were used for repair and maintenance of Kildoney and Kilbarron churches, while Kildoney lands supported the clergy. These independent monastic churches provided the church structure until in 1178 Flaithbhearthaigh O'Muldorey invited the Cistercians into the Ballyshannon area. The Cistercians set up at Abbey Assaroe and were given forty out of the forty-four townlands in the parish of Kilbarron.[7] The townlands of Kildoney, Kilbarron, Ballymacaward and Creevy stayed outside Assaroe control, continuing to support Kilbarron church.[8]

Canon Edward Maguire claims Kildoney was the O'Muldorey homeland with the Dun of Kildoney being their main residence.[9] Maguire also claimed that the Kildoney surname McCarthy came from an O'Muldorey chieftain called Maolchartach.[10] The townland has the remains of several large forts, though there is no memory of the O'Muldorey now or in the last century.[11] Memory of the O'Muldorey was deliberately obliterated by the powerful O'Donnell clan after 1380, when they had firmly established themselves as the leading sept of Tir Chonaill.[12]

---

3 ILC, estate of Hugh O'Donnell, LC Record no. 2885.   **4** J.C. Erck, *Irish Ecclesiastical Record* (Dublin, 1830), p. 46.   **5** Edward Maguire, *St Barron* (Dublin, 1927), pp. 28–9. **6** Edward Maguire, *Ballyshannon Past and Present* (Dublin, 1917), pp. 25–8.   **7** Maguire, *St Barron*, p. 28.   **8** Maguire, *St Barron*, p. 28.   **9** Maguire, *St Barron*, p. 27.   **10** Maguire, *St Barron*, p. 29.   **11** Father O'Flanagan (ed.), *Letters containing information relative to the antiquities of the county Donegal collected during the progress of the Ordnance Survey in 1835* (Bray, 1927), p. 152.   **12** Tomás O'Canann, 'A forgotten medieval place name' in *Donegal Annual* (1986), no. 38, pp. 30–9.

When firmly established the O'Donnells modelled themselves on continental renaissance families, equipping themselves with professional families of poets, historians and genealogists. Former O'Muldorey lands, including the church lands of Kilbarron parish, were chosen to maintain these professional families. The Wards went into Ballymacaward and the O'Sgingin into Kildoney and Kilbarron townlands. Kilbarron church was taken over in 1426 as part of this O'Donnell scheme and its lands given to clan supporters. The O'Clearys married into the learned O'Sgingin and succeeded them in Kildoney and Kilbarron.[13] The O'Donnells are well remembered because they, along with the O'Neills, were the last of the independent Gaelic lords brought under English control. When Hugh O'Donnell fled after the battle of Kinsale in 1601 the crown returned most of the clan lands to his brother Rory. In the Ballyshannon area, however, he did not get the 15,000 acres belonging to Abbey Assaroe nor the 1000 acres given over to Ballyshannon castle because monastic and manorial lands were not returned.

Monastic lands were to be used as a way of attracting new settlers into Tir Chonaill so as to keep the new county open. The coarb and erenagh lands of Kildoney and Kilbarron, dating back to the first monastic settlement, were now also regarded as monastery lands. However, O'Donnell gained temporary possession of them until the crown decided how to 'dispose of them'.[14] The scheme that finally developed for Kilbarron parish church lands was that Folliott, the military commander of Ballyshannon castle, would get Abbey Assaroe lands if he resided as landlord, secondly, the remaining church lands would support the new Protestant churches.[15]

From 1603 onwards a string of enquiries were held to see what land belonged to the king and what belonged to the new bishops. Lugbaidh O'Cleary, historian to O'Donnell, told an enquiry that Kilbarron townland was held by the 'sept of the O'Cleary as erenaghs and that Kildoney was in the tenure of the said sept of the O'Cleary, free from any tithe to the bishops'.[16] By emphasising that Kildoney was not factually church land, Lughaidh O'Cleary probably hoped to obtain a lease of the townland himself. All legal problems of whether land belonged to the king or bishop were solved in 1607 when Rory O'Donnell fled the country. Frustrated by a refusal of the lease of the Abbey Assaroe lands and the return of the 1000 acres given over to Ballyshannon castle, along with other setbacks, O'Donnell decided to leave Ireland. Because of his flight all the lands of Kilbarron parish came to the Crown, which in turn passed them to the Church as a free donation.[17]

Land that had supported the previous Catholic clergy was taken up by Folliott leaving nothing to maintain the newly arriving Protestant clergy. By

13 O'Canann, 'Forgotten placename', pp. 38–9.   14 R.J. Hunter, 'The end of O'Donnell power' in William Nolan, Liam Roynane and Mairéad Dunlevy (eds), *Donegal History and Society* (Dublin, 1995), p. 233.   15 J.C. Erck (ed.), *Repertory of the enrolments on the Patent rolls of Chancery in Ireland, commencing with the reign of King James I* (Dublin, 1846), pp. 24–5.   16 Maguire, *St Barron*, pp. 88–9.   17 *Analecta Hibernica* (1931), no. 3, p. 185.

1622 Kilbarron parish did not have a resident clergyman, mainly because there was no living for one. In 1626 the townland or former quarter of Kildoney was recast as Kildoney Glebe; the land and rents would henceforth form the main support for the parish vicar. The attraction worked, and by 1650 a substantial house had been built in the townland just below Kildoney Oldtown.[18]

In 1650 Kildoney Glebe was taken from the Anglican church by the victorious Cromwellian administration. The Cromwellians, anxious to know how much land they had, used the most able and ancient inhabitants to estimate its size and establish its usage. Commonwealth Kildoney was found to be, in Irish land measure, 120 acres. Fifty acres were arable, fifty were pasture, four were meadow and sixteen red bog. Up to 1655 the Commonwealth had not rented out Kildoney, though they stood to get a good rent for it. The rent of Kildoney in 1641 was twenty two pounds compared to five pounds for nearby Kilbarron.[19] In Pender's 1659 census the name 'Glebe' was dropped in favour of the older name of 'Quarter'.[20]

Table 1   Census of Kildoney, 1659

Parish	*Townland*	*No. of People*	*English/ Scots*	*Irish*
Kilbarron	Quarter of Kildoney	10	4	6

This figure of six Irish people seems very low when Ballymacaward, Creevy and Kilbarron had twenty-two, twenty-two, and twenty-one people respectively and when over a quarter of Kildoney was under tillage, which is labour intensive. Also, the native population did not have to move out of their lands in Kildoney under the terms of the Ulster plantation. Kildoney, like other coastal townlands, had attracted English and Scots settlers while the inland ones failed to do so. With the end of the Commonwealth and the restoration of Charles II in 1660, the townland returned to being a glebe, because under the acts of settlement church lands reverted to whoever held them in 1641.

From the 1650s onwards Kildoney developed in three ways. The population increased from the stated ten people in 1659 to 394 in 1841. Over the same period the townland went from having one village in 1655 to three in the 1830s. There were a total of seventy houses given for Kildoney in the 1841 census. Thirdly, the land was worked under a system of partnership farming called rundale, while the glebe house kept a farm in the centre of the townland for itself.

Under partnership farming the townland was set, not to individual farmers, but as a whole. The rental was due from all the people. Kildoney rental in 1814

18 NA, Down Survey, Baronial Maps, county Donegal, no. 5 Tirhugh, v20–115.   **19** *The Civil Survey AD 1654–6*, iii, ed. R.C. Simington (Dublin,1937), pp. 55–7, 68.   **20** *A census of Ireland circa 1659*, ed. Seamus Pender, IMC (Dublin, 1939), p. 43.

was £500, this rent being made up by all according to their holdings. Close to the villages was the cultivated land, which was an open, ditchless, hedgeless field divided up into strips. Each person was given strips of land in different parts of this open field so as to ensure equal quality of soil. Furthermore, and again to ensure fair shares, these strips were re-allocated every now and then. Within this open field the farmers used their own boundary markings. This system could and did lead to disputes over extent of holdings, access and street rights.[21] Land was divided up among the members of families, it was not passed on to just one sole inheritor.

Circling the townland, by the coast and on the borders with Creevy and Ballymacaward, was the grazing land. Families had collops or grazing rights over this land; these rights might be two cows' grass or one cow's grass every alternate year.[22] The grazing land at Lough Mor is still held in partnership and is spoken of as 'the girl's fortune'.[23] In a marriage settlement a farmer gave part of his collop as his daughter's dowry. Hay was saved in areas of natural meadow, such as the low ground east of Magherabui, north of the police barracks at the Ranny and by the stream through Coolcolly.

In the 1830s John O'Donovan, the eminent Irish scholar, visited the townland and reported it as being chiefly under tillage. Yet, when surveyed for the first rateable valuation also in the 1830s, the land was described as a mixture of arable, meadow and pasture. The approximate agricultural division of the townland in 1837 is given in Table 2.[24]

Table 2 Estimated agricultural land use of Kildoney, 1837

Arable	376	acres
Meadow	12	acres
Pasture	113	acres
Waste	2	acres

This mixed agriculture appears to have stretched back over the previous hundred years. In the 1730s sheep and bullocks were grazed up to the river Erne while the drumlin country from Ballintra northwards was tillage.[25] Kildoney, in the middle of these two exclusive agricultural zones, and with its sandy to clayey soil, most likely had both grazing and tillage. The Kilbarron parish diet at the end of the eighteenth century was salt fish and potatoes with milk and butter.

21 *First report from his Majesties Commissioners for enquiring into the condition of the poorer classes in Ireland, with Appendix A and Supplement*, 1835, xxxii, p. 465 (henceforth cited as *Poor Law Inquiry, 1835*). **22** VO, Cancellation Books, Parish of Kilbarron. **23** Danny Coghlan, Kildoney, in conversation with author at Coghlan's Hill, Kildoney, 1995. **24** NA, VO field books, Co. Donegal, Tirhugh Barony, Parish of Kilbarron, OL 4.0382. **25** J.G. Simms, 'County Donegal in 1739' in *Donegal Annual*, iv (1960), p. 206.

The livestock was undoubtedly milk cows and horses for ploughing.[26] After the harvest, livestock was allowed onto the tillage land to graze the stubble and to manure the land. Any deficiency of manure was made up by seaweed, sand and gravel, all of which were available on the shore. Kildoney had a good network of tracks which gave access to the scattered strips of land and also to the shore. Inland townlands such as Tonragee bought their wrack, sand and gravel in Kildoney.[27] The organisation of the townland was left to the people themselves, that is, to allocate field strips, grazing rights, payment of rent, shore rights and working of the fishing. Education was provided by the Gillespies in their school house in upper Kildoney. Disputes were dealt with within the community and failing this the rector's intervention usually sufficed to resolve them. Only occasionally did Kildoney disputes go before the magistrates at Ballyshannon.[28]

A combination of village life, arable land, peat bog and hillgrazing have been identified as the basic land divisions in partnership subsistence farming.[29] In 1655 Kildoney was judged to be one fifth covered in red bog, which if it was fit for turf cutting rather than just bad land, was all used up by the 1830s. When assessed for rates in the 1830s Kildoney farms were allowed one shilling in the pound because there was no turf in the townland. Hillgrazing or booleying, whereby livestock was taken to the high ground for the summer months, seem to be absent from the Kildoney organisation. Rundale or partnership villages have been associated with poor or marginal land but this is not true for Kildoney, which though exposed, has good land.[30]

McCourt has stated that the open arable field was stripped, so as to make sure of equal quality as well as quantity of land to the farmers. Judging by the way that the townland was divided out after the open fields were broken up, and also by the way in which grazing rights were given in proportion to arable land, it is hard to agree that there was total equality of holdings within the townland. Below the rector, the townland gave an appearance of classlessness and equality in the organisation of the townland's affairs. However, classlessness does not mean that there was not a hierarchy within the townland based on wealth.

KILDONEY AND THE AGRICULTURAL REVOLUTION

Arthur Young, traveller and agricultural reformer, came through Ballyshannon in 1775 on his way to stay at Castle Caldwell in Belleek.[31] Young thought that the partnership farms around the area were in a backward state, but then he

---

26 RIA, OS Memoir, Kilbarron Parish, Statistical Survey, Box 21, Donegal 1.   **27** VO, Field books, Tonragee, Kilbarron, county Donegal.   **28** *Poor Law Inquiry, 1835* p. 465. **29** Desmond Mc Court, 'The rundale system in Donegal; its distribution and decline' in *Donegal Annual*, iii, (1954–5), pp. 47–60.   **30** James Anderson, 'Rundale, rural economy and agrarian revolution: Tirhugh 1715–1855' in *Donegal: History and Society*, p. 449. **31** Arthur Young, *A Tour in Ireland in the years 1776, 1777 and 1778,* ed. A.M. Hutton (London, 1892), i, 187.

would do so, as he was preaching the improvements of the agricultural revolution. Young was among the first to introduce the new agricultural ideas to the Ballyshannon region. He was for new farming techniques, the growing of wheat and green crops, land reclamation and closing of the open field system. The open fields, with their scattered strips, were to be replaced by squared in, fenced off fields. For Young, the partnership farming which was general in the Ballyshannon area stood in the way of a rationalised, commercially driven agriculture. After Young, the Royal Dublin Society, the North West Society and the Tirhugh Farmers Society, set up early in the nineteenth century, all preached the new ideas. The changeover to the new farming system happened very fast from 1827 onwards in south Donegal, because so much land was owned or was managed by Alexander Hamilton of Coxtown, who was wholly in favour of the break up of partnership farming.

Hamilton worked out a whole system for organising the land into individual farms, thus breaking up the partnership strips and the villages based on these strips. He justified the changes on the basis that the partnership farming philosophy worked against good agriculture, and that the villages were centres of idleness, gossip, litigation, dispute and disease. The open fields and the scattered pieces of farms meant that progressive farmers could not put down wheat, clover, vetches and other green crops. The new crops would stay in the ground too long, upsetting the partnership system, whereby townland stock were turned out onto arable land on an appointed day to graze the after crop. Therefore, the partnership system had to go.[32]

As centres of disease, Hamilton was referring to the cholera epidemic of 1832, when Kildoney had suffered badly with the loss of fourteen lives.[33] A health board, set up to fight the long outbreak of the disease in the Ballyshannon area, had hired extra doctors, putting one, a Dr Smith, into Kildoney. Smith seems to have been quite successful in his fight against the cholera in Kildoney.[34] These cholera outbreaks and deaths, especially in Kildoney, were the probable cause for the statement in 1835 by the resident Kildoney landlord, Revd George Nesbitt Tredennick, that the best possible way in which to help the poor would be the 'establishment of suitable arrangements for the preventing the spread of disease and all its consequences'.[35]

The rapid changeover from partnership farming generally in south Donegal was not matched on the glebe lands because of frequent changes of clergymen.[36] The problem of short stay clergymen was solved for Kildoney Glebe by the appointment of Revd George Nesbitt Tredennick as vicar of Kilbarron parish in

---

32 *Evidence taken before Her Majesty's commissioners of enquiry into the state of the law and practice in respect to the occupation of land in Ireland*, pt. ii [616], H.C. 1845, xx, pp. 179–80. **33** NA, Board of Health (Cholera Papers) 1832–4, Antrim – Donegal -34, 2144017, letters, 19 August 1832, 29 August 1832, 14 November 1832. **34** *Ballyshannon Herald*, 16 November 1832. **35** *Poor Law Inquiry*, 1835 p. 465. **36** Anderson, 'Rundale' in *Donegal History and Society*, p. 460.

1830, because he was to remain in Kildoney until 1872. Revd Tredennick was aware that his fellow landlords believed progress towards the new agriculture was slowest on the glebe lands. He took his chance at the poor enquiry in Ballyshannon, in 1835, to state that he also was for breaking up the partnership farms. Living as he was on a large glebe and surrounded by a very dense population, exclusively Roman Catholic, Revd Tredennick described the Kildoney people as peaceable and amenable. However, he found that it was not easy to force them out of partnership farming, which he regarded as bad farming practice, because of their 'prejudice and old notions'.[37] By staying with partnership farming, Kildoney people were sticking not only with a farming method but with a way of life that was based on family, kinship and neighbourliness. Tredennick felt that the stubbornness of the Kildoney people made it difficult for him to achieve what he was trying to do; this was the residence of each farm holder on his own 'cut' or individual farm. Along with the resistance of the people to his scheme, the fact that he held Kildoney only during his own lifetime also held him back. He was reluctant to put the necessary money into re-organisation because the estate would not be passed on to his family. The change over from partnership to the new commercial farming needed time, energy, patience and money. Despite his attempt to overturn their whole way of life he felt that there was no animosity in the townland towards him. There were some outrages in other parts of the parish but according to him Kildoney was so perfectly tranquil and free from crime that 'I scarcely think it necessary to lock or bolt my door'.[38] Two years later in 1837, as a result of his action regarding fishing, Kildoney was not a peaceable or tranquil place.

THE KILDONEY BAG NETS, 1837–63

From around 1809 stake and bag nets were brought into Irish estuaries and along sea coasts. That they spread rapidly around the coast is proof of their efficiency. Bag and stake nets differed from traditional nets because they were fixed in place, meaning that they were fishing at all times and in all weathers. Once in place they needed few men to fish them, compared to traditional boats with crews of from four to six men. Bag nets were fished on the coast in the open sea.

In 1837 bag nets were put up at the mouth of the river Erne for the first time and, in common with other parts of Ireland, their appearance caused trouble. In 1837 James Hector, a Scot, came into Kildoney, at the invitation of the Revd Tredennick, to fish for salmon just beyond the limit of the Erne fishery. Tredennick's glebe allowed him access to the waters of Donegal Bay exactly at the point where the river Erne joins it. Tredennick had joined the ranks of a new type of Irish fisherman, the landed gentry. They had discovered that land capable of being fished with stake or bag nets was a source of great wealth.

37 *Poor Law Inquiry,* 1835 p. 465.   38 *Poor Law Inquiry,* 1835 p. 465.

The Erne fisheries belonged to the Conolly estate and in 1837 they were leased by the Shiel family of Ballyshannon. The Shiel family were the most prominent Catholic family in the area. The Tredennick bag nets intercepted returning fish just as they entered the river system in their efforts to spawn. The Kildoney bag nets were a big threat to the survival of the Erne fisheries. John B. Shiel wrote to the *Ballyshannon Herald* in protest and called a public meeting for 'The Protection of the Ballyshannon Fishery'.

Following the Shiel protests, a series of attacks were carried out by large groups of people against Hector and his nets. Kildoney people who held gear for him or helped him were threatened with violence. Hector was given protection and a force of police and water guards were stationed, firstly in the old police barrack, and later in the glebe house. Despite this, Hector was attacked by sea and land all through the salmon season of 1837. His nets were taken from William Gillen's barn and burned, while a boat of his was taken from Bunatroohan and smashed. Later a replacement boat being built outside Nicholas Morrow's house at Lough Mor was broken up and thrown into the sea. The Kildoney people declared that they had no part in these attacks on Hector.[39]

The Ballyshannon fishery was the biggest non-agricultural industry in the area, on which depended anglers, boatmen, gillies, the hotels of Belleek and Ballyshannon, waterkeepers, coopers, curers, fishing crews and the recently orphaned Shiel girls. All these people felt threatened in their livelihoods, as did the fishermen of Bundoran and Mullaghmore. Hector and Tredennick had angered a wide community of interests.

Money was Tredennick's most obvious motivation for engaging in the capture and sale of salmon at Ballyshannon fish market. Yet Joe Morrow, Kildoney octogenarian, farmer and salmon fisherman, maintains that the Revd Tredennick's motivation was the enlightenment of the Kildoney people in how to fish.[40] The stronger townland tradition is that the bag net fisheries made no contribution to the internal economy of Kildoney. The Kildoney bag nets might actually have hindered the salmon fishing that the Bunatroohan fishermen were doing on the quiet, which as it turned out was not illegal before 1863.[41]

John B. Sheil felt that the rector had no need of extra revenue because he had 'ample support from glebe lands and no difficulty about tithes, and should confine himself to the sacred duty of his ministry, and as he does not keep a curate there is enough to employ his time … without speculation on the sea coast salmon fishery'. John B. Sheil continued to engage the Revd Tredennick by letter and pamphlet in an effort to isolate him from Balyshannon society. The burning, smashing and roaming crowds in Kildoney disappeared with the summer of 1837. By 1841 the local gentry had enough of the Tredennick-Shiel wrangle and

39 *Ballyshannon Herald*, 16 June 1837.   **40** Joe Morrow, Kildoney, in conversation with author, spring 1995.   **41** Patrick Daly, Kildoney and Dun Laoghaire, in conversation with author, summer 1996.

declared themselves neutral. This helped to diffuse the row.[42] Living side by side as they did, Simon Sheil in Wardtown Castle and Tredennick in Kildoney glebe house, they needed to and did work together when the potato disease came in 1846.

FAMINE

The 1845 constabulary and resident magistrates' reports on the potato crop stated that the Ballyshannon region, with the exception of the Ballintra area, was not badly affected. Losses were estimated at one twentieth of the 1844 crop which itself was felt to have been a good one. It was not anticipated that there would be any scarcity before May 1846. By November 1845 it was felt that the disease had not taken in the district 'so as to injure the crop in any material degree'.[43]

In March of 1846, despite the fact that half the labourers were unemployed, only 120 out of a possible 500 places were taken up in the Ballyshannon work-house. Also in March, sections of the Ballyshannon merchants tried to set up schemes of public works for the destitute labourers and tradesmen of the locality.[44] Meantime the acreage under potatoes in the Kilbarron parish was increasing.[45]

Table 3   Constabulary return of potato land in Kilbarron parish

1844	2,400 acres
1845	2,600 acres
1846	2,900 acres

The unwillingness of people to use the workhouse caused a problem; until harvest time of 1846 it was unclear just what was the degree of want in Ballyshannon and the surrounding countryside. Dr John B. Sheil argued that there was a great deal of actual want among the labouring classes by September of 1846. This was not an opinion accepted by others of his class, who felt that, since all the places in the workhouse were not taken, there was no real or actual want. What this line of reasoning did not allow for was that the labouring people would rather perish of hunger than go to the Ballyshannon poorhouse.[46] By December 1846 any problem of definition concerning the extent of want was solved: the potato crop had failed totally and the Ballyshannon workhouse was full.

---

42 Francis Hayes, 'The salmon fisheries of the river Erne' (unpublished MA thesis, Maynooth, 1995), pp. 5–17.   **43** NA, Relief Commission, iv/l, Constabulary reports, September 1845 – November 1845, report dated 17 November 1845, 2/442/8.   **44** NA, Relief Commission, ii /3, letter 25 March 1846, 2/442/6.   **45** NA, Relief Commission, iv/l, letter 24 May 1846.   **46** NA, Distress Papers 1846, letter 26 September 1846, D 5559.

Kildoney society consisted of family farms with few landless labourers. Any labourers that there were would have been on the glebe farm. As it was the labourers who suffered first, Kildoney was not immediately touched by the famine. Above the labourers, farmers were able to hold out just a little longer, so that it was not until January of 1847 that Kildoney became affected by the famine. The Revd McMenamin of Ballyshannon, desperately seeking government help, wrote that he witnessed two cases of death from starvation, 'one of them a James McCafferty of Kildoney, tenant to the Revd George Tredennick. Both these cases were manifestly the result of hunger and want of food' and he added that ' it is most heart rendering to witness the scenes of misery and distress that are everywhere to be met with'.[47]

Back in February 1846 Tredennick, believing that legislation was to be introduced to provide for piers and harbours, sought a pier in the port of Bunatroohan at Kildoney. He was too early with his request as the proposed legislation had not yet become law.[48] Tredennick, again writing to the lord lieutenant in September 1846, suggested various public works for the Ballyshannon area and again returned to the topic of piers: 'much useful employment might also be found in the erection of piers and harbours around this part of the coast, of which it is totally destitute and for which many suitable and convenient sites are to be found, which are resorted to by fishermen but which are quite inadequate for the purpose for the want of a moderate outlay'.[49]

That there were many suitable and convenient sites for the building of piers and harbours was not an opinion held by engineers who had looked at the Ballyshannon coastline before him. A coast survey in 1837 had dismissed the whole sweep of shore from Ballyshannon round to Balalt: 'at Ballyshannon the bar shifts and is not easily practicable even for small craft … hence, round Kildoney to the inlet of Balalt is a cliff with foul ground outside'.[50] This coast survey did not even say that there were fishing boats working out of Bunatroohan and Culbeg.

Simon Shiel, of Ballymacaward, received a letter in October 1846 from the Board of Works saying that they could not fund a pier at Bunatroohan. Their engineer, Barry O'Gibbons, stated that Bunatroohan was unsuitable for the construction of a pier or quay, because of its extreme exposure.[51] When O'Gibbons came into Kildoney in December 1846 and saw the density of population, along with the poverty of the district, he changed his mind. He decided that a modification of the design to a slipway would benefit greatly the people of this densely populated area 'by enabling them to haul up their boats with the aid of a capstan'.[52]

47 NA, Relief Commission, ii/2, county Donegal, Baronial, 29 January 1847, 2/442/9. **48** NA, Public Works, Piers and Harbours, 1/8/2 Letter Books, another series, letter 27 February 1846. **49** NA, Distress Papers 1846, letter 17 September 1846, D. 5084. **50** *First report of Commissioners of Inquiry of Irish Fisheries, 1837*, xxii, p. 70 (henceforth cited as Nimmo's coast survey of Ireland). **51** NA, Public Works, Piers and Harbours, 1/8/1 Letter Book General, 8 May 1846–4 July 1848, letter 159, 4 December 1846. **52** NA, see note 48, letter 159.

O'Gibbons costed this modified proposal at £500. George Tredennick offered to pay £125 of this; thus, between O'Gibbon's plea and Tredennick's pledge, the slipway scheme got approval in early 1847.

Work began in July 1847 and continued until the first week of May 1848 when the scheme was wound up.[53] The work was slow, heavy and skilled. The stone from the rocky outcrops above the beach at Bunatroohan was used as the construction material. No record exists of who was employed on the scheme but the Revd Tredennick would most probably have had first choice on who got employment, as he was the sole member of the relief committee.

The second strand in Tredennick's fight against famine was to get Kildoney people to grow green crops, as alternatives to the failing potato crop. In March 1847 Tredennick asked for a variety of green crop seeds out of the government depot at Sligo 'because the poor farmers of this vicinity are unable to obtain them unless through the means of others'.[54] The proposed growing of green crops was in 1847 primarily a guard against the fear of a repeated potato failure. Also, it was a reminder that a change in farming practice was the inevitable consequence of the end of partnership farming.

END OF PARTNERSHIP FARMING IN KILDONEY

The re-organisation and reallocation of the Kildoney land out of partnership was underway by 1835 and completed by 1855. The ideal was that each farm would be squared, have its boundaries at right angles to the roads, and each farm house would be as central to the farm as possible. This is what Tredennick meant by saying that he wanted each farmer on his own 'cut'.

Because George Tredennick held Kildoney Glebe only for his own lifetime, he was not going to help with or subsidise the building of new houses for the farmers on their new consolidated holdings. Therefore, villages remained the dominant settlement pattern in Kildoney. This contrasts with the scattered farmhouses in the rest of the Ballyshannon area. In what must have been a remarkable feat of consultation and distribution, the new farms were allocated in such a way that for all practical purposes the farmers had their houses on their land without having to move their dwellings. In only four cases did Tredennick succeed in prising houses away from the villages.

The glebe farm was increased in size and acted as a hub out of which the new farms radiated spoke-like. To the north and south of the glebe the farms were long, narrow, and rectangular in shape. In the east corner, the Daly and McNeely farms were broader and came closest to being square. On the west side the farms ran east to west because the coastline moves gradually towards the apex of Kildoney point. More importantly, they ran this way to achieve four

---

53 NA, Relief Commission, Co. Donegal, Baronial, 23 March 1847, 2/441/36. **54** NA, Relief Commission, ii/2, Co. Donegal, Baronial, 23 March 1847, 2/441/36.

things; they covered grazing land, arable land, had access to tracks and managed to have each house on its own land. The same idea of having arable and grazing land in each new farm was achieved in the rest of the townland by use of the long rectangular farms. These farms were at right angles to the roads which bisected them. The roads through the middle of the lands gave easy access to the upper and lower portions of the farms.

The increase in size of the glebe farm meant that some houses had to move out to Lugmore. Townland memory is that the Gillespies had to carry their house on their backs, stone by stone, and rebuild at Lugmore. Townland tradition says that as the houses spoiled the view from the glebe house they had to go.[55] What is probably being remembered here is that the glebe house was rebuilt around 1810 and so the two events have become linked.

Only at Lugmore, between Kildoney Upper and Coolcolly, do we see the scattered farm houses that were typical of this re-development in south Donegal. For Lugmore it was necessary to move some houses away from the village of Kildoney Upper, or Fern's Hill as it is called on the Ordnance Survey maps. Had the people stayed in the village, the farms would have run across the hillside instead of up and down it. This would have given an imbalance of good land to those higher up the hillside. It is not known how people were selected to move away from the villages. However, from the evidence there was no general lottery for the new farms. It appears that, as far as possible, people got land beside where they already lived and farmed. Having reshaped the townland according to the new principles, Tredennick found that he was not entirely able to rid the townland of all traces of partnership farming. Out of the thirty eight townland holdings in 1855, eighteen were still held in partnership and twenty in single ownership.[56]

It was with the grazing land on the west coast, above Lough Mór at Coghlan's Hill, that true partnership or rundale holdings survived. Five Dalys held fifteen acres divided up as two cows' places for Michael Daly, the others having one cow's place. Below them Grace Gillespie, Hugh Dawson and Neil Gillespie held eleven acres at two fifths, two fifths and one fifth respectively.[57] These fractions, called collops, translated as the grass of two cows' and one cow's grass. To the east of Magherabui, the McNeelys and McPhelims held four acres of meadow divided in collops according to the size of the farms that each party held.

Eight of the partnership holdings were held by people within the families of Daly, McCarthy, McNeely, McPhelim, Morrow, Doogan, Gillespie and Sheridan. Partnerships across families were between McShee and McCarthy, Coghlan and McCarthy, McCafferty and Quigley and Daly and Duncan. In these cross family partnerships there is no apparent blood relationship; what was common was that the partners lived beside each other in Coolcolly, Halifax, and Kildoney Oldtown. What was new with these partnerships was that the partners had an actual field

55 Patrick Daly, Kildoney and Dun Laoghaire, in conversation with author, summer 1996.   **56** Griffith, *Valuation*, Co. Donegal, Parish of Kilbarron.   **57** VO, Cancellation books, Kilbarron parish.

fenced in by either wall or hedge; the land was not held in strips or rights. Therefore, these fields were the same in actuality as the individual holdings and were passed on in succession to single heirs.[58]

Those holding land for themselves were Michael, Owen and John Daly, Hugh, William and Michael Gillen, James, Patrick and James Junior McCafferty, Patrick and Brigid McNeely, Grace and Neal Gillespie, Hugh and Edward Dawson, William Cooney, John McCarthy and George Tredennick. Hugh Gillan was the only person to hold land in the townland but to live outside in nearby Creevy. Ten of the farms were held at will, which points to the rest being held likewise. Holding without a lease might have been the wish of the people to avoid legal fees and a reflection of the good relationship between landlord and tenant. Therefore, by 1855 the Kildoney landscape had taken on the field pattern it has today. The villages and small house clusters have only recently given way to scattered single dwellings, one hundred and sixty years after George Tredennick wished them to do so.

KILDONEY, 1850–1911

The high number of partnership holdings related to the new single possessions. By 1901 all the farms, except the grazing and meadow partnership sections, were in single possession with the previous partnerships no longer existing. In mid-nineteenth century, when it was realised that this was to be the future and that some people could be displaced late in life, it was sensible to give the land to brother-brother, or brother-sister partnerships. This avoided anyone being excluded or pauperised. In 1901 all but three of the townland holdings were held by individuals, the land having been passed down through the same family. In cases where a branch of a family, or a family name died out, it was the usual pattern for the land to transfer to a relation such as a niece or nephew.

Under the new single possession it was not the first born male who emerged as the sole or even dominant inheritor of the Kildoney farms. In the 1850s the average age of marriage for men was twenty-eight, while that for girls was twenty-two. Twenty-five was the usual age for mothers on the birth of their first child. The child-bearing age usually ran from twenty-five up to thirty-seven.[59] Given the marriage ages and with procreation spread over twelve years, for the older children the only choice was to move out early. There was a constant upcoming of help within the family and when the time came for parents to hand over the farm it was, in a remarkable number of cases, the second son, the second youngest or the youngest boy who received the farm. Because there was a propensity for wives to outlive husbands, farms came into the possession of wives only before being passed on to one or other category of son; that is, women held land

58 VO, Cancellation books, Kilbarron parish.   59 Kilbarron parish register; NA, census of Ireland 1901, Kildoney Glebe, Kilbarron, county Donegal.

between the death of a husband and the coming of age of an upcoming son. It was not until the 1930s that women inherited farms in their own right.[60] For girls, the principal career opportunity was marriage within or outside the town-land, or else emigration.

The new economic organisation brought in social changes. The excess popu-lation had to emigrate and this caused the population to fall from 394 people in 1841 to 154 people in 1901, as can be seen in Table 4. House numbers fell from seventy to forty over the period 1841 to 1911. The average loss of people in each decade over the period 1841–1901 was thirty-six, showing that the size of families stayed high, despite a fall in average household size from six persons per household to four persons over the same period. Between 1861 and 1871 Kildoney had its heaviest fall of people, with the loss of seventy persons in that ten year period. There is no apparent reason for this heavy fall. In these ten years thirty nine females left the townland. This could be the reason that for half of the recorded marriages in this decade the girls came from outside the townland. Conversely, the high number of marriages outside the townland might explain the high number of girls leaving at this time. Although marriage outside the townland was not unusual, the scale of it in this ten-year period is remarkable. In the 1830s going to America was a daily topic of conversation in the Ballyshannon area.[61] Coulter, a visitor to Ballyshannon in the 1860s, found that it was the ambition and boast of every youth that they were for America at the earliest possibility; it was both necessary and fashionable. Along with a falling population, the census returns show that there was a heavy fall in house numbers between 1841 and 1871. A fall of twenty six houses over thirty years would indicate that whole families were moving out of the townland during the period. Yet, Griffith's *Valuation* for Kildoney around 1855 lists forty eight houses, a figure that included the disused police barrack at the Ranny and the glebe house itself. Table 4 gives the nineteenth-century census returns for Kildoney.[62]

Table 4 Census returns of houses in Kildoney

Year	Houses	Uninhabited houses	Population	Rateable valuation
1841	70	1	394	£279
1851	60	0	337	£246
1861	55	0	321	£336
1871	44	1	256	£333
1881	45	0	244	£325
1891	45	4	213	£324
1901	41	3	178	£325
1911	40	2	154	£325

60 VO, Cancellation books, Kildoney Glebe, Kilbarron, county Donegal. **61** H. Allingham and D. Radford (eds), *William Allingham, a diary* (Middlesex, 1985), p. 7. **62** *Census of Ireland*, 1841–1901.

The Griffith *Valuation* figure of forty-eight houses in 1855 must be taken as the more accurate one and makes nonsense of the census figure of fifty-five houses in 1861. Starting with Griffith, around 1855, and working through the cancellation books the house losses can be accurately traced. The house numbers went down very gradually as people died, the land being taken up but the houses left vacant. Between 1855 and 1901, the house numbers fell by eight, giving a total of forty houses in the townland in 1901 and not forty-one as on the census. Also, the 1841 figure of seventy houses for Kildoney appears to be too high. Working from the remarkable amount of houses and remnants still standing, and plotting these against the 1837 mapped survey of the townland, it is a reasonable assumption to see seventy houses as being an overstatement for the townland in 1841.

The census population figures have to be accepted as there is no way of checking their accuracy. Because Kildoney people did not pay tithe there is no Tithe Applotment to give an indication of the population before the 1850s. Still, there is no tradition of whole family emigration or removal from the townland; a movement which the fall of ten houses over the period 1841–51 and of eleven houses from 1861–71 would suggest took place. There was not a fall of eleven houses in Kildoney between 1861 and 1871, despite the census figures. There was emigration of family groups as is shown by the emigration of four Duncan girls to Boston early in the nineteenth century.[63] Also, the village name Halifax indicates emigration to Canada and sits peculiarly with the rest of the townland names which are all in Irish. The name Fern's Hill for the glebe house area is easily explained by the undoubted English origin of at least one rector. There is a townland story about the eviction of a family called Flammock found guilty of stealing turnips.[64] If true, this removal would fit into the post famine period because of the late introduction of that crop to the townland. A Hand family were also in the townland of whom there is no documentary trace. Their disappearance could simply be that they died out. The conclusion then is that there was no whole family emigration, removal or withdrawal from the townland either over the famine years, or subsequently.

Tracing the townland from the 1850s onwards the pattern was that when land became available, always through death, there was no return of emigrants to take up the available farms. Land becoming available went to increase existing farm sizes, while houses were allowed to fall into ruin. Michael McCarthy returned from Scotland around 1872 to purchase a house and garden but went to live in the Back Street in Ballyshannon. John Gettins, also returned from Scotland, moved in with an aunt, while Patrick Morrow returning from America took up neither family farm nor vacant land. House gardens, ranging in size from twenty perches to up to two roods, were also sought after and added to the existing farm land stock.[65]

---

63 Mary Donagher (Mrs Josie), Kildoney-Ballyshannon, in conversation with author, summer 1996.   **64** Jim McPhelim, Kildoney, in conversation with author, summer 1996. **65** VO, Cancellation books, Kilbarron parish.

Along with emigration, which was to America and Scotland, marriage was also strongly tied to the new succession rites. The number of farm holdings practically determined the number of marriages. Over the period 1850–1901, with four exceptions, marriage was based on succession to a farm. Along with marriage within the townland, Kildoney girls married into other townlands both near and far off. Within the limits of a possible thirty-eight marriages, being the number of holdings in Kildoney in 1855, a further restriction on the population was the number of farmsteads where family members choose to remain unmarried. These were the farms on which there lived brothers and sisters, brothers only and farms with sisters only. On these farms there appears to have been a conscious decision not to marry. When the Kildoney census was taken in 1901, the oldest member of brother-sister farms was a sister. In those situations it would seem a deliberate policy for the younger brother not to marry, so as not to displace the parent-substitute sister. The 1901 census shows also that, in the new order, it was unusual for marriages to happen while brothers, sisters or parents were still present in the home. When marriage did happen with sisters still present then they, the sisters, were displaced.

Despite these restrictions on marriage, the Kildoney population fell because of emigration and not because of any dramatic fall in the birth rate over the time 1850–1901. Throughout this period the birth rate stayed constant, as can be seen in table 5.[66]

Table 5 Kildoney marriage and birth returns from Kilbarron parish registers

Years	Recorded marriages	Recorded births
1850s	9	44
1860s	8	36
1870s	10	48
1880s	7	39

The drop in births during the 1860s and 1880s happened because in each of those two decades there was one married couple who were childless. The males of these marriages, at thirty-nine years and forty-two years, were the second and third highest recorded ages for men marrying either known or estimated over the period. By the 1880s the marrying age for men had definitely risen out of the twenties into the thirties, forties and even fifties. For the three decades before 1880 the marriage age for girls had been consistently in the lower twenties. Now, in the 1880s this age moved up into the later twenties and early thirties without lowering the birth rate.

66 Kilbarron parish registers, Parochial House, Ballyshannon, Co. Donegal, courtesy of Revd Britton, since retired as parish priest of Kilbarron.

The Sheridan, Dawson, Quigley, Keenan and Cooney families disappeared from the townland between 1855 and the 1911 census. Within the Sheridan and Dawson families none of the boys married, while Margaret Sheridan and Bridget Dawson married into Daly families. William Quigley succeeded his mother, stayed single and died between 1901 and 1911. The Keenan family were apparently the only landless family in the townland. They may have moved out with the departure of Revd Tredennick in 1872 or Michael Keenan may have died young, with his widow remarrying into another Daly family. There is no explanation for the loss of the Cooney family, since William and Catherine Cooney had three sons born between 1857 and 1862. One family, the Dorrians, moved into the townland in the 1860s as waterkeeper for the Ballyshannon salmon fisheries. That they quickly established themselves, despite their official role, is shown by the marriage of Hanna and Mary Dorrian into established McCarthy and Daly families in 1864 and 1866 respectively.[67]

Working from the 1901 and 1911 census it was clear that certain other Kildoney families and branches of families were going to die out: Michael and John Doogan, Hugh and Edward Dorrian, James and Margaret Morrow, Mary, Anne and Margaret McCafferty, John and Ann McCarthy, Catherine and Brigid McCarthy, William and Margaret Daly, James and Ann McPhelim, Daniel MacShee, William Quigley, and Patrick McPhelim. In 1911 the townland bachelors ranged in age from twenty two to forty four with Alexander Duncan, William Duggan and Francis McNeely being the most senior. Duncan and Duggan, both returned as aged forty in 1911, confirm the trend of late marriages as both went on to marry.[68]

Kildoney in 1901 was a farming community in which the males returned themselves as farmers while the females returned themselves as seamstresses. This occupation owed more to the training that they received in Creevy national school from Miss Doherty than it did to the reality of each of them being employed at the sewing trade. Four men only returned themselves as being engaged in fishing, which was the second most important occupation in the townland after farming.

FISHING, 1860–1933

Writing in 1862, with a keen sense of lost opportunity, William Allingham described the Ballyshannon sea fisheries as being worked in a crude and unsystematic way.[69] At the end of the eighteenth century and into the early years of the nineteenth the Bunatroohan fishermen ranged from Mullaghmore to St John's Point and occasionally into Teelin Bay in search of fish, with forty to fifty

67 Kilbarron parish registers.   68 NA, 1901 and 1911 census, Kildoney Glebe, county Donegal.   69 William Allingham writing the introduction to *The Ballyshannon Almanac, North West Directory and General Advertisers for 1862* (Ballyshannon, 1862), p. 2.

people working the port's seven boats.[70] As the nineteenth century progressed, and with the number of young men in the townland falling, the range for the Bunatroohan fishermen was set closer to home. The periodic failure of the herring fishing also assisted this tendency.[71] Unlike the St John's Point, Mullaghmore and Teelin men, who were fishermen first and farmers when the weather did not permit fishing, the Bunatroohan fishermen were farmers first.[72] Nonetheless, ten boats continued to work out of the port by the 1880s.

The best fishing grounds were on the north of Donegal Bay around Inver and St John's Point. Revd W. S. Green proved this when trawling off Rossnowlagh in the 1890s: he recorded only three species of fish as against eleven off Inver.[73] This accounts for the strong fishing tradition that had north coast fishermen coming into Bunatroohan rather than Bunatroohan men roving over the north bay fishing grounds.[74]

A bad harvest and resulting distress in 1879–80 brought relief schemes into Kildoney again.[75] The earlier slipway had been washed away leaving the ten boats operating out of the bay badly disadvantaged and exposed. Work began in 1880 on a 200 yard long pier, which is the present pier, incorrectly called Creevy Pier. The local fishermen were satisfied with the Board of Works policy of small piers dotted along the coastline as they liked to fish as near as possible to home. This system served their needs much better than large fishing centres drawing crews in from all over Donegal Bay.[76]

However, the present pier and slipway at Bunatroohan ended up being unsuitable to local needs, not because of any misjudgement by the engineer or of the local fishermen, but because of the stubbornness of a member of the Pier Committee.[77] For the slip, a slope of no more than the ratio of 1:6 was recommended. However, it was built with a slope in the ratio of 1:3. The slip, because it was now shortened, had to have an elbow at the top to allow boats up onto the road. Boats reaching the top of the slip, with the aid of landing gear, still had to get across to the platform of the elbow. This problem was never rectified. For the ten boats which belonged to the harbour the slip was perfectly useless on account of its steepness.[78] The Bunatroohan fishermen wanted the slipway removed. However, it was neither removed nor lengthened. What was done instead was the removal of rocks off the pier head, the excavation of the basin to create a spend for the waves and the removal of rocks opposite the steps which

70 RIA, OS Memoir, Kilbarron Parish. **71** Joe Morrow, Kildoney, in conversation with author, spring 1995. **72** Nimmo's coast survey of Ireland p. 73. **73** W.S. Green, 'Survey of fishing grounds on west coast' in *Proceedings of the Royal Dublin Society* (1891–2), no. 128–9, p. 132. **74** *Report to His Excellency the Lord Lieutenant of Ireland regarding Fishery Piers in the County of Donegal, Ireland*, by Thomas Stevenson, [C–4662], lix, 1886, p. 4, Bunatroohan. **75** *Return of all Piers and Harbours built under the Board of Works in Ireland since the passing of the Act 9 Vict, c.3, 1884–5*, lxx, p. 167. **76** *Report on fishery piers, Donegal*, p. 4. **77** R.H. Sankey, *Report of the Donegal Piers and Harbours*, OPW (Dublin, 1884), p. 17. **78** *Report on fishery piers, Donegal*, p. 4.

were causing a recoil. These modifications were recommended by the Bunatroohan fishermen themselves and agreed to by the county engineer.[79]

By the 1901 census only four Kildoney people returned themselves as fishermen, all of them young men, the sons of farmers still living. They were John, Michael and Thomas McCafferty and John McNeely.[80] Even so, this does not mean that people who returned themselves as farmers were not also fishermen. Kildoney fireside ambitions were concentrated not on the development of the sea fisheries, but on the possibility of access to the salmon rich river Erne, which entered the sea on the south west of the townland. The river Erne and its estuary were privately owned by the Conolly estate. Angling was allowed on the river under licence but there was no public fishing allowed on the estuary. Anyone who ever tried to fish inside the bar was prosecuted. In mid nineteenth century Ballyshannon it was held that a successful challenge to Conolly ownership of the river and estuary fishing could come only from the wealth of the town; other communities, especially those living along the estuary, were regarded as too weak to successfully challenge the powerful Conolly family.[81] In 1927 Kildoney fishermen openly and publicly entered the Erne estuary to fish for salmon, thus taking the first step in their ultimately successful attempt to open the estuary fishing. The Erne Fishing Company, which had bought the rights from the Conolly estate back in 1869, fought the Kildoney fishermen through the courts for six years, only to lose what appeared to be an unassailable case. The legal victory of the Kildoney men in 1933, which allowed public access to the Erne estuary, was the high point of the Kildoney fishing tradition.[82]

SINGLE POSSESSION TO SINGLE OWNERSHIP, 1869–1903

Under the Irish Church act of 1869 the lands of Kildoney Glebe were transferred to the Commissioners of Church Temporalities in Ireland to be managed and sold off by them. Fenian activity in America and Ireland had moved prime minister Gladstone to break the connection between the Anglican church and the state in Ireland; this was the motivation for the Irish Church act.[83]

Kildoney tenants were given first refusal to buy their lands, though there was no system of loans or grants forthcoming from the commissioners. Two families, McPhelim and Daly, were willing and able to take up the offer; the rest declined.[84] That these two were able and willing to do so shows that the Kildoney economy had strengthened over the previous twenty-five years. These families also showed an early belief in peasant proprietorship, well before that idea became common.

79 *Report on fishery piers, Donegal*, p. 4.   **80** NA, Census of Ireland 1901, Kildoney Glebe, county Donegal.   **81** *Report from the Select Committee on Fisheries (Ireland) together with the Proceedings of the Committee*, Minutes of Evidence, Appendix, Plans and Index 1849, xiii, pp. 270–2.   **82** Hayes, *Fisheries of the Erne*, pp. 31–9.   **83** R.F. Foster, *Modern Ireland* (London, 1989), pp. 395–6.   **84** NA, ILC, Estate of Hugh O'Donnell, LC record no. 2885.

Thereafter, 170 acres were sold to Dr James D. Condon of Ballyshannon and 171 acres to Hugh O'Donnell, who was either a Donegal or a Derry merchant. Although the Church Temporalities Commissioners material is not yet available, it appears that the Kildoney farmers had a choice over who their new landlords would be.[85] The tenants were able to safeguard their farms against the incoming landlords, Condon and O'Donnell.

By the Irish Church amendment act 1881, Kildoney lands managed by the Church Commissioners were transferred to the Irish Land Commission. By reason of the land acts passed in the Westminster Parliament from 1886 onwards, the Condon and O'Donnell estates were taken back and they along with Land Commission land in the townland were sold on to the Kildoney farmers, making them outright owners of the land their ancestors had occupied for centuries.

85 ILC, estate of Hugh O'Donnell, LC, record no. 2885.

Kilmacud, county Dublin

CHARLES SMITH

I. TOPOGRAPHY

The development of the Dublin suburbs has led to the loss, in many instances, of popular knowledge of the townlands, their names, bounds and local lore, notwithstanding the efforts of dedicated individuals and groups to rescue and to publish the history of their areas. This is a study of the townlands of Kilmacud in south county Dublin, two of the many suburban townlands whose fields have disappeared under roads and houses in the past fifty years.

The civil parish of Kilmacud comprises two townlands, Kilmacud East and Kilmacud West. The total area is small, 287 acres, statute measure (173 acres, Irish). It is bounded on the east by the townlands of Stillorgan South and Waltersland, on the south by Mulchanstown and the line of the old Dublin South-Eastern Railway, on the west by Drummartin (next to Dundrum) and on the north by Callary and Mount Anville. The northern boundary is roughly the Lower Kilmacud Road, which links Stillorgan with Goatstown, Clonskeagh, Miltown and Ranelagh. The land is around 60–70 metres above sea-level. It rises fairly sharply from the Mount Merrion end towards Drummartin and Dundrum. The highest land is a ridge on the boundary between Kilmacud East and West, along the line of the Upper Kilmacud Road to the point where it turns west towards Dundrum. Generally the district is part of a wide valley stretching from Mount Merrion to the foothills of the Dublin mountains. The land is relatively well-drained and fertile. There are no streams above ground now, but there is a sizable one that rises in the grounds of Lakelands (now St Benildus Secondary School) to the south of the upper road, flows north and then east along the Lower Kilmacud Road and across Stillorgan to enter the sea at Blackrock. It was culverted about thirty years ago. The early Ordnance Survey sheets and plans showed a second stream to the west of the upper road flowing through a field called Thorn Field, where rocks and a pond were marked. It joined the first stream near the junction of the lower and upper roads.[1] There are indications that the area was well wooded, almost certainly eighteenth-century plantings. Agriculture seems to have been mainly pastoral, Kilmacud was a source of fresh milk for the district and the city.

---

1 NA, OS 104E 309/310 (control and line plot) and OS 105E 309/310 fair plan. OS c.1833–37.

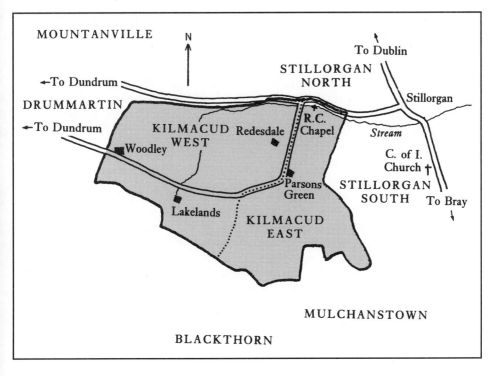

Kilmacud, county Dublin, 1843, 287 acres

   The modern bounds are similar to those described in the *Civil Survey of 1654–56*.[2] The area accounted for, however, was ninety-five acres, Irish measure, little more than half the modern area. In the later Book of Survey and Distribution the area was returned as 150 acres, Irish plantation measure.[3] We can be fairly certain that the two modern townlands correspond largely to the medieval parish. They would have equated to a secular territorial unit, probably fixed by the Anglo-Norman grantees, the de Ridelsfords, but based on an older Gaelic land unit.

II. EARLY HISTORY

Kilmacud was an early church site, although no trace remains on the ground or in local memory. The dedication is to St Mochud. Bishop Donnelly identified him with the early missionary, after whom St Malo in France is named.[4] He is said to have voyaged with St Brendan. Mochud is probably the saint associated with Lismore, County Waterford and also known as St Carthach or Carthage. But there is also a St Mocholmoc or Colman, abbot and bishop of Lismore.[5] He is reputed to have died in 703. Although of east Cork origin, he is closely linked to St Flannan and the O'Briens. It is possible that Kilmacud was founded in the eleventh century when the O'Brien high-kings controlled Dublin. It seems certain that the foundation is late and that Mochud is an intruder. Kilmacud is in the deanery of Taney, whose patron is Nathi. He is associated with the Dal Meisin Corb, an early royal family of Laigin. They lost power in the sixth century and withdrew over the mountains towards the east. A number of other saints associated with south-east county Dublin, such as Begnat of Dalkey, Berchan of Shankill, as well as St Kevin of Glendalough, are said to have belonged to this family, who may have compensated for their loss of power by taking over ecclesiastical offices.[6] The traditional patron of near-by Stillorgan and of much of this part of the county is Brigit of Kildare, another indication of the interest of the royal house of Laigin in the region.

   In the twelfth century, just before the arrival of the Anglo-Normans, the district was part of Ui Briuin Chualann (the modern barony of Rathdown) and was controlled by the MacGiollamocholmog, a minor branch of the royal house and allies of Diarmuid MacMurchada, king of Leinster. They took the Norman side after the capture of Dublin and were absorbed into the new system as minor gentry. Much of the land of Ui Briuin Chualann was granted by Strongbow to Walter de Ridelsford, who also got lands in County Kildare. He founded the

2 *The Civil Survey, 1654–56*, ed. R.C. Simington, (10 vols, Dublin, 1931–61), vol. vii, Co. Dublin, p. 262.   3 RIA *Book of Survey and Distribution,* counties Dublin and Wicklow. 4 Revd N Donnelly, D.D., *Short histories of the Dublin parishes* (Dublin, 1905, reprinted Blackrock, county Dublin, 1977) pt. 3, p. 93.   5 *Martyrology of Tallaght*, ed. Revd Matthew Kelly, D.D. (Dublin, n.d. but *c.*1857) pp. xiii, 60.   6 P. Ó Riain (ed.), *Corpus genealogiorum sanctorum Hiberniae* (Dublin, 1985) 181.14.

convent of Graney or Grane in that county about 1200. Among other endow-
ments, he granted it the church and tithes of Kilmacud. The church seems to
have survived until the Reformation although whether it continued to function
until then is, perhaps, debatable. It is noted in the *Crede Mihi*, a thirteenth
century list of the churches of the diocese, and in the *Repertorium Viride*, lists of
the churches of the diocese compiled by Archbishop John Alen in the early
sixteenth century.[7] Alen was keenly interested in the properties, rights and
privileges of his diocese and collected much material to that end. The entry in
Repertorium Viride suggests that his interest in Kilmacud's status as a dependant
church of a convent in county Kildare related to a dispute with the bishop of
Leighlin about the boundaries of the dioceses.

An entry in *Alen's Register*, clearly interpolated after his time, lists seven
churches created as parish churches after Grane was suppressed in 1536.[8] Kilmacud
is not among them. It is not mentioned in the royal visitation of Dublin in 1615
nor in Archbishop Bulkeley's visitation of 1630.[9] Clearly it ceased to exist very
soon after the onset of the Reformation. It may well have been closed earlier.
The indications are that the population was very small and there were churches
close by in Stillorgan and Dundrum. As stated earlier, no trace of the old church
remains. It is possible that it was on the ridge near the present Carmelite convent,
where the Upper Kilmacud Road swings to the west. Early maps show a house
called 'Parson's Green' at that point, but that may be just a coincidence.

By the fifteenth century the de Ridelsfords' manor of Thorncastle, of which
Kilmacud was part, had passed into the hands of the Cruises. Inquisitions taken
in 1537 and 1540, after Grane was suppressed, showed that the tithes were held
by the chaplain, Walter Cruce or Cruise and by Thomas Boyce, merchant, and
his wife, Alison, under a lease made in 1519 for twenty years from 1521 for £20
a year.[10] Alison was a Cruce and probably a sister or other relative of Walter.

III. SEVENTEENTH AND EIGHTEENTH CENTURIES

From the Cruises the lands passed to the Fitzwilliams, to whom they were
related by marriage. The Fitzwilliams became the wealthiest and most powerful
family in the south county. They survived the wars and confiscations of the
seventeenth century. Their lands stretched from the modern Merrion Square
through Donnybrook, Sandymount, Ringsend, Merrion, Booterstown, Mount

---

7 J.T. Gilbert (ed.), *Crede Mihi* (Dublin, 1897), p. 138; Newport B. White (ed.), 'Repertorium
Viride' in *Analecta Hibernia*, x (1941), p. 192.   **8** Charles McNeill (ed.), *Calendar of Archbishop
Alen's Register c.1172–1534* (Dublin, 1950), p. 278 (hereafter cited as *Alen's Reg*).   **9** Myles V.
Ronan (ed.), 'Royal visitation of Dublin, 1615' and 'Archbishop Buckeley's visitation of
Dublin 1630' in *Archivium Hibernicum*, viii (1941), pp. 1–98.   **10** Margaret C. Griffith (ed.),
Calendar of Inquisitions, county Dublin (Dublin, 1991), H viii 96, 130 (hereafter cited as
Inquisitions).

Merrion and inland to Dundrum. The estate still exists in part as the Pembroke Estate. From the sixteenth century the Archbolds held Kilmacud under lease from the Fitzwilliams.[11] The Fitzwilliam rentals show that in the 1760s John Archbold was paying a chief rent of £2 10s. a year in two instalments, due on 25 March and 29 September.[12] They were an old settler family, which had considerable property interests in south-east Dublin and north Wicklow as well as in north and west Dublin and in county Kildare. In 1615 Patrick Archbold, his son, Maurice, and Edmond Archbold divided the lands of Kilmacud between them, half to Patrick, with succession to Maurice, and half to Edmond.[13] The *Civil Survey* showed Maurice Archbold and a William Archbold, probably Edmond's son, as the holders in 1641. The Book of Survey and Distribution shows that after the restoration Maurice's grandson and heir, Richard Archbold of Mapas, Cheshire, a Protestant, and the duke of York, later James II, each got seventy-five acres. The Archbolds rented James' part and continued to work the land. It is not known where they lived or, indeed, if they lived in the area. Later members of the family seem to have done so; they were buried in Taney churchyard in Dundrum. In 1713 James Archbold was described in a court case as of Kilmacud and the court decree of £102 10s. against him was ordered to be paid out of the lands of Kilmacud. Incidentally, the other party, his brother-in-law Peter Toole, said he was a 'powerful person of great wealth'.[14] In 1756, this branch of the family died out.[15] As a result of mortgages the property passed to a Lt.-Col. John Arabin. Griffith's *Valuation* a century later, showed that the Arabins still had property in Kilmacud, seventy-two acres in the eastern half and ninety-seven acres in the western part.

Data on the population and on the economy begin to become available only from the seventeenth century. The first information we have on the quality of the land comes from the seventeenth century surveys. In the *Civil Survey* the area was recorded as a plough land and a half or 95 acres, 'estimate of the country', of which sixty acres were arable and fifteen were in meadow. The value was assessed as £50, or about 10s. 6d. an acre. The neighbouring townland of Stillorgan's 166 acres were valued at £90, or 10s. 10d. an acre. In an assessment for tax purposes in 1661 Kilmacud was valued at £5 and Stillorgan at £10, broadly confirming the earlier relationship. Seventeenth-century surveyors differed, however, in their estimates of area. An extract from the Philips Ms. in the National Archives, which, according to its title, was a survey of the county Dublin taken in 1658, gives an area of 240 acres.[16] The Book of Survey and Distribution has 150 plantation acres, all profitable.

---

11 F. Elrington Ball, *History of the county of Dublin* (Dublin, 1902), pt. 1, p. 132 (hereafter cited as Ball). **12** NLI, Fitzwilliam rentals, microfilm, pos. 943. **13** Griffith (ed.), *Inquisitions*, appendix no. 15. **14** Historical Manuscripts Commission, *House of Lords*, new series, x (1712–14), pp. 34–5. **15** Ball, p. 133. On the face of it this conflicts with the Fitzwilliam rentals where Archbold is recorded as paying rent in the 1760s. **16** NA, M 2475, Survey of county Dublin, 1658.

The taxation return for 1661, when parliament granted a subsidy to the newly-restored Charles II, shows that Richard Archbold was in possession. He paid tax of 19*s*. 10*d*. on his lands, which, as mentioned earlier, were valued at £5.[17] He was still there in 1664 and 1666 when the hearth money rolls show that he paid tax on one hearth.[18] His neighbour, James Wolverston of Stillorgan, had seven hearths. This shows that he was, at most, a minor gentleman, not much better off than his tenants. In 1664 they were Richard Barlow, John Bradford and Francis Knibe. One hearth was said to be 'waste'. The 1659 'census' had also shown four hearths and had returned thirteen inhabitants, eleven of them English, that is, Protestant. Since young children were not counted, the true population may have been around twenty, assuming a mean household size of five. By 1666 the number of taxpayers had gone up to six, each paying for one hearth. Barlow had gone but Morgan Birne, Thomas Doyle and Thomas Pierce were living there. Byrne and Doyle are old Gaelic names in south county Dublin and their appearance indicates a return to relative calm after the Commonwealth as well as some revival of the economy.

The next piece of information on population is from the religious census of April 1766. This returned twelve Protestant and twenty Catholic families in the united parishes of Stillorgan and Kilmacud (thirty-two families as against twenty-two in the hearth money roll for 1666), making fifty-seven Protestants and 138 Papists of whom eight Protestant and three Popish families 'reside the greater part of the year in Dublin'.[19] The area was sharing in the economic growth of the eighteenth century, when Dublin in particular experienced rapid development as the capital city of colonial Ireland. The return confirms a particular form of development that was taking place throughout county Dublin, that is, the growth of small villa estates for the well-to-do gentry and professional classes of the city. The potential of the south county in this respect was appreciated quickly by the major landowners, who exploited it with alacrity. Viscount Fitzwilliam built a grand house at Mount Merrion. The Allens of Stillorgan built an equally fine one in Stillorgan House and encouraged building on their estates. It is no surprise, therefore, that two-thirds of the Protestant families in 1766 were only occasional visitors, residing mainly in the city. The Catholics were the permanent residents and would have provided most of the farm labour and the tradesmen of the district.

Kilmacud was popular in the eighteenth and nineteenth centuries because of its pleasant aspect and good air. Seward in his *Topographia Hibernica* (1795) described it as standing on a rising ground and having a pure and wholesome air. Fifty years on Lewis wrote that it was in a high state of cultivation and 'from the salubrity of its air and the beauty of its marine and mountain views. is a

17 NA, M 2478, Return of the subsidy (eighth) granted by parliament to King Charles II, 1661. **18** 'Extracts from the hearth money rolls, county Dublin' in *The register of the union of Monkstown, county Dublin, 1609–1786* (Parish Registers Society of Dublin), vi (1908), pp. 86, 91. **19** NA, M 2478, Religious census.

favourite spot for country residences'.[20] It became an area of small estates, not grand enough or big enough to attract the nobility (although there were the exceptions of Lord Redesdale, the lord chancellor, around 1800, and Archbishop Whately in mid-century, both of whom took Redesdale House, the largest estate in the district) but attractive to the rising professional and merchant classes. We have brief descriptions of two of these demesnes about 1800. One, probably Kilmacud House, was said to be 'a good house, pleasantly situated, with a demesne of forty acres, well wooded and improved, good gardens well laid out, and the whole well enclosed'. Another house was described as 'a good house, beautifully situated, commanding an extensive view of the sea, and a fine improved country. The demesne is about twenty-five acres.'[21]

IV. POPULATION AND ECONOMY IN THE NINETEENTH CENTURY

The villas had all been built by the early nineteenth century. The pattern of estates then established continued well into the twentieth century. The tithe applotment for Kilmacud parish in 1826 shows that its 280 acres were shared by ten landowners. The main estates were Redesdale, St Margaret's, Parson's Green, Lakelands and Woodley. Redesdale was the largest with seventy-two acres. The next largest had forty acres. The smallest had four acres.[22] The applotment did not give a full picture of the inhabitants; that was revealed only in the primary valuation *c.*1850.[23] There were still ten estates but the list also disclosed five gate lodges (one vacant) and three other small houses (one vacant). The total number of occupiers was sixteen. According to the 1841 census, however, there were 26 families living in 24 houses. Should one assume then that the number of houses fell by 25 per cent in a decade? Almost certainly not. There are problems about the population, especially between 1841 and 1851, which will be considered later. A list of the demesnes and of their occupiers, in so far as it can be gleaned from the sources, will be found in the appendix.

With one, or maybe, two exceptions the demesnes seem to have been too small to have been run as serious farming businesses. Their owners' main income was derived from business and professional activity in the city, from estates in other parts of the country or, perhaps, from inherited wealth. Even in the case of Redesdale House, the largest estate, the surveyor observed in 1869 'buildings all too large as farm premises but all held in medium order'.[24] They were 'gentlemen's seats' surrounded by parkland, whither the owners could withdraw at the weekend to rejoin their families and to escape the noise and dirt of the

---

20 Samuel Lewis, *A topographical dictionary of Ireland* (2 vols. and atlas, London, 1837), ii, 168. **21** Joseph Archer, *Statistical survey of the county Dublin* (Royal Dublin Society, Dublin, 1801), pp. 103–4 (hereafter cited as Archer).   **22** NA, TAB 9/73 no. 35.   **23** NA, fiche 5f 10, primary valuation, county Dublin.   **24** VO, Valuation lists, county Dublin, Rathdown no. 1, Kilmacud.

city. They usually maintained a town house where they resided during the week and in the 'season'. With the opening of the Dublin and South-Eastern Railway from Harcourt Street in 1853 it became possible to travel to and from the city daily quickly and comfortably. There were stations in Dundrum and Stillorgan. Chief Baron Palles, who lived in Mountainville House, in the next townland to Kilmacud, from 1885 (he had a town residence at 28, Fitzwilliam Place) travelled by rail from Dundrum to Harcourt Street in half an hour and then took a tramcar to the Four Courts.[25] The railway is gone and it would take him longer to travel the distance to-day by road during rush-hour!

The houses were commodious and comfortable and well-staffed with servants. In the census of 1841 fifty out of a permanent population of 172 were classified as servants, 29 per cent. In 1901 there were thirty-six out of a population of 108, exactly a third. The properties may not have been serious farms but in their heyday they were intended to make the family largely self-suficient in vegetables, fruit, including exotics, flowers, milk and butter. Woodley House was ordered by the Land Judges to be sold on 9 May 1890. The rental and particulars of sale described the house as 'a handsome commodious two-storied residence erected so as to command beautiful undulating landscape views of a most picturesque description'. There were four reception rooms, a study, six bedrooms, two servants' rooms, bathroom, water closets, kitchen, wine cellar, dairy, coal stores, scullery, pantries, laundries, force pumps 'with unlimited supply of spring water of excellent quality'. The out-offices in an enclosed yard consisted of two loose stables for five horses, cowshed for five cows with troughs etc., two coach houses and harness room, hay lofts, piggeries and a fine compact walled-in paddock. The lawn in front 'would make a most suitable tennis ground'. Two conservatories adjoined the house. There was a large walled-in fruit and vegetable garden, with melon pits etc.. The main entrance was from the Goatstown Road where there was a cut granite gate lodge. The approach was by a long winding avenue about a quarter mile in length through the centre of the grounds. The lands were studded with fine large old beech, oak, chestnut, elm, ash and other forest trees. There was a two room one-storey cottage on land known as Woodley Farm. The lands were of excellent quality, suitable for tillage or pasture. They were said to be within about three miles of Dublin on the Dundrum and Stillorgan roads (which seems to be an under-estimate) and about three-quarters of a mile of Dundrum railway station.[26]

The apparent continuity masked a degree of consolidation and the gradual conversion of estates to institutional use. It is possible that some land was always set to farmers but evidence is not available before mid-century. From the 1860s there are indications of decline in some demesnes, accompanied by consolidation

25 V.T.H. Delany, *Christopher Palles, his life and times* (Dublin, 1960), pp. 109–10. **26** NA, M 449, Land Judges, sale of Chapman estates, 1890. For more on the importance of the kitchen garden see Mary Davies 'High-class horticulture' in *The Irish Garden*, v, no. 6 (Nov–Dec., 1996), p. 31.

of land for farming. This could lead to its separation from the house. Thus the primary valuation recorded Thomas Wilson as holding thirty-nine acres, a house, gate lodge and two small houses. By the 1860s Joseph Wilson had increased the holding to eighty-eight acres. Clonmore House, one of the estates he had acquired, was said to be vacant, in bad repair and occasionally occupied by a herdsman. Kilmacud Manor, where Wilson had let the house but retained the lodge and, presumably, the land, may also have been in some disrepair because in 1874, after the Carmelite nuns had taken possession, the surveyor reported that it was much improved. Henry Clarke had taken the leases of the Redesdale House lands, Kilmacud House and Hazelwood by the 1860s. Subsequently a William Buckley seems to have acquired most of these lands in the 1890s. His family held them until after the second world war when they were sold for housing. The Buckleys were farmers and their interest was in the land; Redesdale House was leased out. They did not live in the area but in Churchtown, about two miles away.[27] The existence of Woodley Farm was noted earlier. It comprised just short of thirteen acres and had obviously been carved out of the estate. It was held by Patrick Quinn at the yearly rent of £52 payable quarterly in advance, over and above all taxes.

Figure 1 shows the population at each census from 1841 to 1911.

Figure 1 Kilmacud Population, 1841–1911

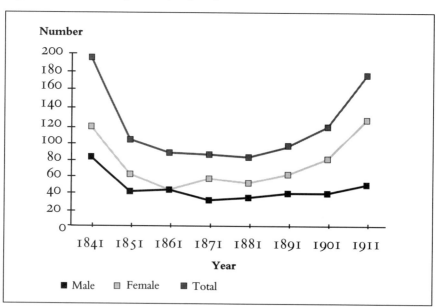

Table 1 shows the housing figures from the census along with the population figures.

27 VO, Valuation lists, county Dublin, Rathdown no. 1, Kilmacud.

Table 1 Kilmacud Housing and Population, 1841–1911

Year	Male	Female	Total	No. of houses
1841	78	114	192	24
1851	40	59	99	19(5)
1861	42	44	86	20(4)
1871	30	53	83	16(1)
1881	31	49	80	16
1891	37	60	97	20(3)
1901	37	76	113	14
1911	48	125	173	26

(Figures for 1911 include Catholic curate and female housekeeper reclassified from Stillorgan North. Figures in brackets denote vacant houses.)

Before discussing this table it may be useful to look at the 1841 data in more detail. The number of servants, fifty, was mentioned earlier. There were also twenty visitors, fifteen female. Twenty-four boys and thirty-two girls were under fifteen years of age. The standard of housing seems to have been good. The twenty-six families lived in twenty-four houses, eighteen of which were rated first and second class and the rest third class. The level of literacy was also high for both sexes, a little higher for the females. Of those aged five years and upwards only about 15 per cent were illiterate, as Table 2 shows.

Table 2 Literacy in Kilmacud, 1841

Sex	Read & Write	Read only	Illiterate	Total
Male	48	6	10	64
Female	67	22	15	104
Total	115	28	25	168

The occupational breakdown in the 1841 census is unsatisfactory. Instead of a list of occupations the numbers engaged in certain activities, such as food, lodging, clothing, medicine, were given. It would not be safe to assume that the nineteen males and two females engaged in food were farmers or agricultural labourers. Likewise the fourteen males described as 'unclassified' could include those of independent means. Or the latter could have been included under 'no specific occupation', where there were seventeen males and forty-eight females. These two categories together must include male and female servants and the large number of females engaged in home duties. When occupation by family is considered it emerges that fifteen of the twenty-six families were chiefly employed in agriculture, three were engaged mainly in manufacturing or trade and the remainder were unclassified. But when one looks at the data on means of support, fifteen families derived their income from directing the labour of others and only six were dependent on their own manual labour. If one abstracts the upper and middle-class families of the mansions and villas and their servants, the number of working-class families was small. But how many were unemployed, under-employed or worked as casual unskilled labourers is impossible to say. D'Alton, however, stated that in 1834 the population of the united parishes of Kilmacud and Stillorgan was 2,145, that about 240 were said to be labourers and that half of them had constant employment.[28] Obviously, economic conditions in the district were good. The main sources of employment would have been agriculture and building (D'Alton commented that the ground around Stillorgan was chiefly let in building or ornamental lots).[29] There was little or no industrial employment apart from Mr Darley's brewery in Stillorgan.

There is no information on living conditions in the area but Archer described the situation in the county generally in his time. There is no reason to think that conditions were much different in Kilmacud or that they had changed that much between 1800 and 1841. Cottagers lived generally in thatched, mud-walled cabins Their rent was three to four shillings a year near the city. In remoter parts farmers sometimes gave labourers free cabins or else they paid a small rent. Archer commented that for the 'lower orders' fuel was scarce. If turf was not available locally the hedges are demolished without mercy'. In many places dung was collected in the fields, dried and burnt. Even straw was used as fuel. The food of cottiers was mainly potatoes and milk. Archer reported that, when he wrote, potatoes were so dear that bread was sometimes used but he added the poor had suffered severely during the previous two years (there was heavy price inflation during the Napoleonic wars, followed by depression in the 1820s).

Labourers earned 6s. to 9s. a week, if fully employed. Temporary workers got 9s. 9d. a week but more at harvest. Potatoes were planted on a piecework system at 4d. a perch of twenty-one feet in length ten feet broad for ridge and furrow. Sometimes the seed was included. Turnips were hoed twice at a guinea an acre. The rate for digging loose ground was 3d. to 7d. a square perch (forty nine square yards). On easy ground ditches were dug for 2s. 2d. to 2s. 9d. a perch. A ditch was dug four feet deep, five feet wide at the top and sloped to two feet at the bottom. A double row of whitethorn quicks was laid on the breast. The rate for mowing hay varied from 6s. 6d. to 10s. an acre. At harvest time wheat was threshed for a shilling a barrel but oats and barley were only 5d. Labourers worked from five in the morning to six in the evening. There was a half hour for breakfast and an hour for dinner. During the harvest they worked from sunrise to sunset and in winter as long as there was light.[30]

28 John D'Alton, *The history of the county Dublin* (Dublin, 1838, reprinted Dublin, 1976), p. 421. **29** Ibid., pp. 420–1. **30** Archer, pp. 110–12.

Returning to the table of population, it will be observed that there appears to be a 50 per cent fall between 1841 and 1851. One could be excused for thinking that this was typical of the Ireland of the day, the effect of the famine. But the population of county Dublin increased in the period as did the population of the barony of Rathdown. What seems to have happened is that in 1851 a new district, Newtownpark town, was introduced, which took population from Stillorgan and from other areas of the district electoral division/union, which cannot now be elucidated. It seems reasonable to conclude that a substantial number of people, close on one hundred, classified as Kilmacud in 1841, disappeared into the new area or other parts of Stillorgan, there remained and cannot now be traced. This hypothesis is supported by the fact that there is a reference in *Thom's Directory* for 1851 to a number of detached cottages (it does not follow that they were in the Kilmacud townlands; the directory is not always accurate in that respect). More important support comes from the separate appearance in the 1911 census of Kilmacud Road, containing forty-nine cottages and from the misclassification in that census of the Catholic curate and his housekeeper from Kilmacud to Stillorgan North.

There were two other important developments that affect the comparability of the data. In 1874 the Carmelite sisters came to Kilmacud Manor. The impact on the figures for 1881 and 1891 is unknown but in 1901 there were fourteen nuns, one female boarder and three female servants. In 1911 the total was seventeen. By the same census Redesdale had become the Irish Training School of Domestic Economy under the Department of Agriculture and Technical Instruction for Ireland and had thirty students, five teachers and five servants, all female. When the data are corrected for these distortions, it will be seen that the population was stable through the nineteenth century and was growing slightly in the early years of this century.

V. THE TWENTIETH CENTURY

Because the individual returns for 1901 and 1911 have survived, there is considerable information on the composition of the population in those years.

Table 3. looks at the gender breakdown for Kilmacud.

Table 3 Kilmacud in the 1901 & 1911 Censuses

Year	Male			Female		
	Adult	Minor	Servant	Adult	Minor	Servant
1901	16	10	11	35	16	25
1911	29	18	1	76	21	28

The reason for the steep fall in the number of male servants is unclear. More of them may have been living in cottages on the estates or may have been living locally.

The district was dominated by a handful of families. In 1901 they were Verschoyle (Woodley), McCrea (Hazelwood), Hamilton (Lakelands), Pilkington (Westbury), Gregg (unknown) and Daly (Kilmacud House). The only change in 1911 was that McCrea had been replaced by a Mr Bladen. Verschoyle was a land agent; in earlier times a family of that name had been agents for the Fitzwilliams. In 1826 a Verschoyle was living at Stillorgan Park and was a commissioner for the tithe composition in Kilmacud. They may have been the only family in the group who could claim to be local. Gregg was also a land agent but, in addition, by 1911 he was a director of a railway company. Pilkington was a director of the Bank of Ireland. Hamilton was a dairy farmer and Daly described himself as a gentleman farmer.

When one probes further one finds that seven other households lived on Pilkington's land in 1911. One was Gregg, but the others were obviously employees. They had small houses with from one to four rooms. One was a coachman, another a groom and, proof that the twentieth century had arrived in Kilmacud, one was a chauffeur-mechanic. The rest were gardeners. Daly had one gardener, who lived on the estate. The convent seems to have had a general labourer, who had a cottage. In Kilmacud West Verschoyle had a coachman, a yardman and a gardener. The last two were married and were living in two three-roomed cottages on his land. Hamilton had three employees, labourers and yardman, on his farm and Bladen had a gardener.

The picture that emerges is of a small elite on whom the rest of the population were totally dependent for work and housing. And as if to emphasise the divide the elite were 100 per cent Protestant (Church of Ireland), whereas their servants and other employees were almost entirely Catholic. There was an occasional Protestant nurse or governess and one or two maids or gardeners, but only one family employed entirely Protestant domestic staff.

The elites' economic contribution to the locality was modest. None of the servants were from the area and the same seems to be true for the other staff. Local girls were in service in the district but not in Kilmacud. Indeed, the children of the tenants, especially girls, seem to have found it very difficult to obtain work. One assumes that the majority left the area to seek work in the city, Kingstown and other districts or else emigrated. The leading families themselves were non-local and seldom seem to have lasted in the area for more than a generation or two. The fact is that for a century and probably more Kilmacud was peopled by a shifting population, whose roots were elsewhere.

But there was another Kilmacud. Reference was made earlier to the apparent loss of population after 1841 and to the sudden reappearance of forty-nine cottages on Kilmacud Road in the 1911 census. They were very likely Kelly's Cottages and Moore's Terrace shown on the map on the north side of the lower Kilmacud Road. The road is the townland boundary at that point. Strictly speaking, they were not in Kilmacud but in Stillorgan North. No doubt the inhabitants always regarded themselves as Kilmacud people, regardless of the vagaries of surveyors and census-takers. So, who were they?

The cottages were mostly two-room. There was one one-room and a few three-room. Two hundred and fifty people lived in them – fifty-eight men, fifty-nine women, forty-six boys and forty-two girls. All were Catholics except two families, ten individuals in all, who were Church of Ireland. In twenty-three cases household size was from five to eight. In two or three rooms! The details are in Table 4.

Table 4   Kilmacud Household Size, 1911 Census

No. in household	No. of households
0–2	12
3–4	14
5–6	17
7–8	6

Fifty males and thirteen females claimed to be working outside although some added that they were at the time unemployed. The range of occupations is shown in Table 5.

Table 5   Occupations in Kilmacud, 1911 Census

Occupation	Male	Female
House–Owner	1	
Car Owner	1	
Grocer	1	
Bootmaker	1	
Carpenter	1	
Mason	1	
Plumber's apprentice	1	
Factory engineman	1	
Asylum attendant	1	
Telegraph messenger	1	
Golf caddie	2	
Groom	2	
Gardener	8	
Labourer	28	
Church caretaker		1
National school teacher		3
Dressmaker		4
Domestic/Charwoman		5
Total	**50**	**13**

When allowance is made for women in the home, children and old people there was little unemployment. But, plainly, there was under-employment and much of the available work was seasonal and irregular. Most of the work was menial; only four males had a trade and only three were self-employed or had independent means. Their businesses were small and nobody was wealthy. Otherwise they would hardly have been living in overcrowded cottages. For women and girls the outlook was even worse. The three school teachers and four dressmakers were lucky. The former in particular had some hope of breaking out of their environment and making a better life. One of those girls was the carpenter's daughter. The others were daughters of labourers. The asylum attendant, telegraph messenger and plumber's apprentice must all have seemed to their families to be on the way up, not to wealth but to some very modest security. For girls though the outlook was bleak. The little work open to them was mostly low-grade. That situation would not begin to change for many years, not until the advent of factory and office jobs in the thirties.

Notwithstanding their poverty, the level of literacy was high, even assuming some understating in the returns. Only eight men and one woman acknowledged that they could neither read nor write.

Finally, the question arises was there ever a village in Kilmacud? Archer called it a small village in 1801.[31] But he could have had the cottages in mind. Neither D'Alton nor Lewis refer to it as a village. More recently it was described as a non-nucleated settlement, around a relict graveyard.[32] In fact there is no sign of a graveyard or of the remains of a church. It is most unlikely that there was ever a village in the townlands. In the middle ages and probably until the eighteenth century, the district may have been orientated towards Dundrum because of its owners and the manorial structure. But from the eighteenth century it came fully into the orbit of Stillorgan. One impetus for this would have been the uniting of the parishes in the Established Church. Another would have been the development of Stillorgan under its landlords, the Allens. Finally, there was a road to Stillorgan but the upper road to Dundrum does not seem to have been completed until late in the eighteenth century.

In the Catholic organisation Booterstown, Blackrock, Stillorgan and Dundrum were constituted a parish in 1787. It obviously included Kilmacud. It was not until 1865 that a chapel was built in Kilmacud to serve it and Stillorgan. The Sacred Heart Sisters had come to Mount Anville, where they opened a school for poor girls. The existing national school on the Lower Kilmacud Road was adapted and extended to make the chapel and a priest's house was also built. When Dundrum became a separate parish, Kilmacud was a chapel of ease. It became part of the new Mount Merrion parish in 1948 and was made a separate parish in 1964. Subsequently a very large new church was built. The old chapel,

31 Archer, p. 92.   32 F.H.A. Aalen and Kevin Whelan (eds), *Dublin, city and county: from prehistory to the present* (Dublin, 1992), pp. 99, 117.

which was a fine cut-stone building of some character, is now used partly as a funeral parlour and partly as a greengrocer's.

The chapel was dedicated to Saints Lawrence, Brigit and Cuthbert. The last was a mistake for Mochud; in fact the English Cuthbert was the patron in medieval times of Kilmacudrick, near Clondalkin. There used to be a fine three-light stained-glass window behind the altar (it was damaged after the building was deconsecrated). It depicted St Laurence of Rome, St Brigit and St Cuthbert. The new church, however, is dedicated to St Laurence O'Toole. Some believe he gave his name to Stillorgan but this is wrong. The pre-Reformation patron of Stillorgan was Brigit, to whom the present-day Church of Ireland parish church is dedicated.[33] There can be no doubt that the intention was to provide a Catholic church for the Stillorgan area. The chapel and national school failed to become the focus of a chapel village and shops and services remained largely in Stillorgan.

VI. CONCLUSION

Kilmacud's rural vista of small estates and cottages would not survive two world wars and the achievement of national independence. By mid-century the villas had become institutions or had been demolished, local authority housing had largely replaced the cottages and the fields were fast being covered by the semi-detached houses and bungalows of suburbia. The name survives and still defines a territory quite different from a thousand years ago but still a living space.

33 *Alen's Reg.*, p. 256.

APPENDIX

ESTATES AND THEIR OCCUPIERS

Estate	Redesdale	Westbury	St Margaret's	Parson's Green
Year	Occupier	Occupier	Occupier	Occupier
1826	Bourne	Epinase	Hone	Magee
1841	Not Known	Wilson	Mooney	Magee
1851	Whately	Wilson	Mooney	Curley
1861	Not Known	Wilson	Fitzpatrick	Wilson
1864	Clarke	Not Known	Not Known	
1874				Carmelites
1875				Carmelites
1889			Curley	Carmelites
1890	Buckley	Pilkington	Buckley	Carmelites
1901	Farrell	Pilkington	Daly	Carmelites
1911	Trg. School	Pilkington	Daly	Carmelites

Estate	Clonmore	Lakelands	Hazlewood	Woodley
Year	Occupier	Occupier	Occupier	Occupier
1826	Not Known	Boileau	Not Known	Leslie
1841	Fulton	Boileau	Not Known	Leslie
1851	Wilson	Leathley	Not Known	Leslie
1861	Eames	Maunsell	Not Known	
1864	Not Known	Maunsell	Mulvaney	Not Known
1874	Vacant			
1875	Purdon			
1889				
1890	Hopkins	Verschoyle		
1901	Hamilton	Mc Crea	Verschoyle	
1911	Hamilton	Bladen	Verschoyle	

Lacken, county Wicklow

SÉAMAS O MAITIÚ

I

A benchmark a couple of paces away from the only shop in the townland of Lacken informs the passerby that he is 793.5 feet above sea level. This is some five feet higher than the highest benchmark in Roundwood, county Wicklow, which claims to be the highest village in Ireland.[1] This question of altitude is, as we shall see, a crucial determinant in the history of this townland on the western flanks of the Wicklow mountains. The townland of Lacken is in the civil parish of Baltyboys, barony of Talbotstown Lower, county Wicklow and is found on the Wicklow Ordnance Survey sheets 5 and 10. It is just under three miles south-east of Blessington (see map 1).

In 1841 the townland consisted of 1,543 acres, but in 1939/40 it lost 48 per cent of this beneath the waters of the Poulaphouca reservoir.[2] The townland is dominated by the slopes of Black Hill to its east and Lugnagun Great to its north where it rises to over 1,000 feet. Before its partial inundation the townland sloped to the south west as far as the banks of the King's river and Cock brook at 570 feet. It now meets the shores of the reservoir near the 600-ft. contour line. The irregular southern boundary of the townland is formed by the Ballynastockan brook, which is the name of the neighbouring townland to the south; this flows into the Cock brook before joining the King's river. Another stream bisects the townland from the high ground to the east and flows directly into the King's river.

The townland name is a reflection of its all-important altitudinal aspect. The word leacain, when used in a topographical context, means the side of a hill and so aptly describes the townland. Liam Price, the great authority on Wicklow placenames, gives the name 'Lacavalyvary' as at one time applied to the townland. He suggests that it contains a corrupt form of some name beginning with *baile*. He remarks that it is curious that Lacken is the only placename in county Wicklow to which the surveyor of the Down Survey has added the word 'towneland'.[3]

---

1 Many thanks to Mattie Lennon of Kylebeg for pointing this out to me and for sharing his deep knowledge of the area with me. **2** Fiachra Mac Gabhann, 'The water was the sheriff: the land beneath the Poulaphouca reservoir', in Ken Hannigan & William Nolan (eds), *Wicklow: history and society* (Dublin, 1994), p. 931. **3** Liam Price, *The placenames of county Wicklow*, iv (Dublin, 1953), p. 241.

II

The evidence for most prehistoric settlement in Wicklow is found on the western slopes of the great granite massif which divides the county in two. The narrow coastal strip between the mountains and the sea was marshy, heavily wooded in places, and isolated, precluding settlement, while the western slopes were connected to the population centres of the interior.[4]

The core area of settlement in Wicklow is this area of north west Wicklow and south Dublin with their passage graves. Evidence suggests more favourable climatic conditions on this high ground more conducive to habitation than today.[5] Lacken has its fair share of evidence of early settlement. A possible site of a cist burial is found at SMR 95/96 (map 2) and the remains of a passage grave were investigated in 1927.[6]

Despite the notorious difficulty of dating them, a certain continuity of settlement is suggested by the presence of four ring forts, one just outside the townland boundary, all now under the waters of the reservoir (SMR 6, 7, 8 and 9). The three ring forts in Lacken townland were excavated in 1939 prior to their inundation. Finds were meagre and the excavators concluded that they were inhabitation sites of poor families in the early Christian period.[7]

Most early Christian sites in Wicklow are found to the west of the mountains also. In the east of Lacken townland is a small graveyard called Templeboodin (SMR 11), possibly of early Christian origin. Boodin, possibly originally Boadán according to Price, was reputedly to have been a bishop, and local folklore refer to him as such. He is said to have been buried under a slab still pointed to in the graveyard. Some remnants of what is said to be a church are still to be seen in the graveyard. A number of bullauns, locally referred to as 'wart stones' are found in the area, one in a stream just outside the boundary of Templeboodin, and are typically associated with an early Christian site like Templeboodin.

The original name for Templeboodin was Kilbodan and in the middle ages it was one of the possessions of Glendalough. It was commonly associated in medieval records with a neighbouring ecclesiastical site called Kilgarrcon (variously spelt). In 1172 Strongbow granted to Thomas, the nephew of Lawrence O'Toole, the abbey of Glendalough and its possessions; among these were Cellboedain and Cellugarrcon.[8] In 1192 King John granted to 'abbot Thomas the abbey of St Peter of Glendaloughe and its possessions'; among its possessions was 'Kelbodane' and 'Kelugarconn'.[9]

When the dioceses of Glendalough and Dublin were amalgamated, all these Wicklow possessions came into the hands of the archbishop of Dublin, where

---

4 Price, *Placenames*, vii (Dublin, 1967), p. v. **5** Geraldine Stout, 'Wicklow's prehistoric landscape' in Hannigan and Nolan (eds), *Wicklow*, p. 7. **6** 'Note on a rude stone monument at Lacken, county Wicklow' in *JRSAI*, no. 15, vol. 19 (1929), pp. 68–9. **7** 'The excavation of three earthen ring-forts in the Liffey valley', *JRSAI*, vol. 74 (1944), pp. 53–60. **8** C. Mc Neill (ed.), *Archbishop Alen's register* (Dublin, 1950), p. 2. **9** Ibid., p. 21.

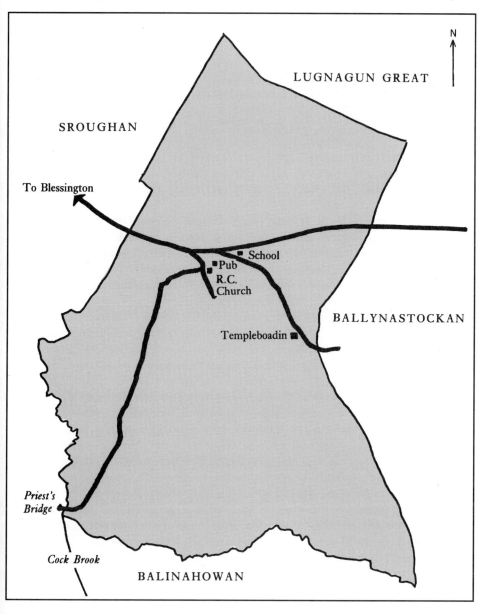

Lacken, county Wicklow, 1908, 1,543 acres

those in west Wicklow became associated with his manor of Ballymore. In the 'names of Feoffees by deed in the tenement of Ballymor' we get a glimpse of the heavily wooded mountains around Kilbodane:

> Hugh Ilim has to him and his heirs for 30 years from 1280 land called Clonmathun in the mountains by Kilarsan with a certain pasture of the wood of Kilgarthane and the adjoining mountains round about, and wood from Kylgarchane to make houses in that land and enclosures for himself, and old wood for firing, by view, however of the forester, for 8*s.* a year paying … ½*d.* of increment. Philip Obery has to him and his heirs all the land Neyuinus Obery, his father, had in Klibodan as one carucate, and thirty acres in Belim Clenedrin to graze his own beasts, two and a half mks.[10]

This Philip Obery was in 1256–66, along with the other tenants of the manor of Ballymore, paying wax-rent; his assessment was a half pound.[11]

By the 1280s this had all changed. The records of the lands of the archdiocese speak of Kilbodan being 'parum aut nichil propter guerram'.[12] The extent of the change is seen in an extent of the manor of Ballymore made by John le Brett in 1326, late sheriff of Dublin; the story is of castles thrown down, granaries burnt and pasture of no value due to war with the Irish. Woods of 40 acres each are recorded in Kilgarthan and Kilbodan, but they were of 'no value, being among the Irish'.[13] Rents had also dried up; 8*l.* 5*s.* in decrease of rent of 3 carucates and 37 acres at Kilbodan, Kilgargan and Balirothan, 'which Henry Gefferey and the Irish held there, waste and in the hands of the Irish'.[14]

Half a mile to the west of Templeboodin is St Boodin's Well (SMR 10). It was much resorted to for cures, especially for warts, but was inundated by the reservoir. The ESB, who are responsible for the reservoir, piped the water from the well to the lake shore and built a new well for the benefit of the devout. It never replaced the old well in the hearts of the local people and when the waters of the artificial lake were very low due to drought in 1975, huge crowds again visited the original well.

Fernand Braudel has seen mountain areas as places of refuge from soldiers and pirates from early times where sometimes the refuge becomes permanent.[15] At the time of the Norman invasion the kings of Ui Fhaelain in north Kildare, centred on Naas, fled to the Wicklow mountains and their descendants, the O'Byrnes have become inseparably associated with the Wicklow mountains.[16] It appears that many of the O'Tooles of Ui Muireadaig, to the south-west of Ui Fhaelain, fled to the mountains in similar fashion and Ui Mail, anglicised as the Glen of Imail, became their stronghold.[17]

---

10 Ibid., p. 189.   11 Ibid., p. 125.   12 John Gilbert (ed.), *Crede Mihi* (Dublin, 1897), p. 142.   13 Ibid., p. 189.   14 Ibid., p. 192.   15 Fernand Braudel, *The Mediterranean and the Mediterranean world in the age of Philip the Second,* i (London, 1972), p. 31.   16 Price, *Placenames,* vii, p. xli.   17 Ibid., pp. xxxvii–xl.

In 1521 Kilbodan was one of nine churches in the area which were regarded as mensal rather than appropriate.[18] Twenty-six years later its advowson, the right of appointing its parish priest, along with that of 'Ballybought', 'Boyseton' and 'Uske', was granted to various members of well-known Pale families such as the St Lawrences, Eustaces, Plunkets, Dillons and Barnwalls.[19]

III

While there is much evidence of prehistoric, early Christian and troubled medieval settlement in west Wicklow the origin of the modern peasant settlement is open to question. It is possible that transhumance or 'booleying' was a precursor to permanent settlement in the area. 'Boley' or 'booley' – a summer milking place – is a common element in placenames in the area, for example, Oldboleys and Woodenboley; it has also been shown that many nearby placenames such as Ballyknockan and Ballynastockan were originally Bolinknockan and Bolenastokane and so once summer milking places.[20]

The placename 'Boleyhemushboy' has been written in a lease of 1663 as James Boys Boley. Boys was a retainer of Gerald, 8th earl of Kildare and was given land in this area some time before 1513. The family name is found in the parish name of Boystown in which Lacken is situated. It is interesting that in the sixteenth century it was the practice on large estates for transhumance to be practised. From 1553 much of the parish of Boystown was in the possession of McDonnells, who were gallowglasses brought from the north by the earl of Kildare to act as his men as justiciar of Ireland.[21]

A map of the 'plott of Killbegg with Booly Ultagh and James Boyds (*recte* Boyce's?) Booly in the parish of Boystown' among the records of the archbishop of Dublin shows that the area was partly wooded still.[22] This would appear to be a remnant of the wood which gave Kilbeg its name. Kilbeg is pronounced *Kylebeg* locally, signifying a wood rather than a church.

The Books of Survey and Distribution classify 402 acres in 'Lackinstowne Land' as profitable and 117 acres as bog. It was described as being in the bishop's lordship.[23] In the Down Survey the lands are divided into lordships reflecting a residual medieval land organisation (map 3).

Being impractical for the archbishop of Dublin to manage his vast but patchy holdings in counties Dublin, Kildare and Wicklow (he owned over 40 per cent of the land of county Dublin) it became the custom to lease them to middlemen,

---

18 *Alen's register*, p. 279. **19** 'Calendar of Christchurch deeds', in *Appendix to twentieth report of the deputy keeper of public records of Ireland*, p. 118. **20** F.H.A. Aalen, 'Transhumance in the Wicklow mountains' in *Ulster Folklife* 10 (1964), p. 70. **21** Liam Price, 'Place-name study as applied to history' in *JRSAI*, vol. lxxix, pp. 26–9. **22** Now in the RCB Library, Churchtown, Dublin. **23** NA, Books of Survey and Distribution, barony of Talbotstown Lower, county Wicklow.

usually members of his own family. The depositions of 1641 show that William Bulkeley, son of the then incumbent, was tenant 'by lease of about 84 years of the lands of Glassnimucky, Ballyknockan and Lacken.'[24] The depositions show that the mountains were a refuge for rebels: Hugh Doran of 'Ballyknockan' and Anthony McDonnell of 'Boysetowne' were branded as rebels in the Tallaght depositions.[25]

The 20-year leases of the archbishop's land were turned into perpetuities by legal chicanery. This was done by renewing them every year. The rents were low but the renewal fine was high. This meant that a new bishop on coming into the see would find a sheaf of 20-year leases on his hands. He could either refuse to renew them and let them run their course but forego most of his income, or go along with the annual custom.

The next detailed map of county Wicklow, Jacob Neville's 1760 map for the grand jury, shows the infrastructural deficiencies of the area. Neither this map nor its revision, surveyed by Neville's nephew A.R. Neville in the 1790s, shows a road through Lacken. A Cobbe estate map and terrier for 1777 give us a closer look at communications in the area; this indicates that there was a road between Blessington and Lacken which was obviously not important enough for the Nevilles to notice. It states in relation to Ballyknockan 'the road throe [*sic*] this farm and the former (the townland of Ballinastockan which lies between Lacken and Ballyknockan) should be presented and made passable for cars which at present only back loads can pass except to Lacken from which is a tolerable road to Blesinton'.[26] The road which was eventually continued to Ballyknockan and beyond runs largely between the 700- and 800-ft. contours dividing the mountain pastures and outfields on the hill from the meadow and cultivated infields in the river valley; the settlement in this classic nucleated cluster landscape lies on the middle ground between the two.

The Blackmore Hill camp was one of four strategic camps held by the west Wicklow and Kildare rebels in 1798.[27] An outcrop of this hill is known as Whelp Rock and Joseph Holt, the rebel leader, refers to it in his memoirs as a place often used by him. Although there is some confusion in Holt's writing about places – he was writing many years later – the Whelp Rock mentioned by him seems to have been that in Lacken townland; he says that it was

> situated in the centre of this dreary and inhospitable district, and was fixed on by me as a position almost unapproachable to the military; here I con-sider myself safe in my own little territory, and by judicious arrangements and, prudent cautions, was enabled to hold out against the united efforts of the King's army and the yeomanry of the country for so long a period.[28]

24 TCD, Ms. 809, deposition of Myles Williams of Tallaght.   **25** William Nolan, 'Society and settlement in the valley of Glenasmole *c*.1750–*c*.1900' in Ken Hannigan and Nolan (eds), *Wicklow*, p. 187.   **26** Cobbe estate rental, NLI, microfilm. pos. 4033.   **27** Thomas Pakenham, *The year of liberty* (London, 1972), p. 184.   **28** T. Crofton Croker (ed.), *The memoirs of Joseph Holt* (London, 1838), p. 139.

He later speaks of being pursued to Whelp Rock by the 89th Regiment together with the Blessington and Donard cavalry.[29] At the time of the Irish folklore Commission schools' survey in the 1930s a well on top of the hill was still known as the 'camp well' and a house used by the soldiers was still pointed out.[30]

Considering its antiquity, Templebodan has very few headstones and none legible of any great age. The earliest, that of John Lawlor, has a date of 1810. Surnames from the early nineteenth century are predictable enough, Browe, Gallagher, Langton, Lawlor, Osborne and Twoomy being recorded. Some of these names would have come from outside the townland.[31]

A Cobbe estate map and terrier of 1777 show ownership of land in Lacken as follows:

> This farm is divided into three holdings and has several fine cabins on each holding and lies about three miles south east of Blessington. The land is mostly good arable meadow and pasture and very capable to receive a great improvement. Lime may be easily brought from Blessington, which is the most proper manure for these lands adjoining Ballystockan; there is good blue marl which is very excellent manure for the dry ground.

Table 1 Land Ownership in Lacken, in 1777

	Acreage	
1. Maurice and Henry Walsh and James Lawler		
(good arable and pasture as now laid out)	270	
Red bog in common.	138	
Templebooden quarter; Widow Mc Daniel		
(good arable and pasture as now laid out).	105	
Course pasture and sheep walk.	90	
Red bog in common.	1	
Red bog in common.	0	(sic)
Templebooden upper quarter; Widow Mc Daniel.	16	
Templebooden upper quarter; Widow Mc Daniel.	10	perch
Templebooden upper quarter; Widow Mc Daniel.	3	
Rocky moory pasture.	104	
Total acreage	**817**	

A possible dispute with the landlord's surveyor is hinted at by a comment appended that 'a man of the name of Parker (?) surveyed this for the tenants and made 839 odd acres'.

---

29 Ibid., p. 146. **30** UCD, Department of Irish folklore, schools collection, Lacken school, county Wicklow. **31** Brian J. Cantwell, *Memorials of the dead*, iv. p. 156 (no date or place).

IV

The Tithe Applotment Books of 1834 list the owners of land in Lacken as Michael Walshe, Patrick Lawlor, the representatives of James Walshe, and Philip Molly and their respective partners. The land was divided into three types: 316 acres of coarse rocky pasture, 356 acres of bog and 9 acres waste or untillable. £6 12s. 10d of the tithe composition went to the rector and £4 6s. 4d. to the vicar. Charles Cobbe was listed as the occupier of Blackmoor hill, 160 acres of 'rocky mountain and pasture'.[32]

A rental of the late 1830s show four owners each paying £64 12s. 3d. Michael Walsh owns one quarter, John Lawler another, James Walsh another and Bryan Browe the last. At this time the great grandson of Cobbe was paying £145 7s. 8d. rent for these mountain lands but a yearly renewal fine of £241 15s.[33]

Michael Walshe seems to have been an influential man as he was known as the King of the Parish and 'The Walshe of the four corners of Lacken'. An instance of the independent and self-sufficient spirit of the mountain people is recorded during the period when Fr Keoghan was parish priest in the early nineteenth century. A dispute arose between two neighbours and Fr Keoghan called a council of the principal men of the parish consisting of James Mahon, Annacarney, James O'Reilly, Garryknock, James Brady, Ballynultagh with Walshe of Lacken presiding. The case was heard with litigants and witnessess and satisfactorily decided.[34]

A renewal of the lease of Charles Cobbe is recorded for the year 1835, the annual rental being £3761 7s. 9d. Although Cobbe noted that these lands 'were a valuable interest which should not be neglected' they were sold off to Baron Henry Joy in 1837.[35] In order to maximise profits one of the first actions of the Joy family was to enclose much of the lower land of Lacken on the expiry of leases in 1839.[36]

As might be expected in this marginal land, the people of the townland of Lacken have been from the beginning of the recording of such matters entirely Catholic. Indeed the whole parish of Boystown or Baltyboys had not a single Protestant residing in it at the time of Archbishop Bulkeley's visitation in 1630. Its market town of Blessington and the good farmland surrounding it have largely been in Protestant hands however. In 1831 it was estimated that the parish of Blessington had 401 Protestants out of a total population of 2,182. Most of these were in the town itself, the administrative core of the estate of the

32 NA, TAB, Baltyboys parish, county Wicklow. 33 Cobbe estate rental (NLI, microfilm pos. 4033). 34 T.M. O'Reilly, 'Blackditches: its traditions and its pastors,' reprinted in Valleymount parish newsletter, Christmas, 1990, pp. 14–17. 35 Marie & John McGuirk, 'Baron Henry Joy, Lord Chief Baron of the Exchequer and Privy Councillor – a Wicklow landowner' in Valleymount parish newsletter, 1995. 36 UCD, Dept. of Irish folklore, Seán O Súilleabháin, 'Scraps of folklore from Lacken, county Wicklow', p. 143; The Poulaphuca survey.

marquis of Downshire, and the surrounding good farmland. The parish of Baltyboys had only 83 Protestants out of a total of 3,235.

Fr Michael Keogan recorded in the parish records observations on the extent of his mountain parish of Boystown: 'the parish is 21 miles long, the two extreme points being Woodend on the north and Oakwood in the south. No estimate can be given of the width because of the hills and mountains'.[37] A chapel existed at Woodend to serve parishioners at that end of the parish but shortly after the arrival of Fr Michael Keogan as parish priest in 1810 he decided to look for a new site for a chapel. Woodend was inconvenient and had been chosen at a time when the chapels were built in remote places. Several sites were suggested for the new chapel and the archbishop of Dublin, Dr Troy, appointed three priests to examine them. Their report states that they were:

> of the opinion that the most intelligent place is in Lacken, as the greatest number of people by far will be accommodated and the subscriptions more cheerfully given, except by very few, besides the almost impossibility of the priest serving the parish with effect if obliged to go to Old Court on Sundays and Holydays, as the road is long and difficult.[38]

A chalice used in Lacken bears the inscription 'presented by Judith Healy, 1802'. The date seems to have been added later. It would appear that the chalice may have come from the old chapel at Woodend. The land for the chapel was given to the parish by Charles Cobbe (see figure 1). The baptismal font used in Lacken bears the date 1441; so it may have come from the old church at Templeboden.[39]

The building of the chapel-of-ease at Lacken was part of the pre-famine wave of chapel-building in the re-invigorated Irish church.[40] The main parish chapel at Valleymount had replaced a penal structure on marginal hilly land around 1803. The site of the new chapel appears to have been a green site one and the name of Valleymount, which appears around the time of the chapel opening, may have been coined for the new site. A typical 'chapel village' developed with school, shop, pub, forge and parish hall following. When the chapel at Lacken was built there may have been a cluster there already. It was common for chapels to be built at a crossroads, as Valleymount was. Lacken was also and, as we have seen, had a hedge-school and national school; James Tipper's forge was there by 1852 and a shop and pub soon followed.[41] Figures collected by the commiss-ioners of public instruction in 1834 show the need for such a chapel of ease. One of the chapels, which was presumably the main chapel at Blackditches, now known as Valleymount, had a usual attendance on the sabbath at Mass of 700 and the other, presumably the chapel of ease at Lacken, had an attendance of 500.[42]

37 Joseph Brady, *In Monavalla* (Dublin), p. 177.   **38** *Valleymount parish newsletter*, Christmas 1990, p. 42.   **39** Ibid., p. 43.   **40** Kevin Whelan, 'The Catholic parish, the Catholic chapel, and village development in Ireland' in *Irish Geography*, vol. xvi (1983), pp. 4–6.   **41** VO, House book, townland of Lacken, county Wicklow.   **42** *Commission of public instruction,*

The small bridge over the Cock brook was known as 'the priest's bridge' and a record of its construction at a total cost of £3 18s. is found in the parish accounts of the Revd Thomas Finney for January 1831. A carpenter and labourer cost £1 8s.; timber for the wooden bridge cost £2 and nails, staples and locks cost 10s.[43] This bridge would have greatly facilitated Finney on his journey from Valleymount to Lacken to celebrate Mass. The inscription 'Finney's Bridge 1828' on a small cut-stone structure over a stream in Lockstown in the parish would indicate that it was also built by the Father Finney who was parish priest from 1827 to 1833. As was common in pre-famine times a number of priests in the parish were involved in landownership and farming, and one even owned a public house which caused controversy; as we have seen the Revd Finney, at least, was involved in bridge-construction also.

In Griffith's *Valuation* the 1543 acres of the townland were valued at only £367 12s., which represents a value of less than 5s. an acre. The quality of the land, on which the livelihood of the community of Lacken largely rested, was well characterised by the Valuation Office surveyors who compiled the field and perambulation books for the district. The 1842 field book describes the land of Lacken as largely 'boggy, heathy pastures with course grass', with the adjectives 'sour' and 'cold' also prominent, but it also had some 'detached pieces of rocky arable'.[44]

Thomas Mulrenin of the Valuation Office visited Lacken in November and December 1852. He found that all the various holdings were devoted to a mixture of pasture and tillage. Not a single tenant had a lease, but all held their property at will. Lady Joy herself held over two hundred acres of mountain pasture and let it to the tenants of the townland at £10 a year. Ninety acres of turbary were also let by her on a yearly basis and it brought in £30 annually. However, it was not fully let and was capable of earning a further £15 a year. The tenants themselves used the greater part of the turf cut but an amount to the value of £10 was sold to outsiders in 1852. Land was being reclaimed from the hill and Thomas Broe had twelve acres of such land recently brought into cultivation. As well as their rent, many tenants shouldered a double tax burden. Those holding land over, in most cases, about seven acres had to pay county cess and poor rate, at the ratio of about two to one. For instance, Joseph Commins paid 16s. 3d. cess and 8s. 1d. poor rate on his twenty-four acres.[45]

Ireland, diocese of Dublin, parish of Baltyboys, p. 86b. **43** Parish accounts held in the presbytery, Valleymount, county Wicklow.   **44** VO, Field book, parish of Boystown, barony of Talbotstown Lower, county Wicklow, pp. 41–41.   **45** VO, Perambulation book, parish of Boystown, barony of Talbotstown Lower, county Wicklow, pp. 53–62.

Figure 1 Landholding in Lacken in 1854.

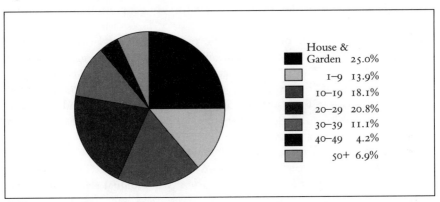

	House &	
■	Garden	25.0%
▨	1–9	13.9%
■	10–19	18.1%
▦	20–29	20.8%
▧	30–39	11.1%
■	40–49	4.2%
▨	50+	6.9%

Due to changed post-famine social conditions and pressure from a more comm-ercialised agricultural system the practice of sub-division of land was in decline at the time of Griffith's *Valuation*. However, it is possible to see evidence of it by noting contiguous holdings of land occupied by people with the same surname.[46] In Lacken five cases of this occur involving the Walsh, Broe, Lawler families and the Carrolls in two separate places.

There is very little movement of new names into the townland. Less than twenty holdings of land changed surname occupier in the period from the primary valuation to the turn of the century. Without a detailed look at parish records it is not possible to say how many of these represent marriage:

Table 2 Changes in surnames of occupiers based on Cancelled Books in VO.

1. Walshe > Carroll 1869	9. Carroll > Zeller★ (1893)
2. Walshe > Meyley★ (1869) > Balfe (1882)	10. Walshe > Kearns > (1894)
3. Reade > McDonald 1869	11. Carroll > Walshe (1905)
4. Carroll > Farrell 1866	12. Kearns > Zeller★ (1896)
5. Browne > Lawler > Walsh 1882	13. Lawler > Maguire★ (1894)
6. Mackey > Miley★ (1879)	14. Anderson > Miley★ 1905
7. McMahon > Sivell (1883)	15. Kelly > Cullen (1888)
8. Bermingham > Cummins (1881)	16. Farley > Byrne (1888) > McDonald (1901)

★ represents surname not in Primary Valuation

46 William J. Smith, 'Landholding changes, kinship networks and class transformation in rural Ireland: a case study from Co. Tipperary' in *Irish Geography*, vol. xvi (1983), p. 21.

This represents four new surnames in 48 changes of occupancy in a fifty-year period; two of the surnames (Miley and Kearns) are common in neighbouring townlands.

A number of tenants held more than one piece of land and the general pattern was that one plot was on the hill above the road and another in the valley near the river. The 'ladder landscape' pattern was the general layout, with the holding running in long strips down the hill. This was to ensure that each holding had access to the commonage on the hill, road frontage and a mixture of high land and low land. Some of these strips could be ridiculously long and narrow. The field of Mary Brown, comprising 2 acres, 1 rood and 25 perches, was approximately 90 yards wide but nearly a quarter of a mile long![47]

Table Two shows a typical population decline in the townland over the nineteenth and early twentieth centuries with an eventual stabilising of the household size to 4.8 from 1891.

Table 3   Lacken Population & Housing, 1841–1911

Year	Population	Houses	Persons per house
1841	550	82	6.7
1851	483	78	6.2
1861	440	73	6.0
1871	369	68	5.4
1881	345	70	4.9
1891	315	66	4.8
1901	285	61	4.8
1911	233	58	4.8

These figures are further illustrated in Figure 2.

47 VO, Valuation map, Lacken, county Wicklow.

Figure 2 Lacken Population & Housing, 1841–1911

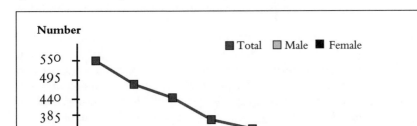

On 2 June 1867 the townland of Lacken was sold by auction in the Landed Estates Court and bought by Elizabeth Smith of Baltyboys. The Smith family owned the contiguous estate of Baltyboys; Elizabeth is known for the detailed journal she has left behind of the famine years in west Wicklow.[48]

Fifty seven holdings were recorded in the townland at the time of the sale and the tenants were described as being 'solvent and respectable'.[49]

V

When Elizabeth Smith obtained possession, one of the first things she did was to set up a school there because, as she explained to the Board of Education, 'the people of the locality are proverbially rude and ignorant'.[50] She and Lord Waterford, another landowner in the area, provided one third of the cost and they applied to the board for the remainder. While she expected 100 males and 60 females to enroll, she envisaged an average daily attendance of 30 and 20 respectively. Smith had, in 1834, built a school in Baltyboys, which catered for girls and small infants. An indication of the primitive nature of the infrastructure

48 Dermot James & Séamas Ó Maitiú (eds), *The Wicklow world of Elizabeth Smith* (Dublin, 1996). **49** NA, Landed Estates Court, rental, map and particulars of Lacken, county Wicklow, 1867. **50** NA, ED 1/97 no. 30, Lacken school, county Wicklow.

in the area is illustrated by her remark in her application for the Lacken school; she stated that it was intended to build small bridges near the King's river to enable the older boys in Baltyboys to attend the school in Lacken.

Her school did not inaugurate education in Lacken as it replaced a 'wretched hedge school' (as she called it) which was nearby and whose location was still remembered at the time of the schools' folklore project in the 1930s. In 1834 there were seven hedge schools in the parish catering for 210 children. The one at Lacken was conducted by a Peter McNally. It was built of stone and mud and was thatched and cost between £5 and £10 to build. McNally taught 11 males and 9 females and received £8 10s. per year for his exertions together with an acre of land and grazing for a cow.[51] It would appear that the pay school had a long life in Lacken and would seem to have had clerical backing. The parish priest, Fr Arthur Germaine, rented a house in Lacken in the 1860s and this was later used as a schoolhouse.[52] There is no apparent reason why Fr Germaine would need a house there for himself and the most likely explanation is that it was for the use of the hedge school master. There is much evidence in the journal of Elizabeth Smith that Fr Germaine was a supporter of the numerous pay schools in the parish. Mrs Smith, in her application for her own school, recommended that 'a commodious and tasteful building should be erected as a model for other school houses as that are much required in the neighbourhood'. This was carried out and the school is a fine structure of the local granite bearing an inscription dedicated to the indefatigable Mrs Smith.

John McDerby, the principal, and Lizzie McDerby were joined by an assistant teacher in 1873. They had 80 males and 55 females on the roll at this stage.[53] McDerby enters the pages of the journal of Elizabeth Smith, which she kept from 1840 to the end of her life and which provide such an insight into the social life of this area in the famine years. He had taken over her school in Baltyboys in 1849. He was a native of Athy and had himself attended a national school and been trained in the model school in Marlborough Street. At this time he was courting a young schoolteacher and no doubt she is the present Lizzie McDerby.[54] In 1875 we find Peter and Kate Jones in charge of the school with no assistant teacher, as the number on the roll had dropped to 69 males and 58 females. The original intention of having a largely male school had been eroded over the years.[55]

Elizabeth Smith became the first resident landlord to obtain possession of Lacken. Long before this her interest in such a place was connected to the political ambitions of her husband, Colonel Henry Smith, who was nominated for the election of guardians to the Naas Poor Law Union in 1840. Mrs Smith reports in her journal that her husband refused to canvass 'some respectable farmer in Lacken' as they knew that his name had gone forward and that was

51 Commission of public instruction, op. cit.   52 VO, Cancelled books, Lacken, county Wicklow.   53 NA, ED 1/97 no. 45, Lacken school, county Wicklow.   54 Patricia Pelly & Andrew Tod (eds), The highland lady in Ireland (Edinburgh, 1991), pp. 460–2.   55 NA, ED 1/97 no. 49, Lacken school, county Wicklow.

enough; his attitude was 'if the blackguards elect him he will do his best for them, but he won't solicit one of their most sweet voices'. Not surprisingly Smith lost the election. The fact that this part of west Wicklow was placed in the Naas Union in neighbouring county Kildare was a recognition of the fact that the human unit here encompassed both east Kildare and west Wicklow.

Fourteen occupations were listed in the townland in 1901; these were:

Farmer	*Shepherd*	*Stonecutter*
Farm labourer	*Schoolteacher*	*Housekeeper*
Mason	*Publican*	*Quarryman*
Blacksmith	*Barmaid*	*Labourer*
Carrier	*Trader*	

VI

Only a tiny proportion of the inhabitants of the townland had been born outside of county Wicklow in 1901. The largest number were farm servants or farm labourers. Three had come from county Dublin and two from Queen's county. Four nurse children, three of them with the one family, had come from county Kildare. Four of one family had been born in Dublin city, but whether the family had moved from there or the mother had been in one of its maternity hospitals for her births is not known. In the Zeller household, the wife was from Dublin and two of the children had been born in England. The single Protestant in the townland was the trader from Sierra Leone who was staying in Zeller's hotel.[56]

The tradition of the area surrounding Lacken being a place of refuge continued up to the time of the War of Independence and Civil War. When 160 republican prisoners escaped from Newbridge barracks on the night of 14 October 1922, a group of them made for west Wicklow and continued to fight the Free State forces in the hills for another six months.[57] The leader of this band was Neil 'Plunkett' O'Boyle from Donegal, and one of the safe houses where he and his men often stayed was that of Christopher and Mary Lambert, schoolteachers in Lacken school. Many barracks and big houses continued to be attacked by O'Boyle's men until he was surrounded and shot dead by Free State soldiers in nearby Knocknadruse in May 1923.[58]

Lambert is remembered in the area as being instrumental in obtaining employment for the boys of Lacken school. A number of them obtained employment in Maynooth and Clongowes Wood colleges in the kitchens and as cleaners. He found employment for others as barmen in Dublin and some of them went on to become successful businessmen.[59]

56 NA, Census returns, Lacken, county Wicklow.   **57** Pádraig Ó Baoill, *Óglach na Rossan: Niall Pluincéad Ó Baoighill* (Baile Átha Cliath, 1994), p. 252.   **58** Ibid., p. 291.
59 Mrs White, 'Lacken' in *Valleymount parish newsletter* (Christmas, 1990), p. 46.

The hotel had been much frequented by fishermen and fowlers and was a stopping-off point for the hillmen on their way to the fair in Blessington; it was owned by the Walsh family. Mary Walsh went to England and met and married a Swiss sea-captain – which seems a contradiction in terms – in Aintree, Liverpool. Alfred Zeller rose in the public life of the area becoming chairman of Wicklow County Council and chairman of the Naas No. 2 Rural District Council, whose area included Lacken.

A number of field names have been recorded in the townland. These are: Mooneenowly, Coolyamoon, Gornamona, the Russawn, Farnathray, Cruthacreeld, Kishnagollyeen, Coolree, The Clorenawn (a place where unbaptised children were buried), Gornathroe (there is a mass rock in this field), The Lacken Faw (the south-west part of Lacken).[60]

The only two commercial establishments in Lacken are a shop and Zeller's pub. Zeller's was described by T.M. O'Reilly in 1906. It had recently been erected as a Highland Hotel;

> the Hotel – a pretty building in the Swiss style – stands in its own grounds, from which a splendid view of the adjacent mountains is obtainable. The interior is up to the appearance of the exterior, as the place is very handsomely and artistically furnished with old Chippendale of considerable value, while it contains as well some very good pictures and curios of every description, including old china, Wedgewood ware, Japanese placques, West African work etc.[61]

The landlord era came to an end in Lacken, as it did in much else of Ireland under the provisions of the Wyndham land act (1903) when Elizabeth G. Stannus, wife of Capt. Stannus, a grandson of Elizabeth Smith, vested the townland in the Land Commission, who in turn vested it in some forty tenants.[62] The family left for England in 1905, ending a family association with the west Wicklow area going back to the early 1700s. Ninette de Valois, the stage and pen name of Edris Stannus, daughter of Elizabeth Stannus, has left a vivid account, as seen through a child's eye's, of an Anglo-Irish family departing from its ancestral home

> As a ripple on a quiet stream, we children began to realize that life was preparing for a big change for us. Our parents and grandmother spoke more often of England; we began to hear something of the needs of big houses, and the necessity of only rich people living in them. Servants threw out hints, the younger ones spoke of emigration and the older ones were seen to weep.[63]

60 Michael O'Connor, 'Local placenames in west Wicklow' in *JRSAI*, vol. 68 (1938), p. 160. 61 T.M. O'Reilly, *Guide to tourists and sportsmen visiting Blessington and its environments* (Naas, 1906). 62 E.C. 5649, Land Commission Office, Dublin. 63 Ninette de Valois, *Come dance with me* (second edition, Dublin, 1992, p. 17).

On the morning of 3 March 1940 at 10 a.m. the sluice gate at the new dam at Poulaphuca was dropped and the history of Lacken and all the surrounding townlands again changed forever. Six thousand acres stretching in extent for nine miles were flooded to roughly the 600-ft. contour to provide electricity and water for Dublin.[64] Lacken lost 15 households and 36 holdings of land.[65] Most of those removed from Lacken resettled on farms bought with compensation money nearby in county Wicklow or county Kildare.[66] This massive state scheme took place at a time when the sensibilities of ordinary people did not weigh much against a glamorous state enterprise. Families were compulsorily moved from the low-lying area of Lacken bottoms. Many received news of the scheme with disbelief and retained hope of remaining on their ancestral patch until the waters were literally lapping around them. The scheme was deeply resented by the local people, who saw it tear the heart out of their parish and lose neighbours who had lived with them for generations. Bitterness against the reservoir was reinforced tragically when two local boys, Alfie Zeller and Tommy McDonald, were drowned in its waters.[67]

---

64 *Valleymount parish newsletter* (Christmas, 1990).   **65** Mac Gabhann, 'The water was the sheriff', p. 931.   **66** Ibid., p. 948.   **67** Mrs White, Knockerin, 'Lacken' in *Valleymount parish newsletter* (Christmas, 1990).

Index

Act of Explanation 13
Act of Settlement 13
Addie, John 98
Aldworth, Richard 20, 23, 29, 31, 39
Alen, Archbishop, John 189
Alen's Register 189
Aleyn, Walter 48
Allen Family, Stillorgan 191, 200
Allingham, William 182
America 85, 87, 155, 179, 181, 184
Anderson, John 22
Anglesey, Marquis 46
Annals of Four Masters 97
Arabin, Lt.-Col. John 190
Archbold, Edward 190
Archbold, James 190
Archbold, John 190
Archbold, Maurice 190
Archbold, Patrick 190
Archbold, Richard, duke of York
    190, 191
Archbold Family 190
Arthur, John 104
Arthur, Thomas 105, 107, 108
Aylmer, Charles 52
Aylmer, George 50, 51
Aylmer, Michael 52, 54, 55
Aylmer, Richard 50, 51
Aylmer, Thomas 51
Aylmer Family 43

Baker, Richard 20
Ballesky, Anne 123
Ballesty, Michael 123, 128
Ballinger, William 112
Ballyshannon Castle 167
Ballyshannon Fishery 173, 182
Ballyshannon Herald 173
Barlow, Richard 191

Barnwall Family 207
Bermingham, Bridget 79, 81
Bermingham, Ellen 81
Bermingham, Thomas 150, 151
Bianconi, car 22
Bindon, David 103
Bindon, Nicholas 103
Birne, Morgan 191
Biron, James 145, 146
Biron, Revd Edward 146
Biron, Robert 146
Bladen, Mr 198
Blake, John 21
Blessington Cavalry 208
Bligh, Thomas, Major General 144
Blood Family 103
Blundell, Revd Dixie 49
Blundo, William 61
Board of First Fruits 39
Boggan, Sarah 60
Boggan, John 58
Bond, John 20
Bond Family 21, 22
Book of Armagh 10
Book of Fermoy 18
Book of Lismore 16
Books of Survey and Distribution 13, 19, 51
Boyce, Alison 189
Boyce, Thomas 189
Boyds, James 207
Bradford, John 191
Brady, James 210
Braudel, Ferdinand 206
Brazier, Kilner 25
Brian Boru 114
Bridewell School 155, 156
Brien, Charles 27
Broning, John 48
Bronx, U.S.A. 80

Brown, Mary 214
Browne, Bryan 210
Browne, Revd Thomas 78
Browne Family 209, 213
Buckley, William 194
Bulkeley, Archbishop 189, 210
Bulkeley, William 208
Bunloe, George 41
Burke, Catherine 158
Burke, Michael 79
Burns, Michael 26
Burns, William 26
Butler, Matilda 50
Butler, Pierce 98, 99
Butler, Sir Theobold 50
Byrne, Ann 145
Byrne, Peter 63

Canada 180
Carey, Mary 123
Carmelite Friary 49–50
Carmelite Nuns 194, 197
Carney Family 125
Carroll Family 213
Caughlin, John 37
Caulter, Henry 77
Clongowes Wood College 217
Charles II, King 191
Cheshire 190
Church of Ireland 76
cholera 171
Cistercians 166
Clare election 102
Clarke, Anne 173
Clarke, Thomas 123
CLARE
    Balingaddy East 99, 101
    Ballycullinan 93, 96, 105, 111, 112
    Ballycullinan Lake 94, 111
    Bushy Park 104
    Clonroad 101
    Cloonagh 105
    Cloonfeaghra 94, 97, 108, 109

CLARE (*contd.*)
    Cooga 96, 97, 98, 99, 100, 101, 105,
        107, 108
    Corofin 99, 103, 105, 111, 112
    Craugaunboy 103
    Cregmoher 97, 98, 108, 109
    Drumcavan 11, 93–112 *passim*
    Drumfinglas 96, 97
    Dysert O'Dea 93, 105, 106
    Errinagh Lake 112
    Inchiquin barony 93, 96
    Kilkee 111
    Kilkee West 96, 97, 98, 100, 105,
        107, 108, 109
    Killeen 97, 100
    Kilnamona Parish 98
    Kilrush 104
    Lehinch 111
    Liscannor 99
    Mahonburg 9
    Miltown Malbay 111
    Quin 101
    Rath Parish 93, 97, 105
    Ruan 102, 105, 106, 111, 112
    Ruan Parish 93, 94, 105
    Shanvalley Lough 94, 100, 101,
        105, 111
    Spancilhill 101
    Tubber 101
Cleary, John 123
Clonbrock, Lord Robert 145, 150
Cloncurry, Lady 53
Cloncurry, Lord 52, 53, 56, 57, 58, 62, 68
Cloncurry, Lord Valetine 46, 54, 62
Clonfert diocese 142
Coates, Arthur 53
Coates, Sam 54, 55
Cobbe, Charles 210, 211
Cobbe Estate 208, 209
Cogan, Fr Anthony 113
Coghlan, Jerry 27
Colgu, Abbot of Cloncurry 44, 47
collops 169

Colman, Abbot, Bp 88
Commins, Joseph 212
Comyne, John 98
Condon, Dr James 185
Condon Family 19
Condons and Clangibbon Barony 18,
   19, 31
Congested District Boards 76, 79, 86
Connacht, Composition of 96
Connell, Paul 11
Conolly Estate 173, 184
Conroy, Charles 27
Conroy, F. 37
Cooke, Sir Charles 144
Cooney, Catherine 182
Cooney, William 178, 182
Cooney Family 182
Coppinger, Thomas 19
Corcoran, Mark 80
CORK
   Aghacross 17, 38
   Annes Grove 20
   Ballyvoddy 14, 16, 19, 20, 24, 25,
      32, 33, 37, 38
   Ballyenahan 25
   Ballyhooly 22
   Ballyhoura Mts 18
   Ballynahalisk 11, 14–42 *passim*
   Bandon 37
   Bowenscourt 31, 40
   Carrigleagh 14
   Carrigdownane 14, 20, 37, 38, 39
   Castletown Roche 22
   Cloyne 71
   Cork 9
   Cullenagh 25
   Derriordane 9
   Derrynabourky 9
   Derryvillane 32
   Farahy 21, 31, 40
   Fermoy 14, 18, 22, 23, 29, 30
   Fermoy Barony 19, 31
   Funcheon River 14, 16, 17, 23, 25, 31
   Galtee Mts 18

CORK (*contd.*)
   Glanmire 23
   Glanworth 22
   Kildorrery 14, 19, 21, 40, 28, 30,
      32, 33, 38
   Kinsale 167
   Labbamolaga 17
   Lackybrack 21
   Lisnagourneen 14, 32
   Mallow 3, 22
   Millstreet 20
   Mitchelstown 18, 22
   Munster Blackwater 14, 18
   Nagle Mts 18
   Nathlash 14, 16, 17, 19, 22, 24, 35,
      37, 38, 39, 40
   Oldcastletown 25
   Queenstown 41
   Ransborough 14, 25
   Rockmills 16, 20, 21, 23, 24, 25, 26,
      28, 29, 38, 39, 40, 41, 42
   Scart 25, 38
   Shanballymore 22
   Templemolaga 17, 37
Corley, Dominick 156
Cormick, John 49
Crannagh River 141
Crede Mihi 189
Crisham, Sabina 81
Crisham, Peter 80
Cronin, Denis 11
Cronin, Maurice 27
Cronin Family 36, 37
Cross River 141
Cruise, Walter 189
Cullinan, Andrew 80
Cullinan, John 75
Cullinan, Walter 80
Curtin, Constance 105, 106, 107
Curtin Family 36
Curtis, Thomas 106
Cusack, Robert 48

Dal Meisin Corb 188
Daly, Michael 177, 178

Daly, John 178
Daly, Margaret 182
Daly, Owen 178
Daly Family 176, 177, 182, 184
Daly Family (Kilmacud House) 198
Dargan, Michael 182
Davenport, Mary 99
Davitt, Michael 111
Dawson, Bridget 182
Dawson, Catherine 58
Dawson, Edward 178
Dawson, Hugh 177, 178
Dawson, James 60
Dawson, Lizzie 60
Dawson Family 182
Day, Christianna 74
Day, Elizabeth 74, 75
Day, Frances Benmina 76
Day, Isabella 74, 75
Day, John 74, 75
Day, Dr John, Robert 76
Day, Robert 74, 76
Day, William 74, 75
Day, Dr William 76
de Beaumount, Gustave 77
de Burgh, Richard, Earl of Ulster 116
de Clare, Richard 93, 105
de Coquebert, Charles 52
de Hereford, Adam 50
de Hereford, Stephen 50
de Hereford Family 48
de Lacy, Hugh 114
de Lacy, Walter 116
de Ridelsford, Walter 188
de Ridelsford Family 188, 189
de Sandford, John
de Tocqueville, Alex 77
de Valois, Ninette 218
de Verdon, Sir Thomas 116
Degnan, Luke 154
Degnan, Thomas 154
Delaney, Edward Revd 23
Devon Commission 74, 83

Diegnan, John 154
Diegnan, Thady 154
Dignum, Christopher 123
Dillion, Daniel 112
Dillon, Luke 144
Dillon, Richard 144
Dillon, Robert 144
Dillon, Thomas 144
Dillon Family 148, 149, 160, 207
Dineen, Daniel 37
Dixon, Christopher 53
Dixon, Edward 49
Dixon, Mathew 59
Dixon, William 49
Doherty, Miss 182
Donard Cavalry 209
Donegan, Christopher 54, 55
Doneraile, Lord 23
Donnellan, James 86, 87
Donnellan, Patrick 155
Donnellan, Thomas 81, 155
DONEGAL
  Balalt 175
  Ballintra 169, 174
  Ballymacaward 164, 166, 167, 168,
    169, 175
  Ballyshannon 167, 170, 171, 174,
    175, 180, 184
  Bunatroohan 164, 173, 175, 176,
    182, 183, 184
  Coghlan's Hill 177
  Coolcolly 164, 173, 177
  Creevy 168, 169, 178, 182, 183
  Culbeg 175
  Donegal 217
  Donegal Bay 183
  Erne River 164, 169, 172, 184
  Fern's Hill 177, 180
  Halifax 164, 177, 180
  Inver Point 183
  Kilbarron, Parish 166, 167, 168,
    171, 174
  Kildoney 11, 164–85 *passim*

DONEGAL (*contd.*)
  Kildoney Glebe 166, 168, 171, 174, 176
  Kildoney Oldtown 168, 177
  Lough Mor 164, 169, 177
  Lugmore 164, 169, 177
  Magherabui 164, 169, 177
  Mullaghmore 173, 182, 183
  Ranny 169, 179
  Rossnowlagh 183
  rundale 170
  Scotland 180, 181
  St John's Point 182, 183
  Teelin Bay
  Tonragee 170
  Wardstown Castle 174
Doogan, John 182
Doogan Family 177
Doran, Edward 54, 55
Dorian, Edward 182
Dorian, Hugh 208
Dorrian, Hannagh 182
Dorrian, Hugh 182, 208
Dorrian, Mary 182
Dorrian Family 182
Douglass, Revd Archibald 49
Dowell, Philip 144
Dowlan, Roger 150
Dowlan, Thomas 150
Dowllan Families 148, 149, 154
Down Survey 13
Downshire, Marquis of 211
Doyle, Thomas 191
Doyle Family 148, 149
DUBLIN
  Artane, 116
  Blackrock 186, 200
  Booterstown 189, 200
  Callary 186
  Churchtown 194
  Clondalkin 201
  Clonskeagh 186
  Clontarf 114

DUBLIN (*contd.*)
  Darley's Brewery, Stillorgan 196
  Donnybrook 189
  Dublin 9, 48, 53
  Dun Laoghaire 126
  Dundrum 186, 189, 190, 193, 200
  Goatstown 186, 193
  Harcourt St 193
  Huntstown 9
  Kilmacud 11, 186–202 *passim*
  Kilmacudric 201
  Kingstown 62, 198
  Lakelands 186
  Lakelands Estate 192, 198
  Luttrellstown 9
  Marlborough Street 216
  Merrion Square 189
  Milltown 186
  Mount Anville 186, 200
  Mount Merrion 186, 189, 190, 191
  Mulchanstown 186
  Newcastle Lyons 52, 57
  Newtown Park 197
  Ranelagh 186
  Rathdown, barony 188, 197
  Rathmines 75
  Ringsend 189
  Sandymount 189
  St Thomas' Abbey 116
  Stillorgan 186, 188, 189, 190, 191, 193, 197, 199, 200
  Stillorgan Park 198
  Terenure 69
  Trinity College Dublin 106
  Waltersland 186
  Warrenstown 9
  Westbury 198
Drummartin 186
Dublin, Diocese 204
Dublin Southeastern Railway 186
Duggan, William 182
Duncan, Alexander 182
Duncan Family 177, 180

Dunn, Bridget 54
Dunne, Catherine 64
Dunne, Joseph 64

eels 78, 86
Egan, Revd Andrew 49
Elphin 12
Elphin Diocese 142
Encumbered Estates Court 145, 146
Erne Fishing Company 184
Eustace Family 207
Evans, William 128, 129

Faley, Luke 81
Fallon, Daniel 145, 146, 150
Fallon, John 150
Fallon, Mary 145
Fallon, Mathias 150
Fallon, Thomas 155, 159
Fallon Families 148, 149, 154
Feeney, Christina 59
Feeney, John 59
Feeney, Patrick 59
FERMANAGH
    Belleek 170, 173
    Castle Caldwell 170
Feidhlimidh, King of Cashel 44
Fenians 184
Finnegan Family 126
Finney, Revd Thomas 212
fishing 172, 182
Fitzgerald, Catherine 145
Fitzgerald, George 145
Fitznicholas, John 50
Fitznicholas, Ralph 50
Fitzpatrick, Patrick 27
Fitzwilliam, Viscount 191
Fitzwilliam Family 189, 198
Flammock Family 180
Flanagan, James 100
Flax Field 46
Fleming, John 81
Fleming Family 18

Folliott, Commander 167
Ford, Catherine 80
Ford, Margaret 79, 80
Forde, Honoria 83
Forde, Jeremiah 83
Forde, Mary 83
Foster, Andrew 50
Foster, Edward 50, 51
Fox, James 32
France 53, 188
Franks, Mansfield, Mary 31
Franks, Mansfield, Thomas 31, 32
Fraser, Capt. 50
Frazier Family 32

Gacquin, William 11, 12
Gallagher Family 209
Garland Sunday 157
GALWAY
    Ballybane 74
    Carantanlas 81
    Clare River 69, 72, 75, 78, 82
    Clashroe 70
    Clonbrock 144
    Clonfert 71
    Clonmore House 194
    Cloonbrictan 144
    Cloonfush 11, 12, 69–92 *passim*
    Galway 75
    Connemara 70
    Headford 77
    Kilbannon 71, 73, 74
    Killaunty 70, 73, 74
    Kilmore 74, 81
    Lissavelly 81
    Newpark 74
    Tuam 11, 69, 70, 73, 77, 79, 84, 141
Galway Bay 62
Gavagan, Edward 129
Gavagan Family 129
Gefferey, Henry 206
Geraghty, John 55, 56
Germaine, Fr Arthur 216

Gettins, John 180
Gillen, Hugh 178
Gillen, Michael 178
Gillen, William 173, 178
Gillespie, Grace 177, 178
Gillespie Family 170, 177
Gillespie, Ned 177, 178
Gilligan, Thomas 81
Gladstone, William 75, 184
Glass, John 145
Gleatowe, Thomas 144
Glennon, Bartle 155
Golburne, Christopher 48
Goold, William 20, 21
Gould Family 37
Grace, John 37
Grady, James 27
Graham, Redmond 20
Graney Convent 189
Green, Revd W.S. 183
Gregg Family 198
Grier Family 148, 149
Griffith, Richard 12
Gurhy, Pat 156
Gurhy, Thomas 150, 156
Gurhy, William 156
Gurhy Families 148, 149, 154, 156

Halahan, Murty 106, 107
Haly, Revd Francis 64
Haly, Luke 53
Hamilton, Alexander 171
Hamilton Family 198
Hamrock, Bridget 159
Hamrock, Patrick 159
Hand Family 186
Hannin, Daniel 27
Hanrahan, John 111
Hanrahan, Thomas 107, 112
Harbrig Thomas 51
Hare, William 56
Harmer, Capt. William 19, 20
Harris Family 60

Hart, Edward 55
Hayes, Frank 11
Hayes, Laurence 107
Hazelwood Estate 194, 198
Healy, Judith 211
Hector, James 172, 173
Hennessy, F. 36
Hewelson, Catherine 145
Hickey, Donagh 100
Higgins, John 101
Higgins, Matthew 83
Higgins, Patrick 155
Higgins, Thomas 83, 155
Highland Hotel 218
Hogan, Edmund 99, 102, 104
Hogan, Honara 98
Hogan, Patrick 97, 98
Hollywood, Elizabeth 116
Hollywood, Robert 116
Holt, Joseph 208
Holton, Karina 11, 12
Hughes, Bartholomew 144, 146
Hughes, Terrence 144

Ilim, Hugh 206
Inchiquin, Earl 98
Irish Land Commission 12, 112, 146, 185
Irish Language 35
Irish Training School of Domestic
        Economy 197
Ivers, Henry 98, 99

Jackson, Joseph 37
Jones, Kate 216
Jones, Peter 216
Joy, Baron Henry 210
Joyce, John 101

Keaghan, Fr 210
Kearney, Dennis 21
Kearney, James 20
Kearney, Mary 20
Kearney, Michael 32

Kearney, Thomas 54, 55, 56, 58
Kearney Family 36, 37
Kearney's Well 38
Kearns Family 214
Keating, Geoffrey 43
Keaugh Family 148, 149
Keefe, David 27
Keefe, William 100
Keefe Family 36
Keenan, Michael 182
Keenan Family 182
Kein Family 148, 149
Kelliher, Michael 106, 107
Kelly, Archbishop of Tuam 78
Kelly, Bryan 150, 156
Kelly, Frank 150, 156
Kelly, Fr James 129
Kelly, John 155
Kelly, Mary 158, 159
Kelly, Michael 81
Kelly, Pat 150
Kelly, Thomas 156
Kelly Families 58, 148, 149, 154
Kelly's Cottages 198
Kenna, Thomas 56
Keogan, Fr Michael 211
Keogh, Laurence 145
KERRY
    Ardfert 71
    Tralee 75
Kiernan, Simon 127
Kildare Diocese
Kildare, Gerald, 8th earl, 207
Kildare rebels 208
Kildare Street Society 64
KILDARE
    Athy 53
    Ballinakill 43, 46, 53, 54, 55, 56, 57,
        65
    Ballycahon 55
    Ballycarn River 63
    Ballyvoneen 43, 46, 53, 54, 55, 56,
        57, 65

KILDARE (*contd.*)
    Cappagh 55, 62, 65
    Carbury 53
    Cloncurry 11, 12, 43–68 *passim*
    Cloncurry Castle 51
    Donadea 59
    Grand Canal 62
    Grange 55
    Hortland 63
    Johnstownbridge 63
    Kilbrook 56, 57, 58, 63
    Kilcock 56, 61, 63
    Liffey 43
    Naas 53, 206, 216, 218
    Newbridge 217
    Newtown 59, 64, 65,
    Royal Canal 11, 56, 82
Kilgarriff, John 79
Kilkenny 49
Killaloe, Bishop 99
Killian, James 124
Killian, Mary 122
Killian Family 125
Kilmacud House 192, 198
Kilmacud Manor 194, 197
Kilroy, Hugh 56
King, George 145, 152, 154
Kingston, Lord 19, 32
Knibe, Francis 191

Lacken School 216
Lally, Archbishop 73
Lambert, Christopher 217
Lambert, Mary 217
Land League 111
Land War 129
Lane, James 38
Langton Family 209
Lawler, James 209
Lawler Family 209, 213
Lawless, Sir Nicholas 52
Lawless, Valentine 53
Lawless Family 43

Lawlor, John 209, 210
Lawlor, Patrick 210
Le Brett, John 206
Leader, Thomas 21
Lestrange, Patrick 129
Lestrange, Thomas 123
LEITRIM
   Oughteragh 10
Lindsay, Charles, Bishop of Kildare 49
LIMERICK
   Abington 57
   Kilmallock 20, 22, 23, 29
   Limerick 29, 53, 103
Liverpool 218
Longford 120, 145
Loorame, Thomas 122
Lowe, Anthony 42
Lucas, Col. Benjamin 99
Lucas, John 99, 104, 106, 107
Lucas, Samuel 99
Lucas, Mr 117
Lucas Diary 12
Lyne, William 38
Lyons 50
Lyster, Elizabeth 145
Lyster, Mathew 145, 150
Lyster, P.L. 29

Mac Bruaideadha, Conchobhar 97
Mac Bruaideadha, Ualgharg 96
Mac Fhaolain Family 47
Mac Giollamocholmog 188
Mac Murchada, Diarmuid 188
Magelan, Cornelius 47
Mackelan Family 47
Macken, Mick 106, 107
Mackey, Patrick 112
Magauen, Denis 53
Magelan, Felix 47
Magelan, Fin 47
Magelan Clan 65
Maguire, Canon Edward 166
Mahon, James 210

Mahon Family 125, 126
Mahony, Patrick 36
Malachy the Great, King 114
Marshall, Isabella 73, 74
Marshall, John 73
Marshall Day Family 69, 74, 75, 76,
   79, 82
Martyrology of Donegal 44, 114
Martyrology of Tallaght 114
Maybury, Isabella 75
Maybury, Dr Thomas 75
Maybury-Marshall, John 76
Maynooth College 217
MAYO
   Castlebar 77
   Newport 10, 73
MEATH
   Athboy 114
   Baconstown 65
   Ballyskeagh 49, 50
   Clonard 43
   Enfield 43, 56, 61, 63
   Meath County 120
McBrady, Michael 10
McBrady Family 97
McCafferty, Anne 182
McCafferty, James 175, 178
McCafferty, John 184
McCafferty, Margaret 182
McCafferty, Mary 182
McCafferty, Michael 184
McCafferty, Patrick 178
McCafferty, Thomas 184
McCafferty Family 177
McCarthy, Ann 182
McCarthy, Brigid 182
McCarthy, Catherine 182
McCarthy, John 178, 182
McCarthy, Michael 180
McCarthy Family 166, 177, 182
McCrea, Family 198
McDerby, John 216
McDerby, Lizzie 216

McDermott, Joseph 10
McDonald, Tommy 219
McDonell, John 106, 107, 111
McDonnell, Anthony 208
McDonnell, Gallowglasses 207
McDowell, Walter 144
McEaghagh, Brandubh 44
McEntire, Mary 145
McMahon, Peter 112
McMenamin, Revd 175
McNeely, Brigid 178
McNeely, Francis 182
McNeely, John 184
McNeely, Patrick 178
McNeely Family 176, 177
McPhelim, Ann 182
McPhelim, James 182
McPhelim, Patrick 182
McPhelim Family 177, 184
McQuay, George 20, 21
McShee, Daniel 182
McShee Family 177
Meade, Nicholas 20, 21
Meade Family 36
Meehan Ann 126
Medlicott, Isabella 73
Meehan, James 126
Meehan, Katherine 126
Meehan, Patrick 123, 126
Meehan Family 126, 128
Mehir, John 112
Midland and Great Western Railway
    56
Miley Family 214
mill 61
Molloy, Thomas 123, 124
Molly, Philip 210
Monaghan Family 59
Moore's Terrace 198
Morris, James 73
Morrow, James 182
Morrow, Joe 173
Morrow, Margaret 182

Morrow, Nicholas 173
Morrow, Patrick 180
Morrow Family 177
Mounrag, Roger 117
Mount Carmel, Order of 49
Mountain Villa House 193
Mountjoy Jail 129
Mulrenin, Thomas 212
Murchadh Mor, king of Leinster 47
Murphy, Catherine 37
Murphy, James 55, 57, 111
Murray, Thomas 122
Murray Family 60, 126

Naas Union 216–17
Nagle, Johanna 29
Nagle, John 26
Nagle, Richard 19
Nagle Family 36
Nally, Matthew 127
Nally, Kate 128
Napoleonic Wars 128, 196
National Archives 13
Nestor Family 125
Netterville's Map of Aylmer Estate 51,
    61, 65
Neville, A.R. 208
Neville's Map of Wicklow 208
New York 28
New Zealand 46
Neylon, Daniell, Bishop of Kildare 96
Niall, King of Ireland 44
Nicholson, John 81
Noble and Keenan's Map of Kildare 52
Norbury, Lord 53
Norry Family 36
Nugent, Andrew 116
Nugent, Andrew General 124, 128
Nugent, Christopher, 14th Baron of
    Delvin 116
Nugent, James, 10th Baron of Delvin
    116
Nugent, John 117, 124

Nugent, Katherine 116
Nugent, Lavallin 116
Nugent, Sir Robert 116
Nugent, Richard, 15th Baron of
    Delvin 116
Nugent Family 116, 128, 129

Ó Braonain, Micheal 141, 142
Ó Briain, Muircheartach 93
O Briain, Murchadh 96
Ó Dalaigh, Aengus 19
Ó Dálaigh, Brian 11, 12
Ó Dea, Conchobhar 93, 105
Ó hOgain, Giollapadraig 96
Ó hOgain, Conchobhar 96
Ó hOgain, Aodh 96
Ó Maitiu, Seamus 11
O'Boyle, Neil, Plunket 217
O'Brien, Bridget 60
O'Brien, Charles 26
O'Brien, Conor 26
O'Brien, Ellen 37
O'Brien, Henry, Earl of Thomond 102
O'Brien, Michael 38, 112
O'Brien, Murrough the Burner 98
O'Brien, Patrick 37
O'Brien, Thomas 60
O'Brien, Bishop of Cloyne 38
O'Brien Family 36, 37
O'Brien Family 188
O'Byrne Family 206
O'Cleary, Lughaidh 167
O'Cleary Family 167
O'Connell, Hearman 20
O'Connor, Gabriel 11
O'Connor, Michael 81
O'Connor Clan 72
O'Connor Family 142
O'Donnell, Hugh 167, 185
O'Donnell, Rory 167
O'Donnell Clan 166, 167
O'Donovan, John 16, 18, 70, 72, 105,
    141, 169

O'Fallon Family 142
O'Gibbons, Barry 175, 176
O'Keefe Family 18
O'Melaghlin, Murchadh 114
O'Melaghlin Family 116
O'Muldorey, Flaithbhearthaigh 166
O'Neill Clan 167
O'Reilly, T.M. 218
O'Reilly, James 210
O'Rourke, Revd John 70
O'Sgingin Family 167
O'Shaughnessy, Stephen 87
O'Toole, Thomas 204
O'Toole Family 206
Obery, Neyuinus 206
Obery, Philip 206
Oliver, Charles 29, 30
Oliver, C.D. 30
Oliver Family 37
Ormond, Earl 51
Ormond Estates 43, 50
Osborne Family 209

Palles, Chief Baron 193
Parnell, Charles 111
Parson's Green Estate 192
Pembroke Estate 190
Phibbs, Mathew 101
Pierce, Thomas 191
Piers, Sir John 53
Pilkington Family 198
Pippard, William 50, 116
Pippard, Alice 50
Plunket Family 207
Portugal 106

Quigley, William 182
Queen's County 217
Quigley Family 177, 182
Quinn, Patrick 194

Radford, Ebenezer 20
Radford, William 19
Red Book of Ormond 43

Redesdale, Lord 192
Redesdale Estate 192, 194, 197
Reeves, William
Register of St Thomas Abbey 48
Reilly, Mary 80
Reilly, Patrick, 83
Remage, Lockhart 124, 127
Repertorium Veride 189
Report on State of Popery 49
Representative Church Body 128
Rhyne, Philip 100
Robinson, Edward 55
Roche, John 49
Roche, Patrick 10, 26
Roche Family 18, 36, 37
Rooney, Hugh 156
Rooney, Roger 156
ROSCOMMON
    Athlone barony 141, 144
    Brideswell 141, 142, 144, 150, 151,
        155, 158
    Cam Cemetery 144, 145, 154, 156
    Cam parish 141, 145, 146, 150,
        154, 155, 159, 160
    Cam Townland 142, 151, 152
    Carrantober 150
    Carrick 144
    Carrick Townland 156
    Castlesampson 152, 154
    Cornageeha 145, 146
    Crannagh River 141
    Curraghboy 141, 151, 156
    Derryglad 141, 145, 155, 156
    Dysart parish 159
    Eskerbaun 11, 141–163 *passim*
    Gortacoosan 145
    Kiltoom Parish 154, 155
    Lough Funshinagh 141
    Lysterfield 9
    Milltown 152, 154
    Poll Sheoin 142
    Pollalaher 146
    Shannon River 141
    Taughmaconnell 145

Royal Dublin Society 171
Ryan, Edward 54
Ryan, Mary 57
Ryan, Patrick 82

Ryan, Thomas 53, 54, 55, 58
Ryan Family 53
Ryly, Patrick 64

Sacred Heart nuns 200
salmon 78
Savage, Andrew 117
Savage-Nugent Family 117, 124
schools 64, 85, 87
Scotland 126
Scott, W.G. 145
Shaughnessy, Jeremiah 83
Shaughnessy, John 83
Shaghnessy, Kate 81
Shaghnessy, Mary 80
Sheeghan, Thomas 103
Sheehan, David 20
Sheehan Family 36
Sheil Family 173
Sheridan, Margaret 182
Sheridan Family 177, 182
Shiel, John B. 173, 174
Shiel, Simon 174, 175
Sierra Leone 217
Slayne, Richard 50
Smith, Bartholomew 53
Smith Charles 11
Smith, Elizabeth 215, 216, 218
Smith, Col. Henry 216
Smith, Patrick 155
Smith, Dr 171
Smith Family 37
Smythe, Ralf 145
Song of Dermot and the Earl 47
Southeastern Railway 193
St Barron 166
St Begnat, Dalkey 188
St Benen 71

St Benildus School 186
St Berchan, Shankill 188
St Boodin's Well 206
St Brendan 71, 188
St Brigid 157,188, 201
St Carthach 188
St Colman 71, 114
St Cuthbert 201
St Flannan 188
St Jarlath 70, 71
St Jarlath's Seminary 75
St Kevin, Glendalough 188
St Laurence O'Toole 201, 204
St Laurence of Rome 201
St Lawrence Family 207
St Leger, Chichester 23
St Maelduin 166
St Maeltuile 114
St Malo 188
St Margaret's Estate 192
St Martin 48
St Martin of Tours 46
St Mary 48
St Mocholmoc 188
St Mochud 188, 201
St Molaga 16, 37, 38
St Nathi 188
St Nathlash 14, 16, 18
St Nicholas 18
St Ninian 44, 46, 48
St Patrick 46
St Thomas Abbey 48
Stackpole Family 36
Stanley, Arthur 145
Stanley, James 144, 145
Stannard Family 20
Stannard's Grove 31
Stannus, Edris 218
Stannus, Elizabeth G. 218
Stannus, Capt. 218
Stillorgan House 191
Strafford Survey 70, 72
Strongbow 50, 188, 204

Studdert of Cregmoher 108, 112
Sweeney, Bryan 26
Sweeney, Maurice 26
Synge Census of Elphin 12, 144, 146, 148, 160

Taafe, Martin 107
Taafe, Helena 112
Taylor's Map of Kildare 52
Thompson, Joseph 51
Thompson, Richard 51
Thorncastle Manor 189
Thornfield 186
Thornton, John 83
Thornton, shopkeeper 50, 60, 63
Tipper, James 211
TIPPERARY
    Cashel 18
Tir Chonaill 166, 167
Tirhugh Farmer's Society 171
Toole, Peter 190
Tortola, West Indies 117
Tredennick, Revd George Nesbitt 171, 172, 173, 174, 175, 176, 177, 178,182
Troy, Archbishop of Dublin 211
Trumble, Morgan 101
Tuam Corporation 78
Tuam Herald 69, 80
Tuam Town Commissioners 83
Tullamore Jail 129
Twoomy Family 209

Uí Briuin Chualann 188
Uí Faolain 43, 44, 47, 50, 65, 206
Uí Mail 206
Uí Maine 141, 142
Uí Muireadaig 206
Uí Neil 44
United Irish League 129
Upton, Ambrose 103

Vaughan, Fr Jeremiah 112
Vaughan, Revd James 107

Verschoyle Family 198
Vesey-Nugent, John 117, 128

Wade, Richard 122, 123
Wall, Thomas 156
Walsh, Henry 209
Walsh, James 210
Walsh, Mary 218
Walsh, Maurice 209
Walsh, Michael 210
Walsh, Nicholas 48
Walsh, Fr Paul 113
Walsh, Thomas 59
Walsh Family 213, 218
Walshe, Roger 48
Warren, Margaret 122
Warrington 80
Watch, Edward 154
Watch, Thomas 154
Waterford, Lord 215
WATERFORD
    Lismore 30, 188
Watson, William 150, 154
Webb, Thomas 124
Weldon, William 48
Welsh, John 100
Welsh, Revd Laurence 49
West Clare Railway 110
WESTMEATH
    Athlone 48, 141, 145
    Barretstown 122
    Blackwater, Leinster 43, 63
    Castletown-Geoghegan 113, 122
    Cro Inis 114
    Dun na Sciath 114
    Dysart 11, 113–140 *passim*
    Lough Ennell 113, 114
    Moyashel and Magheradernan
        barony 113, 114
    Mullingar 113, 116, 122, 128
    Tobar Multilly 114
    Whitepark 129
WEXFORD
    Ballydermod 9

WEXFORD (*contd.*)
    Cushenstown 9
    Rochestown 9
    Trillok 9
    Wexford 9
Whately, Archbishop 192
White, Richard 123, 124
Whiteboys 31, 41
Wicklow rebels 208
WICKLOW
    Annacarney 210
    Balirothan 206
    Ballinastockan 208, 209
    Ballyknockan 208
    Ballymore 206
    Ballynastockan 203
    Ballynultagh 210
    Baltyboys 203
    Black Hill 203
    Blackditches 211
    Blackmore Hill 208
    Blessington 203, 208, 210, 218
    Boleyhemushboy 207
    Booly Ultagh 207
    Boystown 207
    Cellboedain 204
    Cellugarrcon 204
    Clonmathun 206
    Cockbrook 203, 212
    Finney's Bridge 212
    Garryknock 210
    Glassnimucky 208
    Glen of Imail 206
    Glendalough 204
    Kilarsan 206
    Kilbodan 204, 205, 206, 207
    Kilgargan 206
    Kilgarrcon 204
    Killbegg 207
    King's River 203, 216
    Knocknadruse 217
    Lacavalyvary 203
    Lacken 11, 203–19 *passim*

WICKLOW (*contd.*)
    Lugnagun Great 203
    Manor Kilbride 58
    Oakwood 211
    Oldboleys 207
    Poulaphouca Reservoir 203, 219
    Roundwood 203
    Talbotstown Lower Barony 203
    Templeboodin 204, 206, 209, 211
    Valleymount 211, 212
    Whelp Rock 208, 209
    Wicklow Mts 52
    Woodenboley 207
    Woodend 211
Wigan 80, 81
William of Cloncurry 48

Williams, Charles Wye 62
Williamson, D. 82
Williamson, Revd John 49
Wilson, Joseph 194
Wilson, Thomas 194
Wogan, Katherine 51
Wolverston, James 191
Woodley Estate 192, 198
Wrexham 80
Wyndham Land Act 33, 104, 218

Young, Arthur 170, 171

Zeller, Alfred 218, 219
Zeller Family 217
Zeller Hotel 217, 218